KANJI CLUES: A MNEMONIC APPROACH TO MASTERING JAPANESE CHARACTERS

T0403333

Kanji Clues: A Mnemonic Approach to Mastering Japanese Characters introduces a novel approach to character acquisition that combines the ancient practice of memory enhancement with a modern appreciation for active learning.

By placing phonology at the center of the reading-writing process, the learner establishes an essential link between sound and meaning before addressing each character's orthography, much in the way native speakers do. Another prominent feature of these volumes is that the lessons are organized thematically according to components in order to enhance their retention and to distinguish between similar looking kanji. As a result, character order is determined by the frequency of their primary elements or components. Once a character is learned, it retains the same meaning when it appears as an element in other characters. There is thus an internal recycling of components and characters throughout the course that serves as an additional aid to their retrieval. Proceeding from components and characters, each lesson then introduces ten new compounds, half of which appear in sentences. Here again, the learner actively forges meaningful links by responding to the clues provided. Indeed, the entire learning sequence is based upon mnemonic principles, such as attention, association, and elaboration, which, when employed together, comprise a memory-enhancing network that facilitates accurate recall and retention.

Designed for students who wish to master the Japanese reading/writing system, each volume is comprised of a year's worth of lessons, which can be used alongside a primary textbook, as well as for self-study, reference, or review. Upon completion of the course, the learner will have not only mastered all the 2,136 everyday use characters, but also be familiar with more than 1,200 kanji compounds and the most common sentence patterns in the Japanese language, thereby providing a deep understanding of the inner workings of the language and the tools to decipher new words.

Volume 1 is an ideal supplementary resource for students throughout their first year of Japanese-language study.

John Esposito is Professor in the School of Global Studies at Chukyo University, Nagoya, Japan.

KANJI CLUES: A MNEMONIC APPROACH TO MASTERING JAPANESE CHARACTERS

Volume 1

John Esposito

Routledge
Taylor & Francis Group

LONDON AND NEW YORK

First published 2020
by Routledge
2 Park Square, Milton Park, Abingdon, Oxon OX14 4RN

and by Routledge
52 Vanderbilt Avenue, New York, NY 10017

Routledge is an imprint of the Taylor & Francis Group, an informa business

British Library Cataloguing-in-Publication Data
A catalogue record for this book is available from the British Library

Library of Congress Cataloging-in-Publication Data
A catalog record for this book has been requested

ISBN: 978-0-367-44152-4 (hbk)
ISBN: 978-0-367-44150-0 (pbk)

Typeset in Times New Roman
by Apex CoVantage, LLC

CONTENTS

Appendixes

INTRODUCTION

Mastering kanji is a formidable task, especially for those who do not reside in an environment where they are exposed to the characters on a daily basis. For native speakers of Japanese, formal kanji instruction begins in the first grade of elementary school. By the end of high school, students are expected to have learned the 2,136 everyday use or *jooyoo* kanji. This involves twelve years of regular study, most of which centers on learning through repetition, including reading and writing. Formal study is inevitably reinforced by exposure to the writing system through the mass media and other channels of quotidian communication. The number of hours devoted to the study of kanji is significant and cannot be easily replicated by non-natives residing outside of Japan. For those who come to Japan to learn the language, it is not feasible to allot twelve years to reading and writing instruction before beginning advanced-level study.

The methods that have been developed for second-language learners tend to follow those used in Japanese public schools. In short, they involve a sequential approach to the characters based on frequency of usage or received academic standards. As new characters are introduced, rote memorization is the primary method used for achieving fluency. This entails memorizing lists of characters through constant repetition, primarily copying and writing the individual strokes of each character in the correct order. Such methods inform the typical second-language learner course, although recently there has been more emphasis placed on learning characters in context as either parts of compounds or in short sentences.

Regardless of the method employed, learning kanji place inordinate demands on the memory. Mnemonic techniques have thus become a common component of kanji course books and learning manuals as they allow for more efficient learning of large amounts of new material. When such techniques appear in kanji textbooks, they are invariably applied in a linear fashion without much regard to the principles involved. Simply making connections between the orthographic and semantic properties of the characters, for instance, does not address the needs of learners to establish their own mental associations when attempting to encode new information. If memorization of thousands of characters in order to achieve native-like fluency is the primary goal, then an approach that respects how factors such as association, elaboration, imagination, and organization facilitate learning because they support specific memory processes ought to be followed. These are, in fact, some of the guiding principles that inform the mnemonic network method used in this book.

Elements of a mnemonic network

In contrast to established mnemonic techniques, the organizing principle of a mnemonic network is meaning. Simply put, what is rendered meaningful in a person's mind is what is usually remembered. Meaning has been found to facilitate deep levels of cognitive processing, whereby new information is either connected to existing knowledge or becomes the basis of an incipient semantic network. In this case, the sound of a Japanese character is linked to a core concept in English via the creation of an acronym whose letters comprise a clue to the character's meaning. The meaning, therefore, is not provided but must be deduced from the clues. Extending cognitive effort in such a manner addresses the primary factor associated with forgetting, which is a lack of attention at the time of encoding.

This initial focus on meaning is complemented by introduction to the character's pronunciation, both of which operate interactively when reading. The purpose here is to mimic the way in which native speakers first encounter kanji, namely, with a rudimentary knowledge of their meaning and pronunciation. Moving in the opposite direction from step one, the learner is provided with the core concept and the first letters of the acronym and must complete the clue, thereby reinforcing the semantic and phonetic links of a character before being introduced to its orthography. This last point is especially important due to the plethora of homonyms in Japanese, and the high probability of interference occurring during retrieval as similar sounding characters become confused. Thus, the significance of the acronym as a semantic clue in itself and its concrete connection to the graphic elements of the character help to distinguish it from other homonyms.

Due to their visual complexity and unfamiliarity, except to those who are raised in a kanji environment, identifying their primary elements by performing a componential analysis is the next step. Focusing on a character's essential parts has been found to facilitate learning even for native speakers. It has the benefit not only of simplification but also of establishing patterns that begin to bring clarity to the mysterious agglomeration of strokes. Putting flesh on the kanji's bones, as it were, is then enhanced through a deliberate form of writing repetition. Rather than mindlessly reproducing the characters, learners are advised to rehearse their pronunciation and meaning at the same time. The effect is that as each character becomes more familiar, it attains a distinct identity in the learner's mind.

To further reinforce the semantic, phonetic, and orthographic links in the network, the acronym, core concept, and main elements of the character are to be integrated into a succinct story that relies on vivid imagery. The creation of such a narrative is not merely one of synthesis but of elaboration that serves to entwine the learner as well into the mnemonic network. Stories that rely on idiosyncratic, experiential, and preferential tendencies best serve the goal of strengthening memory traces, while also establishing multiple paths for recall and recognition. Applying what has been learned is another useful principle, especially when it mimics the encoding process. Reading practice thus involves character clusters whose completion is facilitated by knowledge of their components and pronunciation. The final step is one of evaluation but only after an established period of time. In effect, rest is also a critical component of this method, for there can be no easy way to acquisition without extending much effort—invariably the flip side to a brief period of repose.

There are a number of unique aspects to the mnemonic network method, which marries meaning to pronunciation while activating the learner's innate curiosity and creativity. First, it combines the ancient practice of memory enhancement with a modern appreciation for active learning. It thus demands of the learner commitment and initiative. This method also allows for learner differences. Highly visual and analytical learners benefit from the emphasis on componential analysis of the characters; auditory learners appreciate the alliteration and rhythmic aspects of the clues as well as the extensive use of acronyms; and creative learners can thrive when asked to combine the clues and elements in an unusual or highly idiosyncratic narrative or when required to artistically elaborate on the characters after componential analysis. The entire effort, moreover, is one of collaboration. Whereas the acronym is provided, the learner must link it to the core concept. The word completion task in step two likewise functions as stimuli to self-generation. After the components of a character are identified, the learner is required to bring them to life through their visual imagination. Finally, the acronym, core concept, and character components are incorporated into a story-sketch by the learner to complete the mnemonic network.

From mnemonic principles to practice

The following learning sequence forms the organizing framework of this book. Each week 21 characters are introduced via a crossword puzzle, the clues of which are the words that comprise the acronyms and the solutions the meanings of the target words. The second step involves the use of acrostics to reinforce the semantic-phonologic associations introduced in the acronym. As mentioned earlier, this is accomplished by reversing the process in the first step. Componential analysis of the 21 characters on day three initiates identification and integration of unfamiliar parts into a coherent pattern or whole by assigning significance to each, thereby establishing visual associations between a character and its meaning. The next step consists of writing practice characterized by mindful repetition not only of a character's form, but also its pronunciation and meaning. On day five, all elements are integrated into a memorable story. Character clusters on day six take learners a step back to their components before learning how to combine them into compounds and use them in sentences. The final step is one of rest, as it should be, broken up periodically with a comprehensive review.

While some claim that the entire list of *jooyoo* kanji can be mastered in a matter of weeks if not hours, completion of this course will ideally take about two years—not an unreasonable amount of time given the material to be covered. If one does the math, 21 characters per week multiplied by 50 weeks per year equates to 1,050 characters. The last week's lesson of each year includes 18 characters for a total of 1,068. After two years, the learner will have covered the entire list of 2,136 *jooyoo* kanji. At the end of each five-week sequence, there is a review of 105 characters that entails both reading and writing.

Unlike most texts that follow a character frequency approach, this book is ordered according to the relative rate of component occurrence. Components are the primary meaningful elements of each character, including those traditionally referred to as radicals. The most frequently occurring components are thus introduced first. This principle not only informs the ordering of the chapters but also their composition. Each lesson is composed primarily of characters with the same component(s), thereby fostering their rapid acquisition while helping highlight distinctions between similar looking characters. Such a focus also necessitates proceeding from orthographically simpler to more complex characters. A final benefit to this approach is that there is an internal recycling of components throughout the course that serves as an additional aid to their recognition and character recall.

Weekly course outline

Day	Focus	Activity
1	**M** = Meanings	Crossword Puzzle: Complete the puzzle by inferring core concepts from the clues provided.
2	**A** = Associations	Acrostics: With the core concepts provided, complete each acrostic of the crossword clues by filling in the missing letters.
3	**S** = Symbols	Componential Analysis: Move from acronyms to characters while first identifying and then recording their primary parts.
4	**T** = Traces	Writing Practice: Trace and copy the strokes of each character while repeating its pronunciation and meaning silently.
5	**E** = Elements	Story Sketch: Link clues to components in a personalized narrative, thereby establishing a mnemonic network.
6	**R** = Readings	Character Clusters: Using the clues, complete the characters, compounds, and sentences.
7	**Y** = Yields	Rest and Review: Slow down to allow method to produce results, which are further enhanced through periodic evaluations.

Clue principles as simple as ABC

Clues were developed according to three principles: Accuracy—in terms of the character's core meaning or contemporary essence; Brevity—as few words or syllables as possible so as to not overburden the memory; and Creativity—make as much use of assonance, alliteration, and rhyme to further enhance retention. Accuracy: The clues are not meant to be definitions, per se, although they should lead the learner in the direction of the core meaning. In some cases, clues are analogic, metaphoric, elliptic, iconic, metonymic, or simply poetic. They were made to stimulate the learner's inferential abilities much in the manner of typical crossword puzzles. Rather than simply looking up the meaning of a character or identifying its primary denotation, the cognitive effort involved in discovering its meaning establishes the initial link in the mnemonic network. Brevity: Mnemonics teaches us that less is always better; therefore, every effort was made to keep the clues as brief as possible by combining the letters in the acrostic, for instance, without sacrificing accuracy. In a similar way, monosyllabic words were chosen instead of polysyllabic ones, and words with higher frequency were selected over those with lower frequency as long as the former in both instances did not compromise the semantic accuracy of the clue. Creativity: Repetition of sounds within the clue, just as in poetry and song, is a welcome aid to memory. Again, this was done only when it did not interfere with accuracy or brevity and could effectively complement them.

In regards to phonetics, the acronyms that function as clues are the Romanized equivalents of the Japanese *on* (Chinese) reading according to the Hepburn system, wherein long vowels are rendered by a doubling of the vowel. The acronym for direction [方], for instance, is *hoo* (not *hou* or *hō*). Moreover, due to the paucity of words in English that begin with the letter *k* (or the hard *c* sound) and the large number of words in Japanese that do, all English words beginning with the hard *c* (in addition to those beginning with a *k*) are used in the clues where a *k* is needed. For example, Komplete Alteration is the clue for the character [化] whose *on* (Chinese) reading is transliterated as "*ka*."

How to make best use of this book

The study of human memory is ultimately about the intimate relations between time and forgetting. That which is unattended to at first is seemingly lost forever; conversely, once something receives attention through rehearsal, for instance, it has the potential to be retained for a virtual unlimited duration. What happens between initial exposure to new material, in this case, kanji, and the time it takes to encode it in a meaningful manner is the key to remembering. The dynamic nature of the processes involved, like all organic phenomena, develops within certain temporal constraints. There are exceptions, of course, but this book has not been designed for those with extraordinary cognitive capabilities. The method upon which it is based presumes that mastery of a large amount of new information places an inordinate burden on normal memory functions, which can best be lessened by utilizing certain mnemonic principles. Establishing meaningful associations, taking heed of complexity, and creating novel connections all take time. Transgressing these steps in pursuit of some mad dash to mastery is a prescription for frustration and forgetting. The following suggestions, therefore, are meant to keep you moving along this mysterious path at a propitious pace.

Day 1

Approach this activity as you would any puzzle, that is, with a sense of curiosity and attentiveness. Try to finish the puzzle in one sitting if possible, and do not look ahead for the answers, which, by the way, are the clues for the acrostics on Day Two. Due to the unorthodox nature of the clues, constrained as they are by the acronyms from which they originate, the first letter for seven in each puzzle is provided. Proceed to the next step only after the puzzle is (nearly) complete, preferably on the following day or in preparation for the next lesson if this book is being used as part of a class. Remember that just as the cognitive effort dispensed in this step establishes the initial links in the network, the power of discovery provides the heat necessary to fuse them. That said, don't get overheated if you cannot fill in all the blanks; rather, treat those empty spaces as pause for reflection.

Day 2

Once you confirm that the crossword puzzle is completed correctly, fill in the missing letters of the acrostics, which should proceed rather quickly because they have just been encountered as clues on Day One. Next, review the core meanings and pronunciations of the words. Again, please do not work ahead. It is important to forge connections between the semantic and phonetic aspects of the characters before being introduced to their complex orthography.

Day 3

The typical kanji appears at first as an abstract conglomeration of lines or marks. The purpose of dividing each character into its constituents and labeling them in a consistent manner is to lend a certain familiarity to recurrent patterns. Some of these components are characters unto themselves. For example, the kanji for *moon* [月] often appears in other characters, such as [明], which combines *sun* and *moon* to indicate *bright*. The denotations of the characters are not always so straightforward due in part to their lengthy etymologies. The kanji for *crumble* [崩] appears to be comprised of a *mountain* [山] and two *moons*. However, [月] is an element that also designates *body* or *flesh* being derived from the character for *meat* [肉]. When to distinguish between *moon* and *body* or *flesh* is one of the goals of componential analysis. Consistently labeling each component in a meaningful manner, moreover, will decrease the memory load while enhancing a character's long-term retention. Often, the components are not characters but simply distinct elements of a character, like [艹] which indicates *plants*. While conventionally known as radicals, such graphemic constituents will also be referred to as components. In addition to stand-alone characters and conventional radicals, there is a third group of components that have been devised exclusively for this course to facilitate recall and recognition. Criteria for their inclusion is that they must appear as distinct elements in at least three characters and their consolidation is consistent with the meaning of the characters in which they appear. To illustrate, [畐] is composed of three parts, *one* [一], *mouth* [口], and *field* [田], which when combined, connotes a sense of fullness derived from "enough food from field to fill one mouth." Therefore, whenever [畐] is encountered as part of a character, rather than divide it further, *full* is rendered as its meaning.

Componential analysis thus consists of the following steps. The character is first divided into its primary components each of which is given a meaningful designation (refer to examples from Lesson 1 below).

Course Number	**Kanji**	ON Reading(s)*	Primary Components***	Kanji Canvas
		Core Concept(s)**		
0017	日	NICHI, JITSU	Sun with spot	日
		day; sun		
0018	白	HAKU	⟋ (accent)^{K2} + 日 (sun)^{17}	白
		white		

* Refer to Appendix Two for secondary *on* pronunciations and their acronyms. For characters without an *on* reading, the primary *kun* reading is used.
** Core concepts and secondary meanings are separated with semicolons. Refer to Appendix Three for secondary meanings and their acronyms.
*** Components rendered in italics indicate orthographic variation. Those rendered in italics whose meanings are not in parentheses appear only once or twice in the course.

When a component is also a character, as is the case for [日] in 0018 [白], its course number appears in superscript for cross-referencing. If a component is not a stand-alone character, then its numeric designation begins with a 'K' (for Komponent). In this case, record the entire character in the list in Appendix One. For characters such as 0017 [日] comprised of a single symbolic image, usually referred to as pictographs, simply review its description. In either case, the next step is one of creative elaboration. With the character isolated in a box on the right, try to fill in the space either pictorially or semantically as a means of embellishing or emphasizing its meaning in an idiosyncratic manner. In doing so, approach each kanji canvas and the lines therein as a sketch, outline, or first draft of a potential artistic production.

Day 4

There is a reason that kanji are ideally suited to calligraphy: their internal balance and distinct set of strokes lend themselves to creative expression. Although aesthetic excellence is not the goal here, the approach is quite similar. First you need to learn some general rules about how their anatomy is properly constructed. Stroke order proceeds from top to bottom and left to right. Horizontal strokes are usually written before vertical ones, although there are some notable exceptions: [田] [由] [王] [里]. The center stroke is written first except when it runs through the middle of a character as in [中] or [車]. And in kanji that contain an outer frame, such as [回] or [国], the left side, then top and right side (one stroke) of the frame come before the center strokes with the bottom of the frame written last. In addition to stroke order, the size of each stroke is also important. Simply put, size is a function of number. The more strokes, the smaller they will be given the fact that they must coexist on the same kanji canvas, or in what some call an imaginary box. Compare [七] to [鬱], for example, the former comprised of two strokes and the latter twenty-nine. Obviously, internal balance of the elements is important, which brings us back to method. Writing practice should commence by first saying out loud the character's pronunciation. Try to get into a rhythm when writing—one whose repetition induces relaxation. Such heightened concentration is not only a useful memory aid, but also emulates the artistic intent of the calligrapher.

Day 5

Now is your opportunity to collaborate in an act of creative synthesis. Given the clues, core concepts, and components of each character, combine them into a succinct memorable story-sketch no longer than an average sentence. Try not to break up the acronym, while connecting the words in a meaningful manner. When possible or appropriate, make use of alliteration, assonance, and rhyme, as well as vivid and interactive imagery. What is memorable or meaningful for one person is not necessarily true for another. No need, therefore, to invoke the bizarre and ugly unless doing so is sure to make a lasting impression. The following is a select sample of story sketches beginning with course number and character for each.

0026	工	**Work** with cutting tool Keeps One Occupied.
0157	東	Looking **east** TOward Orient, sun rises behind tree.
0251	荒	KOmpletely Overgrown plants run **wild** along dead river.
0330	宝	HOard of Opulent jewels under one roof is **treasure**.
0446	釜	Father's metal **kettle** Kooks A Meal Accordingly.
0560	剣	Discreet cut with **sword** Kills ENemy.
0636	波	On seawater's skin witness Hesitant Advance of **waves**.
0775	暗	At Night the **dark** sound of day.
0837	郎	In good village woman's ROmantic Other is her **husband**.
0928	矢	Take this **arrow** and SHoot It toward the heavens.
1010	光	Kandle Offers One small boy **light**.
1160	匂	Nose Identifies Odor of person sitting wrapped in **smelly** clothes.

1222	眠	People's eyes are closed and Mind INactive when they **sleep**.
1389	咲	**Bloom** of heavenly flowers opens Spring Activity.
1493	娠	Seed Held INside fertile woman who is **pregnant**.
1547	賭	Person with money tries to Tempt Odds by **gambling**.
1664	集	Small birds **gather** in tree where Some HUddle Under the leaves.
1775	劇	**Drama** Greatly Enacts KIlling of tiger tearing pig into pieces.
1867	航	**Navigate** boat in straight line to Kross Over Ocean.
1951	変	Have Entirely New dance routine after **changing** steps again.
2085	触	SHOulder Karessed Undressed is **touched** by horny insect.

Day 6

Think of the character clusters as involving a complex progression from components and characters to compounds and sentence comprehension. In some respects it mirrors the learning process itself, although their primary purpose is to reinforce existing networks in order to further expand them. Please do not approach them as you would a test—that is for later. Rather, attend to them as you did to the crossword puzzles. Instead of boxes to fill in, now there are blanks.

Day 7

Finally a chance to rest and reflect upon what has been learned. Reviews are scheduled every five weeks for a reason. If done too soon, they lose their evaluative function, and, if too late, they fail to live up to their names. Surely, approach them as you would a formal exam but with the caveat that they are not all that different from anything you've done thus far. This is a chance to evaluate your mnemonic strengths and identify what may need further attention. Keep in mind that the reviews recycle material from previous lessons to build upon what has already been learned, so if you don't get it now, make an effort to do so, preferably in the intervening weeks before the next review.

For love of kanji

What if through the study of kanji one learned more than a complex orthographic system? What if, in addition, it instilled an attention to detail, an appreciation of harmony, a facility for artful expression, and an inner calmness through repetition and concentration? In other words, what if the study of kanji cultivated all of those qualities that outsiders find most admirable in the Japanese people? Kanji, that is, might be thought to embody the cultural and linguistic spirit of the people in a manner quite distinct from other ethnic groups who also use them. The suggestion dating back to some prominent education reformers during the Meiji restoration that they could or ought to be replaced by an alien script such as the Roman alphabet displays a critical lapse in cross-cultural understanding not to mention a lurking linguistic imperialism parading under the banner of logic and efficiency. If, instead, we were to replace that banner with one of respect and diversity, then the study of kanji might begin to be seen for what it is—an ineluctable labor of love.

Lessons

1

BY THE NUMBERS

Day one: crossword puzzle

Across

1. Nearly Identical
3. Significant ENumeration (T)
5. Square HIghlights
8. Multiple Added Numbers (two words: T/T)
11. Standard UNit
12. Hole Atop Corresponding Hole Integer
14. NIght CHanges Into
16. Conveys HOrrific Outlook
17. Robust YOur KUre
18. Standard HAs Komparative Unit
19. Sake HOlder Ordinarily (M)
21. Sex Has Its CHeating Itch

Down

2. HAs Kolor Unclouded (W)
4. Kat Years Up Until
6. Initial CHinese Integer
7. Historical Years Armed Konflicts Undertaken (H)
9. JUdged Utmost
10. Transfers Oil (D)
13. Grasping Ones (F)
15. Stool Appendage Number
20. ROund KUbe

Day two: acrostics

1 Two: N _ _ _ _ _   I _ _ _ _ _ _ _ _

2 White: H A _   K _ _ _ _   U _ _ _ _ _ _ _ _

3 Thousand: S _ _ _ _ _ _ _ _ _   E N _ _ _ _ _ _ _ _

4 Nine: K _ _   Y _ _ _ _   U _   U _ _ _ _

5 Four: S _ _ _ _ _   H I _ _ _ _ _ _ _ _

6 One: I _ _ _ _ _ _   C H _ _ _ _ _   I _ _ _ _ _

7 Hundred: H _ _ _ _ _ _ _ _   Y _ _ _ _   A _ _ _ _   K _ _ _ _ _ _ _   U _ _ _ _ _ _ _ _

8 Ten Thousand: M _ _ _ _ _ _ _   A _ _ _ _   N _ _ _ _ _ _

9 Ten: J U _ _ _ _   U _ _ _ _ _

10 Dipper: T _ _ _ _ _ _ _ _   O _ _

11 Measure: S _ _ _ _ _ _ _   U N _ _

12 Eight: H _ _ _   A _ _ _   C _ _ _ _ _ _ _ _ _ _ _   H _ _ _   I _ _ _ _ _ _

13 Five: G _ _ _ _ _ _ _   O _ _ _

14 Day: N I _ _ _   C H _ _ _ _ _   I _ _ _

15 Three: S _ _ _ _   A _ _ _ _ _ _ _ _   N _ _ _ _ _

16 Sign: C _ _ _ _ _ _   H O _ _ _ _ _ _   O _ _ _ _ _ _

17 Power: R _ _ _ _ _   Y O _ _   K U _ _

18 Measure: S _ _ _ _ _ _ _   H A _   K _ _ _ _ _ _ _ _ _   U _ _ _

19 Measure: S _ _ _   H O _ _ _ _   O _ _ _ _ _ _ _ _

20 Six: R O _ _ _   K U _ _

21 Seven: S _ _   H _ _   I _ _   C H _ _ _ _ _ _   I _ _ _

Day three: componential analysis

Course Number	Kanji	ON Reading(s) / Core Concept(s)	Primary Components	Kanji Canvas
0001	一	ICHI, ITSU / **one**	Single stroke or line	一
0002	二	NI / **two**	Two strokes or lines	二
0003	七	SHICHI / **seven**	Person reclining with arms spread	七
0004	八	HACHI / **eight**	Hole opening	八
0005	九	KYUU / **nine**	Cat with long tail	九
0006	十	JUU / **ten**	Needle	十
0007	力	RYOKU / **power, strength**	Muscular arm	力
0008	万	MAN / **ten thousand**	一 (one)[01] + 力 (power)[07]	万
0009	三	SAN / **three**	Three strokes or lines	三
0010	千	SEN / **thousand**	一 (*one*)[01] + 十 (ten)[06]	千
0011	寸	SUN / **measure; little**	Space between forefinger and thumb	寸
0012	尺	SHAKU / **measure**	Span made by hand	尺
0013	五	GO / **five**	Three fingers extended, thumb up, little finger bent	五
0014	六	ROKU / **six**	亠 (top)[K1] + 八 (eight)[04]	六
0015	斗	TO / **dipper; measure**	Ladle with two drops	斗
0016	升	SHOO / **measure**	ノ (accent)[K2] + 廾 (two hands)[K3]	升
0017	日	NICHI, JITSU / **day; sun**	Sun with spot	日
0018	白	HAKU / **white**	ノ (accent)[K2] + 日 (sun)[17]	白
0019	百	HYAKU / **hundred**	一 (one)[01] + 白 (white)[18]	百
0020	四	SHI / **four**	囗 (enclosure)[K4] + 儿 (boy)[K5]	四
0021	兆	CHOO / **sign; trillion**	Cracks on turtle shell	兆

Day four: writing practice

一	二	七	八	九	十	力
一	二	七	八	九	十	力
万	三	千	寸	尺	五	六
万	三	千	寸	尺	五	六
斗	升	日	白	百	四	兆
斗	升	日	白	百	四	兆

Day five: story sketch

一	one: (single stroke or line) + Initial CHinese Integer
二	two: (two strokes or lines) + Nearly Identical
七	seven: (person reclining with arms spread) + Sex Has Its CHeating Itch
八	eight: (hole opening) + Hole Atop Corresponding Hole Integer
九	nine: (cat with long tail) + Kat Years Up Until
十	ten: (needle) + JUdged Utmost
力	power: (muscular arm) + Robust YOur KUre
万	ten thousand: 一 (one) + 力 (power) + Multiple Added Numbers
三	three: (three strokes or lines) + Stool Appendage Number
千	thousand: 一 (*one*) + 十 (ten) + Significant ENumeration
寸	measure: (space between forefinger and thumb) + Standard UNit
尺	measure: (span made by hand) + Standard HAs Komparative Unit
五	five: (three fingers extended, thumb up, little finger bent) + Grasping Ones
六	six: 亠 (top) + 八 (eight) + ROund KUbe
斗	dipper: (ladle with two drops) + Transfers Oil
升	measure: 丿 (accent) + 卅 (two hands) + Sake HOlder Ordinarily
日	day: (sun with spot) + NIght CHanges Into
白	white: 丿 (accent) + 日 (sun) + HAs Kolor Unclouded
百	hundred: 一 (one) + 白 (white) + Historical Years Armed Konflicts Undertaken
四	four: 囗 (enclosure) + 儿 (boy) + Square HIghlights
兆	sign: (cracks on turtle shell) + Conveys HOrrific Outlook

Day six: character clusters

I   Complete the characters using the clues.

1	亠	ROund KUbe (ROKU)
2	力	Multiple Added Numbers (MAN)
3	口	Square HIghlights (SHI)
4	白	Historical Years Armed Konflicts Undertaken (HYAKU)
5	廾	Sake HOlder Ordinarily (SHOO)

II Compose the compounds using the clues.

1   (SAN) ____   +   (GATSU) 月   =   _____ (March)
                              month

2   (IN) 引   +   (RYOKU) ____   =   _____ (gravitation)
        pull

3   (HAKU) ____   +   (JIN) 人   =   _____ (Caucasian)
                              person

4   (MAI) 毎   +   (NICHI) ____   =   _____ (daily)
        every

5   (NI) ____   +   (KAI) 回   =   _____ (twice)
                              turn, time

III Complete the sentences using the clues.

1   クラスは＿時に始まる。
    Kurasu wa HACHIji ni hajimaru.
    Class starts at eight o'clock.

2   この本は＿円しました。
    Kono hon wa SEN'en shimashita.
    This book cost one thousand yen.

3   どのアイスクリームが＿番好きですか。
    Dono aisukuriimu ga ICHIban suki desu ka.
    Which ice cream do you like the best?

4   時間は＿分にあります。
    Jikan wa JUUbun ni arimasu.
    There is enough time.

5   彼はドレスの＿法をとりました。
    Kare wa doresu no SUNpoo o torimashita.
    He took the dress measurements.

2

WATER WORLD

Day one: crossword puzzle

Across

3. Keen Yearning Upsetting Utterance
5. Kettle Issues
6. Hydrous Advance Nonstop
8. Konsequence ANxiety (S)
11. SHOrt Order
13. Exertion Immersed (S)
16. KOve Opening
17. SHOrt One
20. RIse To SUpport
21. Concavity Harbors Invertebrates (P)

Down

1. Kondition Arid Now
2. Stream Urging Influence (W)
4. Your Underlying Urge
7. Enduring Influence (E)
9. JUice Unflavored (L)
10. HYdrogen Oxygen Ossification
12. Yields Unction (O)
14. Keeps One Occupied
15. Terrain AKcustomed Underwater
18. House AKcommodates Us
19. Seashore Along

Day two: acrostics

1 Dry: K _ _ _ _ _ _ _ _   A _ _ _   N _ _

2 Water: S _ _ _ _ _   U _ _ _ _ _   I _ _ _ _ _ _ _

3 Cry: K _ _ _   Y _ _ _ _ _ _ _   U _ _ _ _ _ _ _ _   U _ _ _ _ _ _ _ _

4 Reason: Y _ _ _   U _ _ _ _ _ _ _ _ _   U _ _ _

5 Steam: K _ _ _ _ _ _   I _ _ _ _ _

6 Overflow: H _ _ _ _ _ _ _   A _ _ _ _ _ _   N _ _ _ _ _ _

7 Everlasting: E _ _ _ _ _ _ _ _   I _ _ _ _ _ _ _ _

8 Sweat: K _ _ _ _ _ _ _ _ _ _   A N _ _ _ _ _

9 Liquid: J U _ _ _ _   U _ _ _ _ _ _ _ _ _

10 Ice: H Y _ _ _ _ _ _   O _ _ _ _ _   O _ _ _ _ _ _ _ _ _ _ _

11 Little: S H O _ _   O _ _ _ _

12 Oil: Y _ _ _ _ _ _   U _ _ _ _ _ _

13 Swim: E _ _ _ _ _ _ _ _   I _ _ _ _ _ _ _

14 Work: K _ _ _ _ _   O _ _   O _ _ _ _ _ _ _

15 Marsh: T _ _ _ _ _ _   A K _ _ _ _ _ _ _ _   U _ _ _ _ _ _ _ _ _

16 Inlet: K O _ _   O _ _ _ _ _ _

17 Small: S H O _ _   O _ _

18 Lodge: H _ _ _ _   A K _ _ _ _ _ _ _ _ _ _   U _

19 Sand: S _ _ _ _ _ _ _   A _ _ _ _

20 Stand: R I _ _   T _   S U _ _ _ _ _

21 Pond: C _ _ _ _ _ _ _ _   H _ _ _ _ _ _   I _ _ _ _ _ _ _ _ _ _ _

Day three: componential analysis

Course Number	Kanji	ON Reading(s) / Core Concept(s)	Primary Components	Kanji Canvas
0022	水	SUI **water**	Streams flow into river	水
0023	氷	HYOO **ice**	丶 (accent)[K2] + 水 (water)[22]	氷
0024	干	KAN **dry**	Clothes rack	干
0025	汗	KAN **sweat**	氵 (water)[K6] + 干 (dry)[24]	汗
0026	工	KOO, KU **work**	Cutting tool	工
0027	江	KOO **inlet**	氵 (water)[K6] + 工 (work)[26]	江
0028	汁	JUU **liquid; juice**	氵 (water)[K6] + 十 (ten)[06]	汁
0029	池	CHI **pond**	氵 (water)[K6] + 也 (serpent)[K7]	池
0030	氾	HAN **overflow**	氵 (water)[K6] + 㔾 (slumped)[K8]	氾
0031	小	SHOO **small**	Three small points	小
0032	少	SHOO **little, few**	小 (small)[31] + 一 (one)[01]	少
0033	沙	SA **sand**	氵 (water)[K6] + 少 (little)[32]	沙
0034	汽	KI **steam**	氵 (water)[K6] + vapors (cf. 2124)	汽
0035	沢	TAKU **marsh; abundant**	氵 (water)[K6] + 尺 (measure)[12]	沢
0036	泊	HAKU **lodge**	氵 (water)[K6] + 白 (white)[18]	泊
0037	立	RITSU **stand**	Person standing on ground	立
0038	泣	KYUU **cry, weep**	氵 (water)[K6] + 立 (stand)[37]	泣
0039	由	YUU **reason**	Barrel	由
0040	油	YU **oil**	氵 (water)[K6] + 由 (reason)[39]	油
0041	永	EI **everlasting**	River with tributary	永
0042	泳	EI **swim**	氵 (water)[K6] + 永 (everlasting)[41]	泳

Day four: writing practice

水	氷	干	汗	工	江	汁
水	氷	干	汗	工	江	汁
池	氾	小	少	沙	汽	沢
池	氾	小	少	沙	汽	沢
泊	立	泣	由	油	永	泳
泊	立	泣	由	油	永	泳

Day five: story sketch

水	water: (streams flow into river) + Stream Urging Influence
冰	ice: 丶 (accent) + 水 (water) + HYdrogen Oxygen Ossification
干	dry: (clothes rack) + Kondition Arid Now
汗	sweat: 氵 (water) + 干 (dry) + Konsequence ANxiety
工	work: (cutting tool) + Keeps One Occupied
江	inlet: 氵 (water) + 工 (work) + KOve Opening
汁	liquid: 氵 (water) + 十 (ten) + JUice Unflavored
池	pond: 氵 (water) + 也 (serpent) + Concavity Harbors Invertebrates
氾	overflow: 氵 (water) + 巳 (slumped) + Hydrous Advance Nonstop
小	small: (three small points) + SHOrt One
少	little: 小 (small) + 一 (*one*) + SHOrt Order
沙	sand: 氵 (water) + 少 (little) + Seashore Along
汽	steam: 氵 (water) + *vapors* + Kettle Issues
沢	marsh: 氵 (water) + 尺 (measure) + Terrain AKcustomed Underwater
泊	lodge: 氵 (water) + 白 (white) + House AKcommodates Us
立	stand: (person standing on ground) + RIse To SUpport
泣	cry: 氵 (water) + 立 (stand) + Keen Yearning Upsetting Utterance
由	reason: (barrel) + Your Underlying Urge
油	oil: 氵 (water) + 由 (reason) + Yields Unction
永	everlasting: (river with tributary) + Enduring Influence
泳	swim: 氵 (water) + 永 (everlasting) + Exertion Immersed

Day six: character clusters

I Complete the characters using the clues.

1	氵	Konsequence ANxiety (KAN)
2	立	Keen Yearning Upsetting Utterance (KYUU)
3	小	SHOrt Order (SHOO)
4	氵	Kettle Issues (KI)
5	十	JUice Unflavored (JUU)

II Compose the compounds using the clues.

1 (JIN) 人   +   (KOO) ____   =   _____ (artificial)
   person

2 (DEN) 電   +   (CHI) ____   =   _____ (battery)
   electricity

3 (HYOO) ____   +   (ZAN) 山   =   _____ (iceberg)
                          mountain

4 (SEKI) 石   +   (YU) _____   =   _____ (petroleum)
   stone

5 (SUI) ____   +   (FU) 夫   =   _____ (sailor)
                          husband, man

III Complete the sentences using the clues.

1 コンビニは＿学校のとなりにあります。
   Konbini wa SHOOgakko no tonari ni arimasu.
   The convenience store is next to the elementary school.

2 東京のホテルに一＿＿しました。
   Tokyo no hoteru ni ipPAKU shimashita.
   I stayed one night at a hotel in Tokyo.

3 スイスは中＿国です。
   Suisu wa chuuRITSUkoku desu.
   Switzerland is a neutral country.

4 私は自＿＿な時間がたくさんある。
   Watashi wa jiYUUna jikan ga takusan aru.
   I have a lot of free time.

5 彼は水＿＿が上手です。
   Kare wa suiEI ga joozu desu.
   He is good at swimming.

3

TREE OF LIFE

Day one: crossword puzzle

Across

4. Hard Admits Nails
7. Span Of Neighbors
9. Softwood Unfurling Green Infinitely (C)
11. BOldly Kept Uncomplicated
13. Means OKUlar
14. Konsequent Action (F)
15. Maturation Incomplete (two words: N/Y)
17. Kutting INstrument
18. SEparate Kompletely Into
20. Mark AT SUmmit
21. Redwoods INdigenous

Down

1. Sheet Assigns The SUm (B)
2. Shape Of Observation (A)
3. Domain ENclosed
5. Has ANtagonism
6. Zebrawood Altered Into (T)
8. Juridical Official Outline
10. Make Another TAke
12. Mountain Occupant KUstomarily
16. Special Ability Innate
19. Kounter Individual (D)

Day two: acrostics

1 Bill: S _ _ _ _ A _ _ _ _ _ _ T _ _ S U _

2 Aspect: S _ _ _ _ O _ O _ _ _ _ _ _ _ _ _

3 Field: D _ _ _ _ _ E N _ _ _ _ _ _

4 Board: H _ _ _ A _ _ _ _ _ N _ _ _ _

5 Oppose: H _ _ A N _ _ _ _ _ _ _ _

6 Timber: Z _ _ _ _ _ _ _ _ A _ _ _ _ _ _ I _ _ _

7 Village: S _ _ _ O _ N _ _ _ _ _ _ _ _

8 Article: J _ _ _ _ _ _ _ _ O _ _ _ _ _ _ _ O _ _ _ _ _ _

9 Cedar: S _ _ _ _ _ _ _ U _ _ _ _ _ _ _ _ G _ _ _ _ I _ _ _ _ _ _ _ _ _

10 Again: M _ _ _ A _ _ _ _ _ _ T A _ _

11 Simple: B O _ _ _ _ K _ _ _ U _ _ _ _ _ _ _ _ _ _ _ _

12 Tree: M _ _ _ _ _ _ _ O _ _ _ _ _ _ _ K U _ _ _ _ _ _ _ _

13 Eye: M _ _ _ _ O K U _ _ _

14 Fruit: K _ _ _ _ _ _ _ _ _ A _ _ _ _ _

15 Not Yet: M _ _ _ _ _ _ _ _ _ I _ _ _ _ _ _ _ _

16 Talent: S _ _ _ _ _ _ A _ _ _ _ _ _ I _ _ _ _ _

17 Ax: K _ _ _ _ _ _ I N _ _ _ _ _ _ _ _

18 Divide: S E _ _ _ _ _ _ K _ _ _ _ _ _ _ _ _ _ I _ _ _

19 Desk: K _ _ _ _ _ _ I _ _ _ _ _ _ _ _ _

20 End: M _ _ _ A T S U _ _ _ _

21 Forest: R _ _ _ _ _ _ _ I N _ _ _ _ _ _ _ _

Day three: componential analysis

Course Number	Kanji	ON Reading(s) / Core Concept(s)	Primary Components	Kanji Canvas
0043	木	MOKU / **tree, wood**	Branches and roots	木
0044	未	MI / **not yet**	一 (one)[01] + 木 (tree)[43]	未
0045	末	MATSU / **end**	木 (tree)[43] + 一 (top)[K1]	末
0046	札	SATSU / **bill**	木 (tree)[43] + 乚 (kneeling)[K9]	札
0047	朴	BOKU / **simple**	木 (tree)[43] + 卜 (divination)[K10]	朴
0048	机	KI / **desk**	木 (tree)[43] + 几 (table)[K11]	机
0049	杉	sugi / **cedar**	木 (tree)[43] + 彡 (pattern)[K12]	杉
0050	条	JOO / **article, clause**	夂 (step)[K13] + 木 (tree)[43]	条
0051	村	SON / **village**	木 (tree)[43] + 寸 (measure)[11]	村
0052	才	SAI / **talent**	寸 (*measure*)[11] + ノ (*accent*)[K2]	才
0053	材	ZAI / **timber; material**	木 (tree)[43] + 才 (talent)[52]	材
0054	林	RIN / **forest**	木 (tree)[43] + 木 (tree)[43]	林
0055	斤	KIN / **ax; weight**	Ax with handle	斤
0056	析	SEKI / **divide**	木 (tree)[43] + 斤 (ax)[55]	析
0057	又	mata / **again**	Right hand	又
0058	反	HAN / **oppose**	厂 (cliff)[K14] + 又 (hand)[K15]	反
0059	板	HAN, BAN / **board**	木 (tree)[43] + 反 (oppose)[58]	板
0060	田	DEN / **field; paddy**	Rice paddy separated by paths	田
0061	果	KA / **fruit, result**	田 (field)[60] + 木 (tree)[43]	果
0062	目	MOKU / **eye**	Vertical representation of eye and iris	目
0063	相	SOO / **aspect; mutual**	木 (tree)[43] + 目 (eye)[62]	相

Day four: writing practice

木	未	末	札	朴	机	杉
木	未	末	札	朴	机	杉
条	村	才	材	林	斤	析
条	村	才	材	林	斤	析
又	反	板	田	果	目	相
又	反	板	田	果	目	相

Day five: story sketch

木	tree: (branches and roots) + Mountain Occupant KUstomarily
未	not yet: 一 (one) + 木 (tree) + Maturation Incomplete
末	end: 木 (tree) + 丄 (top) + Mark AT SUmmit
札	bill: 木 (tree) + 乚 (kneeling) + Sheet Assigns The SUm
朴	simple: 木 (tree) + 卜 (divination) + BOldly Kept Uncomplicated
机	desk: 木 (tree) + 几 (table) + Kounter Individual
杉	cedar: 木 (tree) + 彡 (pattern) + Softwood Unfurling Green Infinitely
条	article: 夂 (step) + 木 (tree) + Juridical Official Outline
村	village: 木 (tree) + 寸 (measure) + Span Of Neighbors
才	talent: 寸 (*measure*) + 丿 (*accent*) + Special Ability Innate
材	timber: 木 (tree) + 才 (talent) + Zebrawood Altered Into
林	forest: 木 (tree) + 木 (tree) + Redwoods INdigenous
斤	ax: (ax with handle) + Kutting INstrument
析	divide: 木 (tree) + 斤 (ax) + SEparate Kompletely Into
又	again: (right hand) + Make Another TAke
反	oppose: 厂 (cliff) + 又 (hand) + Has ANtagonism
板	board: 木 (tree) + 反 (oppose) + Hard Admits Nails
田	field: (rice paddy separated by paths) + Domain ENclosed
果	fruit: 田 (field) + 木 (tree) + Konsequent Action
目	eye: (vertical representation of eye and iris) + Means OKUlar
相	aspect: 木 (tree) + 目 (eye) + Shape Of Observation

Day six: character clusters

I   Complete the characters using the clues.

1	乚	Sheet Assigns The SUm (SATSU)
2	木	Kounter Individual (KI)
3	ト	BOldly Kept Uncomplicated (BOKU)
4	木	Zebrawood Actually Into (ZAI)
5	亠	Mark AT SUmmit (MATSU)

II   Compose the compounds using the clues.

1   (CHUU) 注   +   (MOKU) ____   =   _____ (attention)
    concentrate

2   (KAN) 看   +   (BAN) ____   =   _____ (sign)
    watch

3   (HAN) ____   +   (SOKU) 則   =   _____ (violation)
                                  rule

4   (TEN) 天   +   (SAI) ____   =   _____ (genius)
    heaven

5   (JOO) ____   +   (YAKU) 約   =   _____ (treaty)
                                  promise

III   Complete the sentences using the clues.

1   ケーキの＿＿料はありますか。
    Keeki no ZAIryoo wa arimasuka.
    Do you have the ingredients for the cake?

2   先生は数学の問題を分＿＿した。
    Sensei wa suugaku no mondai o bunSEKI shita.
    The teacher analyzed the math problem.

3   テストの結＿＿はとても良かったです。
    Tesuto no kekKA wa totemo yokatta desu.
    The test results were very good.

4   トムは＿＿来のコンピュータに興味があります。
    Tomu wa MIrai no konpyuuta ni kyoomi ga arimasu.
    Tom is interested in computers of the future.

5   私はその件について父と＿＿談する。
    Watashi wa sono ken ni tsuite chichi to SOOdan suru.
    I will consult with my father on that matter.

4

IN PERSON

Day one: crossword puzzle

Across

1. Just INdividual
3. Torso Appears Intrinsic
7. Sword Holding Individual
10. Simple Help Implies
11. Fasten Upon
13. BATter SUddenly
14. Distinct Age Interval
16. Such Ascendant Nature (M)
18. His Original Notes (B)
20. Kreative Interpretation
21. SEclusion Nurtures (H)

Down

2. Kalmly You Unwind Until
4. Thing Alien
5. But UTtered SUtras (B)
6. Grass Yearning Uddered Ungulate
8. Concerns HUman Union (R)
9. Key Event Now (M)
12. Index (R)
15. Center Has Uniform Unit
17. Komplete Alteration
19. Submits HImself

Day two: acrostics

1 Person: J _ _ _   I N _ _ _ _ _ _ _ _

2 Rest: K _ _ _ _ _   Y _ _   U _ _ _ _ _   U _ _ _ _

3 Body: T _ _ _ _   A _ _ _ _ _ _   I _ _ _ _ _ _ _ _

4 Other: T _ _ _ _   A _ _ _ _

5 Buddha: B _ _   U T _ _ _ _ _   S U _ _ _ _

6 Cow: G _ _ _ _   Y _ _ _ _ _ _ _   U _ _ _ _ _ _   U _ _ _ _ _ _ _

7 Samurai: S _ _ _ _   H _ _ _ _ _ _   I _ _ _ _ _ _ _ _

8 Relationship: C _ _ _ _ _ _ _   H U _ _ _   U _ _ _ _

9 Matter: K _ _   E _ _ _ _   N _ _

10 Support: S _ _ _ _ _   H _ _ _   I _ _ _ _ _ _

11 Attach: F _ _ _ _ _   U _ _ _

12 Rank: I _ _ _ _

13 Attack: B A T _ _ _   S U _ _ _ _ _ _

14 Generation: D _ _ _ _ _ _ _   A _ _   I _ _ _ _ _ _ _

15 Middle: C _ _ _ _ _   H _ _   U _ _ _ _ _ _   U _ _ _

16 Mountain: S _ _ _   A _ _ _ _ _ _ _ _   N _ _ _ _ _

17 Change: K _ _ _ _ _ _ _   A _ _ _ _ _ _ _ _

18 Basis: H _ _   O _ _ _ _ _ _   N _ _ _ _

19 Serve: S _ _ _ _ _ _   H I _ _ _ _ _

20 Performance: K _ _ _ _ _ _ _   I _ _ _ _ _ _ _ _ _ _ _ _

21 Hermit: S E _ _ _ _ _ _ _   N _ _ _ _ _ _

Day three: componential analysis

Course Number	Kanji	ON Reading(s) / Core Concept(s)	Primary Components	Kanji Canvas
0064	人	JIN, NIN / person	Side view standing	人
0065	化	KA / change	亻(person)[K16] + 匕(sitting)[K17]	化
0066	仏	BUTSU / Buddha	亻(person)[K16] + 厶 (self)[K18]	仏
0067	士	SHI / samurai	Man standing erect	士
0068	仕	SHI / serve	亻(person)[K16] + 士 (samurai)[67]	仕
0069	付	FU / attach	亻(person)[K16] + 寸 (measure)[11]	付
0070	他	TA / other	亻(person)[K16] + 也 (serpent)[K7]	他
0071	山	SAN / mountain	Three peaks	山
0072	仙	SEN / hermit	亻(person)[K16] + 山 (mountain)[71]	仙
0073	代	DAI / generation; replace	亻(person)[K16] + 弋 (stake)[K19]	代
0074	休	KYUU / rest	亻(person)[K16] + 木 (tree)[43]	休
0075	牛	GYUU / cow, bull, ox	Head of ox	牛
0076	件	KEN / matter	亻(person)[K16] + 牛 (cow)[75]	件
0077	中	CHUU / middle	Center pierced by line	中
0078	仲	CHUU / relationship	亻(person)[K16] + 中 (middle)[77]	仲
0079	支	SHI / support; branch	十 (ten)[06] + 又 (hand)[K15]	支
0080	伎	KI / performance	亻(person)[K16] + 支 (support)[79]	伎
0081	伐	BATSU / attack; cut down	亻(person)[K16] + 戈 (spear)[K20]	伐
0082	位	I / rank	亻(person)[K16] + 立 (stand)[37]	位
0083	本	HON / basis; book	Base of tree	本
0084	体	TAI / body	亻(person)[K16] + 本 (basis)[83]	体

Day four: writing practice

人	化	仏	士	仕	付	他
人	化	仏	士	仕	付	他

山	仙	代	休	牛	件	中
山	仙	代	休	牛	件	中

仲	支	伎	伐	位	本	体
仲	支	伎	伐	位	本	体

Day five: story sketch

人	person: (side view standing) + Just INdividual
化	change: 亻 (person) + 匕 (sitting) + Komplete Alteration
仏	Buddha: 亻 (person) + ム (self) + But UTtered SUtras
士	samurai: (man standing erect) + Sword Holding Individual
仕	serve: 亻 (person) + 士 (samurai) + Submits HImself
付	attach: 亻 (person) + 寸 (measure) + Fasten Upon
他	other: 亻 (person) + 也 (serpent) + Thing Alien
山	mountain: (three peaks) + Such Ascendant Nature
仙	hermit: 亻 (person) + 山 (mountain) + SEclusion Nurtures
代	generation: 亻 (person) + 弋 (stake) + Distinct Age Interval
休	rest: 亻 (person) + 木 (tree) + Kalmly You Unwind Until
牛	cow: (head of ox) + Grass Yearning Uddered Ungulate
件	matter: 亻 (person) + 牛 (cow) + Key Event Now
中	middle: (center pierced by line) + Center Has Uniform Unit
仲	relationship: 亻 (person) + 中 (middle) + Concerns HUman Union
支	support: 十 (ten) + 又 (hand) + Simple Help Implies
伎	performance: 亻 (person) + 支 (support) + Kreative Interpretation
伐	attack: 亻 (person) + 戈 (spear) + BATter SUddenly
位	rank: 亻 (person) + 立 (stand) + Index
本	basis: (base of tree) + His Original Notes
体	body: 亻 (person) + 本 (basis) + Torso Appears Intrinsic

Day six: character clusters

I   Complete the characters using the clues.

1	イ	But UTtered SUtras (BUTSU)
2	也	Thing Alien (TA)
3	中	Concerns HUman Union (CHUU)
4	イ	BATter SUddenly (BATSU)
5	支	Kreative Interpretation (KI)

II   Compose the compounds using the clues.

1   (MI) 見   +   (HON) _____   =   _____ (sample)
    see

2   (KA) _____   +   (SEKI) 石   =   _____ (fossil)
                             stone

3   (JI) 時   +   (DAI) _____   =   _____ (age, period)
    time

4   (GYUU) _____   +   (NIKU) 肉   =   _____ (beef)
                             meat

5   (KA) 火   +   (ZAN) _____   =   _____ (volcano)
    fire

III   Complete the sentences using the clues.

1   この___事は大変ですよ。
    Kono SHIgoto wa taihen desu yo.
    This work is very difficult.

2   その店は町の___心にある。
    Sono mise wa machi no CHUUshin ni aru.
    That store is in the center of town.

3   ___重はどのぐらいありますか。
    TAIjuu wa dono gurai arimasu ka.
    About how much do you weigh?

4   みんなその意見を___持します。
    Minna sono iken o SHIji shimasu.
    Everyone supports that idea.

5   うちの___近にはスーパーがありません。
    Uchi no FUkin ni wa suupaa ga arimasen.
    There is no supermarket in my neighborhood.

5

SOUTHPAW

Day one: crossword puzzle

Across

1. KOmpletely Oppose (R)
4. KOmprehensive Opening (W)
6. Kolossal Your Obstacle
8. FUnd The SUm
9. Selection Has One Objective
11. Father Unadulterated
14. KArefully Kan Unfold
15. SEparate The SUbstance (B)
16. HAnds Kollide Unified
17. Further Underpin
18. Step Expect To Stumble Upon
19. Keenly You Object (R)
21. Correct HOld On (E)

Down

2. SHoot Up Through SUrface
3. Deliberate Attack
5. SHake Usually
7. Contort Hand Until Uprooted
10. TOss Out
12. TAKe Unmistakably (S)
13. Movement Across Transforms SUrface (E)
20. Given Ingenuity

Day two: acrostics

1 Resist: K O _ _ _ _ _ _ _ _   O _ _ _ _ _

2 Emerge: S H _ _ _   U _   T _ _ _ _ _ _   S U _ _ _ _ _

3 Strike: D _ _ _ _ _ _ _ _ _   A _ _ _ _ _

4 Wide: K O _ _ _ _ _ _ _ _ _ _   O _ _ _ _ _ _

5 Hand: S H _ _ _   U _ _ _ _ _ _

6 Huge: K _ _ _ _ _ _ _   Y _ _ _   O _ _ _ _ _ _ _

7 Extract: C _ _ _ _ _ _   H _ _ _   U _ _ _ _   U _ _ _ _ _ _ _

8 Pay: F U _ _   T _ _   S U _

9 Excerpt: S _ _ _ _ _ _ _ _   H _ _   O _ _   O _ _ _ _ _ _ _

10 Throw: T O _ _   O _ _

11 Husband: F _ _ _ _ _ _   U _ _ _ _ _ _ _ _ _ _ _

12 Select: T A K _   U _ _ _ _ _ _ _ _ _ _

13 Erase: M _ _ _ _ _ _ _   A _ _ _ _ _   T _ _ _ _ _ _ _ _ _   S U _ _ _ _ _

14 Spread: K A _ _ _ _ _ _ _   K _ _   U _ _ _ _ _

15 Break: S E _ _ _ _ _ _   T _ _   S U _ _ _ _ _ _ _

16 Clap: H A _ _ _   K _ _ _ _ _ _   U _ _ _ _ _ _

17 Support: F _ _ _ _ _ _   U _ _ _ _ _ _ _

18 Clumsy: S _ _ _   E _ _ _ _ _   T _   S _ _ _ _ _ _   U _ _ _

19 Refuse: K _ _ _ _ _   Y _ _   O _ _ _ _ _

20 Skill: G _ _ _ _ _   I _ _ _ _ _ _ _ _

21 Exact: C _ _ _ _ _ _   H O _ _   O _

Day three: componential analysis

Course Number	Kanji	ON Reading(s) / Core Concept(s)	Primary Components	Kanji Canvas
0085	手	SHU / **hand**	Hand spread open	手
0086	払	FUTSU / **pay; clear away**	扌 (hand)[K21] + ム (self)[K18]	払
0087	丁	CHOO / **exact; block**	Intersection	丁
0088	打	DA / **strike**	扌 (hand)[K21] + 丁 (exact)[87]	打
0089	技	GI / **skill**	扌 (hand)[K21] + 支 (support)[79]	技
0090	折	SETSU / **break; bend, fold**	扌 (hand)[K21] + 斤 (ax)[55]	折
0091	択	TAKU / **select**	扌 (hand)[K21] + 尺 (measure)[12]	択
0092	抗	KOO / **resist**	扌 (hand)[K21] + 亢 (straight)[K22]	抗
0093	抄	SHOO / **excerpt**	扌 (hand)[K21] + 少 (little)[32]	抄
0094	夫	FU, FUU / **husband, man**	Person with large hairpins	夫
0095	扶	FU / **support**	扌 (hand)[K21] + 夫 (husband)[94]	扶
0096	投	TOO / **throw**	扌 (hand)[K21] + 殳 (club)[K23]	投
0097	出	SHUTSU / **emerge**	山 (mountain)[71] + 山 (mountain)[71]	出
0098	拙	SETSU / **clumsy**	扌 (hand)[K21] + 出 (emerge)[97]	拙
0099	巨	KYO / **huge**	Large pupil	巨
0100	拒	KYO / **refuse**	扌 (hand)[K21] + 巨 (huge)[99]	拒
0101	広	KOO / **wide**	广 (building)[K24] + ム (self)[K18]	広
0102	拡	KAKU / **spread**	扌 (hand)[K21] + 広 (wide)[101]	拡
0103	拍	HAKU, HYOO / **clap; beat**	扌 (hand)[K21] + 白 (white)[18]	拍
0104	抽	CHUU / **extract**	扌 (hand)[K21] + 由 (reason)[39]	抽
0105	抹	MATSU / **erase**	扌 (hand)[K21] + 末 (end)[45]	抹

Day four: writing practice

手	払	丁	打	技	折	択
手	払	丁	打	技	折	択
抗	抄	夫	扶	投	出	拙
抗	抄	夫	扶	投	出	拙
巨	拒	広	拡	拍	抽	抹
巨	拒	広	拡	拍	抽	抹

Day five: story sketch

手	hand: (hand spread open) + SHake Usually
払	pay: 扌 (hand) + ム (self) + FUnd The SUm
丁	exact: (intersection) + Correct HOld On
打	strike: 扌 (hand) + 丁 (exact) + Deliberate Attack
技	skill: 扌 (hand) + 支 (support) + Given Ingenuity
折	break: 扌 (hand) + 斤 (ax) + SEparate The SUbstance
択	select: 扌 (hand) + 尺 (measure) + TAKe Unmistakably
抗	resist: 扌 (hand) + 亢 (straight) + KOmpletely Oppose
抄	excerpt: 扌 (hand) + 少 (little) + Selection Has One Objective
夫	husband: (person with large hairpins) + Father Unadulterated
扶	support: 扌 (hand) + 夫 (husband) + Further Underpin
投	throw: 扌 (hand) + 殳 (club) + TOss Out
出	emerge: 山 (mountain) + 山 (mountain) + SHoot Up Through SUrface
拙	clumsy: 扌 (hand) + 出 (emerge) + Step Expect To Stumble Upon
巨	huge: (large pupil) + Kolossal Your Obstacle
拒	refuse: 扌 (hand) + 巨 (huge) + Keenly You Object
広	wide: 广 (building) + ム (self) + KOmprehensive Opening
拡	spread: 扌 (hand) + 広 (wide) + KArefully Kan Unfold
拍	clap: 扌 (hand) + 白 (white) + HAnds Kollide Unified
抽	extract: 扌 (hand) + 由 (reason) + Contort Hand Until Uprooted
抹	erase: 扌 (hand) + 末 (end) + Movement Across Transforms SUrface

Day six: character clusters

I   Complete the characters using the clues.

1	ム	FUnd The SUm (FUTSU)
2	扌	Contort Hand Until Uprooted (CHUU)
3	少	Selection Has One Objective (SHOO)
4	扌	HAnds Kollide Unified (HAKU)
5	末	Movement Across Transforms SUrface (MATSU)

II   Compose the compounds using the clues.

1   (GAI) 外   +   (SHUTSU) ____   =   _____ (go out)
       outside

2   (KYO) ____   +   (JIN) 人   =   _____ (giant)
                          person

3   (GI) ____   +   (SHI) 師   =   _____ (engineer)
                          teacher

4   (HAN) 反   +   (KOO) ____   =   _____ (resistance)
       oppose

5   (KAKU) ____   +   (DAI) 大   =   _____ (expansion)
                          big

III   Complete the sentences using the clues.

1   バスは六時＿＿度に着きます。
    Basu wa roku-ji CHOOdo ni tsukimasu.
    The bus arrives at exactly six o'clock.

2   あしたはサムが一番＿＿者です。
    Ashita wa samu ga ichiban DAsha desu.
    Tomorrow Sam will be the leadoff hitter.

3   この件について選＿＿の自由はない。
    Kono ken ni tsuite senTAKU no jiyuu wa nai.
    There is no choice in this matter.

4   私もジャックに＿＿票しました。
    Watashi mo jakku ni TOOhyoo shimashita.
    I also voted for Jack.

5   その店はテレビに＿＿告を出した。
    Sono mise wa terebi ni KOOkoku o dashita.
    That store advertised on television.

REVIEW: LESSONS 1–5

I   Given the character and meaning, write the pronunciation.

1 七 seven _____   2 池 pond _____   3 林 forest _____

4 中 middle _____   5 投 throw _____   6 白 white _____

7 小 small _____   8 杉 cedar _____   9 牛 cow _____

10 払 pay _____   11 九 nine _____   12 汽 steam _____

13 斤 ax _____   14 伐 attack _____   15 技 skill _____

16 兆 sign _____   17 沢 marsh _____   18 八 eight _____

19 他 other _____   20 巨 huge _____   21 六 six _____

22 沙 sand _____   23 札 bill _____   24 仕 serve _____

25 折 break _____   26 末 end _____   27 一 one _____

28 油 oil _____   29 田 field _____   30 相 aspect _____

II   Given the character and pronunciation, write the meaning.

1 寸 SUN _____   2 氾 HAN _____   3 板 HAN _____

4 仙 SEN _____   5 拙 SETSU _____   6 四 SHI _____

7 氷 HYOO _____   8 才 SAI _____   9 仲 CHUU _____

10 拡 KAKU _____   11 斗 TO _____   12 由 YUU _____

13 机 KI _____   14 山 SAN _____   15 扶 FU _____

16 升 SHOO _____   17 干 KAN _____   18 朴 BOKU _____

19 士 SHI _____   20 打 DA _____   21 永 EI _____

22 伎 KI _____   23 抄 SHOO _____   24 泊 HAKU _____

25 立 RITSU _____   26 尺 SHAKU _____   27 工 KOO _____

28 夫 FU _____   29 位 I _____   30 人 JIN _____

III Given the meaning and pronunciation, write the character.

1 three	SAN	_____		2 sweat	KAN		_____
3 not yet	MI	_____		4 basis	HON		_____
5 select	TAKU	_____		6 inlet	KOO		_____
7 village	SON	_____		8 change	KA		_____
9 thousand	SEN	_____		10 exact	CHOO		_____
11 little	SHOO	_____		12 divide	SEKI		_____
13 Buddha	BUTSU	_____		14 refuse	KYO		_____
15 cry	KYUU	_____		16 again	mata		_____
17 extract	CHUU	_____		18 eye	MOKU		_____
19 wide	KOO	_____		20 five	GO		_____
21 swim	EI	_____		22 oppose	HAN		_____
23 attach	FU	_____		24 erase	MATSU		_____
25 two	NI	_____					

IV Compose compounds using the following characters.

出 百 件 代 手 万 果 汁 木 日 支 抗 材 体 十 水 条 力 休 拍

1 (SUI) _____   +   (RYOKU) _____   =   _____ (waterpower)

2 (HYAKU) _____   +   (MAN) _____   =   _____ (million)

3 (KA) _____   +   (JUU) _____   =   _____ (juice)

4 (ZAI) _____   +   (MOKU) _____   =   _____ (lumber)

5 (JOO) _____   +   (KEN) _____   =   _____ (condition)

6 (JUU) _____   +   (DAI) _____   =   _____ (teens)

7 (KYUU) _____   +   (JITSU) _____   =   _____ (holiday)

8 (SHI) _____   +   (SHUTSU) _____   =   _____ (expenditure)

9 (KOO) _____   +   (TAI) _____   =   _____ (antibody)

10 (HAKU) _____   +   (SHU) _____   =   _____ (applause)

6

WATCH ONE'S MOUTH

Day one: crossword puzzle

Across

1. Handmade Imports Normally
5. KOnfront One
7. Space ENsconced (O)
9. Most Enunciated Identity
15. Kindred Earlier Influence (two words: O/B)
17. Kount Amount
18. Duplicate Of One
19. GO On (F)
20. Upstanding
21. Klausal Unit

Down

2. Klassic Oration
3. SHOut Order
4. Mouth Intimate (T)
6. Say Harshly IT'S Unpleasant
8. DAIs
10. Keep Open Ordinarily
11. Given Ordinal Order (N)
12. Thrust Out Object (S)
13. Sun Exits Krescent Intense
14. KAn (P)
16. Kount All KUps

Day two: acrostics

1 Goods: H _ _ _ _ _ _ _   I _ _ _ _ _ _   N _ _ _ _ _ _ _

2 Old: K _ _ _ _ _ _   O _ _ _ _ _ _

3 Summon: S H O _ _   O _ _ _ _

4 Taste: M _ _ _ _   I _ _ _ _ _ _ _

5 Face: K O _ _ _ _ _ _   O _ _

6 Scold: S _ _   H _ _ _ _ _ _   I T ' S   U _ _ _ _ _ _ _ _

7 Occupy: S _ _ _ _   E N _ _ _ _ _ _ _

8 Platform: D A I _

9 Name: M _ _ _   E _ _ _ _ _ _ _ _   I _ _ _ _ _ _

10 Mouth: K _ _ _   O _ _ _   O _ _ _ _ _ _ _ _

11 Number: G _ _ _ _   O _ _ _ _ _ _   O _ _ _ _

12 Sword: T _ _ _ _ _   O _ _   O _ _ _ _ _

13 Evening: S _ _   E _ _ _ _   K _ _ _ _ _ _ _   I _ _ _ _ _ _

14 Possible: K A _

15 Older Brother: K _ _ _ _ _ _   E _ _ _ _ _ _   I _ _ _ _ _ _ _ _

16 Each: K _ _ _ _   A _ _   K U _ _

17 Add: K _ _ _ _   A _ _ _ _ _

18 Same: D _ _ _ _ _ _ _ _   O _   O _ _

19 Fit: G O   O _

20 Right: U _ _ _ _ _ _ _ _

21 Phrase: K _ _ _ _ _ _   U _ _ _

Day three: componential analysis

Course Number	Kanji	ON Reading(s) / Core Concept(s)	Primary Components	Kanji Canvas
0106	口	KOO **mouth; open**	Open mouth	口
0107	右	U, YUU **right**	手 (*hand*)[85] + 口 (mouth)[106]	右
0108	古	KO **old**	十 (ten)[06] + 口 (mouth)[106]	古
0109	可	KA **possible**	丁 (*exact*)[87] + 口 (mouth)[106]	可
0110	句	KU **phrase**	勹 (wrap)[K25] + 口 (mouth)[106]	句
0111	加	KA **add; join**	力 (power)[07] + 口 (mouth)[106]	加
0112	占	SEN **occupy**	卜 (divination)[K10] + 口 (mouth)[106]	占
0113	叱	SHITSU **scold**	口 (mouth)[106] + ヒ (sitting)[K17]	叱
0114	台	DAI, TAI **platform, stand**	ム (self)[K18] + 口 (mouth)[106]	台
0115	刀	TOO **sword, knife**	Sharp blade	刀
0116	召	SHOO **summon**	刀 (sword)[115] + 口 (mouth)[106]	召
0117	兄	KEI **older brother**	口 (mouth)[106] + 儿 (boy)[K5]	兄
0118	合	GOO, GAT, KAT **fit, combine**	𠆢 (cover)[K26] + 一 (one)[01] + 口 (mouth)[106]	合
0119	同	DOO **same**	冂 (border)[K27] + 一 (one)[01] + 口 (mouth)[106]	同
0120	向	KOO **face**	丿 (accent)[K2] + 冂 (border)[K27] + 口 (mouth)[106]	向
0121	号	GOO **number; sign**	口 (mouth)[106] + 丂 (emerge)[K28]	号
0122	各	KAKU **each, every**	夂 (step)[K13] + 口 (mouth)[106]	各
0123	夕	SEKI **evening**	Crescent moon	夕
0124	名	MEI **name**	夕 (evening)[123] + 口 (mouth)[106]	名
0125	味	MI **taste**	口 (mouth)[106] + 未 (not yet)[44]	味
0126	品	HIN **goods; quality**	口 (three mouths)[106]	品

Day four: writing practice

口	右	古	可	句	加	占
口	右	古	可	句	加	占
叱	台	刀	召	兄	合	同
叱	台	刀	召	兄	合	同
向	号	各	夕	名	味	品
向	号	各	夕	名	味	品

Day five: story sketch

口	mouth: (open mouth) + Keep Open Ordinarily
右	right: 手 (*hand*) + 口 (mouth) + Upstanding
古	old: 十 (ten) + 口 (mouth) + Klassic Oration
可	possible: 丁 (*exact*) + 口 (mouth) + KAn
句	phrase: 勹 (wrap) + 口 (mouth) + Klausal Unit
加	add: 力 (power) + 口 (mouth) + Kount Amount
占	occupy: 卜 (divination) + 口 (mouth) + Space ENsconced
叱	scold: 口 (mouth) + 匕 (sitting) + Say Harshly IT'S Unpleasant
台	platform: 厶 (self) + 口 (mouth) + DAIs
刀	sword: (sharp blade) + Thrust Out Object
召	summon: 刀 (sword) + 口 (mouth) + SHOut Order
兄	older brother: 口 (mouth) + 儿 (boy) + Kindred Earlier Influence
合	fit: 𠆢 (cover) + 一 (one) + 口 (mouth) + GO On
同	same: 冂 (border) + 一 (one) + 口 (mouth) + Duplicate Of One
向	face: ノ (accent) + 冂 (border) + 口 (mouth) + KOnfront One
号	number: 口 (mouth) + 丂 (emerge) + Given Ordinal Order
各	each: 夂 (step) + 口 (mouth) + Kount All KUps
夕	evening: (crescent moon) + Sun Exits Krescent Intense
名	name: 夕 (evening) + 口 (mouth) + Most Enunciated Identity
味	taste: 口 (mouth) + 未 (not yet) + Mouth Intimate
品	goods: 口 (three mouths) + Handmade Imports Normally

Day six: character clusters

I Complete the characters using the clues.

1	口	Say Harshly IT'S Unpleasant (SHITSU)
2	儿	Kindred Earlier Influence (KEI)
3	未	Mouth Intimate (MI)
4	冂	KOnfront One (KOO)
5	口	SHOut Order (SHOO)

II Compose the compounds using the clues.

1 (GOO) ____ + (KAKU) 格 = _____ (passing)
                    standard

2 (KO) ____ + (DAI) 代 = _____ (antiquity)
                  generation

3 (KYOO) 共 + (DOO) ____ = _____ (collaboration)
   together

2 (KA) ____ + (KOO) 工 = _____ (processing)
                  work

5 (TAI) ____ + (FUU) 風 = _____ (typhoon)
                  wind

III Complete the sentences using the clues.

1 日本の人___はどのくらいですか。
  Nihon no jinKOO wa dono kurai desu ka.
  What is the population of Japan?

2 そのビルへ入る許___をもらっている。
  Sono biru e hairu kyoKA o moratte iru.
  I have permission to enter that building.

3 ヤングさんの電話番___を教えてください。
  Yangu-san no denwa banGOO o oshiete kudasai.
  Please tell me Mr. Young's telephone number.

4 あゆみは上___なドレスを着ています。
  Ayumi wa jooHIN na doresu o kite imasu.
  Ayumi is wearing an elegant dress.

5 京都は古い寺で有___です。
  Kyooto wa furui tera de yuuMEI desu.
  Kyoto is famous for its old temples.

7

HEART TO HEART

Day one: crossword puzzle

Across

3. SExual Instinct (N)
5. KONtemporary
7. Just Individual
10. Be Overly Occupied
12. Have IT SUrely (I)
15. Kharacter Own
16. Bring On Oblivion
18. Section Hidden INside
19. BOrn Obverse
21. Notion ENtails

Down

1. Just Inflicts Nicks (B)
2. KOntinually Occuring (C)
4. Never INdulge
6. Sink Head Into (T)
8. Sentient Existence Is
9. Orally Oppose (R)
11. Sweet Home INside
13. Commit Heart Utterly Upright
14. Single Oxygen KUrrent
17. Kontempt Intense (A)
20. Signifies Heart's Intent

Day two: acrostics

1 Blade: J _ _ _   I _ _ _ _ _ _ _   N _ _ _ _

2 Constant: K O _ _ _ _ _ _ _ _   O _ _ _ _ _ _

3 Nature: S E _ _ _ _   I _ _ _ _ _ _ _

4 Endure: N _ _ _ _   I N _ _ _ _ _

5 Now: K O N _ _ _ _ _ _ _ _

6 Think: S _ _ _   H _ _ _   I _ _ _

7 Self: J _ _ _   I _ _ _ _ _ _ _ _

8 Life: S _ _ _ _ _ _ _   E _ _ _ _ _ _ _ _   I _

9 Respond: O _ _ _ _ _   O _ _ _ _ _

10 Busy: B _   O _ _ _ _ _   O _ _ _ _ _ _

11 Heart: S _ _ _ _   H _ _ _   I N _ _ _ _

12 Inevitably: H _ _ _   I T   S U _ _ _ _

13 Loyalty: C _ _ _ _ _   H _ _ _ _   U _ _ _ _ _ _   U _ _ _ _ _ _

14 Breath: S _ _ _ _ _   O _ _ _ _ _   K U _ _ _ _ _

15 Self: K _ _ _ _ _ _ _ _   O _ _

16 Forget: B _ _ _ _   O _   O _ _ _ _ _ _ _

17 Abhor: K _ _ _ _ _ _ _   I _ _ _ _ _

18 Core: S _ _ _ _ _ _   H _ _ _ _ _   I N _ _ _ _

19 Dead: B O _ _   O _ _ _ _ _

20 Aim: S _ _ _ _ _ _ _ _   H _ _ _ _ _   I _ _ _ _ _

21 Thought: N _ _ _ _ _   E N _ _ _ _ _

Day three: componential analysis

Course Number	Kanji	ON Reading(s) / Core Concept(s)	Primary Components	Kanji Canvas
0127	心	SHIN / **heart**	Beating vibrations	心
0128	必	HITSU / **inevitably**	心 (heart)[127] + *overemphasis*	必
0129	応	OO / **respond**	广 (building)[K24] + 心 (heart)[127]	応
0130	志	SHI / **aim**	士 (samurai)[67] + 心 (heart)[127]	志
0131	芯	SHIN / **core**	⺾ (plants)[K29] + 心 (heart)[127]	芯
0132	己	KO, KI / **self**	Finger pointing at face	己
0133	忌	KI / **abhor; mourning**	己 (self)[132] + 心 (heart)[127]	忌
0134	亡	BOO / **dead, die**	亠 (lid)[K1] + ∟ (corner)[K30]	亡
0135	忘	BOO / **forget**	亡 (dead)[134] + 心 (heart)[127]	忘
0136	忙	BOO / **busy**	⺖ (heart)[K31] + 亡 (die)[134]	忙
0137	刃	JIN / **blade**	Edge of sword	刃
0138	忍	NIN / **endure; stealth**	刃 (blade)[137] + 心 (heart)[127]	忍
0139	今	KON / **now**	𠆢 (cover)[K26] + 一 (one)[01] + 乛 (*corner*)[K30]	今
0140	念	NEN / **thought**	今 (now)[139] + 心 (heart)[127]	念
0141	忠	CHUU / **loyalty**	中 (middle)[77] + 心 (heart)[127]	忠
0142	生	SEI / **life; birth**	Growing plant	生
0143	性	SEI, SHOO / **nature; sex**	⺖ (heart)[K31] + 生 (life)[142]	性
0144	思	SHI / **think**	田 (field)[60] + 心 (heart)[127]	思
0145	恒	KOO / **constant**	⺖ (heart)[K31] + 二 (two)[02] + 日 (day)[17]	恒
0146	自	JI / **self**	Nose	自
0147	息	SOKU / **breath**	自 (self)[146] + 心 (heart)[127]	息

Day four: writing practice

心	必	应	志	芯	己	忌
心	必	应	志	芯	己	忌

亡	忘	忙	刃	忍	今	念
亡	忘	忙	刃	忍	今	念

忠	生	性	思	恒	自	息
忠	生	性	思	恒	自	息

Day five: story sketch

心	heart: (beating vibrations) + Sweet Home INside
必	inevitably: 心 (heart) + *overemphasis* + Have IT SUrely
応	respond: 广 (building) + 心 (heart) + Orally Oppose
志	aim: 士 (samurai) + 心 (heart) + Signifies Heart's Intent
芯	core: 艹 (plants) + 心 (heart) + Section Hidden INside
己	self: (finger pointing at face) + Kharacter Own
忌	abhor: 己 (self) + 心 (heart) + Kontempt Intense
亡	dead: 亠 (lid) + └ (corner) + BOrn Obverse
忘	forget: 亡 (dead) + 心 (heart) + Bring On Oblivion
忙	busy: 忄 (heart) + 亡 (die) + Be Overly Occupied
刃	blade: (edge of sword) + Just Inflicts Nicks
忍	endure: 刃 (blade) + 心 (heart) + Never INdulge
今	now: 𠆢 (cover) + 一 (one) + 𠃌 (*corner*) + KONtemporary
念	thought: 今 (now) + 心 (heart) + Notion ENtails
忠	loyalty: 中 (middle) + 心 (heart) + Commit Heart Utterly Upright
生	life: (growing plant) + Sentient Existence Is
性	nature: 忄 (heart) + 生 (life) + SExual Instinct
思	think: 田 (field) + 心 (heart) + Sink Head Into
恒	constant: 忄 (heart) + 二 (two) + 日 (day) + KOntinually Occuring
自	self: (nose) + Just Individual
息	breath: 自 (self) + 心 (heart) + Single Oxygen KUrrent

Day six: character clusters

I   Complete the characters using the clues.

1	艹	Section Hidden INside (SHIN)
2	忄	SExual Instinct (SEI)
3	白	Single Oxygen KUrrent (SOKU)
4	日	KOntinually Occuring (KOO)
5	亡	Be Overly Occupied (BOO)

II   Compose the compounds using the clues.

1   (KI) 記   +   (NEN) ____   =   _____ (remembrance)
    record

2   (HITSU) ____   +   (YOO) 要   =   _____ (need)
                                necessary

3   (CHUU) ____   +   (KOKU) 告   =   _____ (advice)
                                inform

4   (AN) 安   +   (SHIN) ____   =   _____ (relief)
    peaceful

5   (SHI) ____   +   (KOO) 向   =   _____ (orientation)
                                face

III   Complete the sentences using the clues.

1   白い肌は日光に反＿＿する。
    Shiroi hada wa nikkoo ni hannOO suru.
    Fair skin reacts to the sunlight.

2   ＿＿夜は月がとてもきれいです。
    KONya wa tsuki ga totemo kirei desu.
    The moon is very beautiful tonight.

3   ニューヨークの日常＿＿活は面白いですか。
    Nyuuyooku no nichijoo SEIkatsu wa omoshiroi desu ka.
    Is everyday life in New York interesting?

4   部屋を＿＿分で掃除してください。
    Heya o JIbun de sooji shite kudasai.
    Please clean the room yourself.

5   災害で百人が死＿＿した。
    Saigai de hyaku-nin ga shiBOO shita.
    One hundred people died in the disaster.

8
SUNSHINE

Day one: crossword puzzle

Across
2. Standard Human Attribute
4. Zero Errors
5. Orders Others
6. Surely Halt Individual
10. Bravely Overcome Odds (R)
12. Sky Evening Illuminator
13. Set Exactly Into
15. Obvious Opulence (F)
17. TOward Orient
19. SHines Off Of (C)
20. Globe Eclipses The SUn
21. Twinkles After Nighttime

Down
1. Moon Emits Illumination (B)
3. Envision Koming Incidents (D)
7. Mostly Ambiguous Image
8. Sun HOrizon Over
9. Something Has Importance
11. KOmforting Odor (F)
14. SHine Often On
16. SOOn (E)
18. One Noise

Day two: acrostics

1 Bright: M _ _ _   E _ _ _ _   I _ _ _ _ _ _ _ _ _

2 Person: S _ _ _ _ _ _ _   H _ _ _ _   A _ _ _ _ _ _ _

3 Divination: E _ _ _ _ _ _ _   K _ _ _ _ _   I _ _ _ _ _ _ _

4 Right: Z _ _ _   E _ _ _ _ _

5 King: O _ _ _ _ _   O _ _ _ _ _

6 Stop: S _ _ _ _ _   H _ _ _   I _ _ _ _ _ _ _ _

7 Obscure: M _ _ _ _ _   A _ _ _ _ _ _ _ _   I _ _ _ _

8 Rise: S _ _   H O _ _ _ _ _   O _ _ _

9 Purport: S _ _ _ _ _ _ _ _   H _ _   I _ _ _ _ _ _ _ _

10 Risk: B _ _ _ _ _ _   O _ _ _ _ _ _ _   O _ _ _

11 Fragrance: K O _ _ _ _ _ _ _ _   O _ _ _

12 Star: S _ _   E _ _ _ _ _ _   I _ _ _ _ _ _ _ _ _

13 Correct: S _ _   E _ _ _ _ _ _   I _ _ _

14 Bright: S H _ _ _   O _ _ _ _   O _

15 Flourishing: O _ _ _ _ _ _   O _ _ _ _ _ _ _

16 Early: S O O _

17 East: T O _ _ _ _   O _ _ _ _ _

18 Sound: O _ _   N _ _ _ _

19 Crystal: S H _ _ _ _   O _ _   O _

20 Moon: G _ _ _ _   E _ _ _ _ _ _ _   T _ _   S U _

21 Dawn: T _ _ _ _ _ _ _   A _ _ _ _   N _ _ _ _ _ _ _

Day three: componential analysis

Course Number	Kanji	ON Reading(s) / Core Concept(s)	Primary Components	Kanji Canvas
0148	旦	TAN / **dawn**	日 (sun)[17] + 一 (one)[01]	旦
0149	早	SOO / **early**	日 sun[17] + 十 (ten)[06]	早
0150	旨	SHI / **purport, gist**	匕 (sitting)[K17] + 日 (sun)[17]	旨
0151	昇	SHOO / **rise**	日 (sun)[17] + 升 (measure)[16]	昇
0152	者	SHA / **person**	耂 (old man)[K32] + 日 (sun)[17]	者
0153	月	GETSU, GATSU / **moon; month**	Crescent moon	月
0154	明	MEI / **bright**	日 (sun)[17] + 月 (moon)[153]	明
0155	王	OO / **king**	Crown	王
0156	旺	OO / **flourishing**	日 (sun)[17] + 王 (king)[155]	旺
0157	東	TOO / **east**	日 (sun)[17] + 木 (tree)[43]	東
0158	易	EKI, I / **divination; easy**	日 (sun)[17] + *knives* (cf. 1573)	易
0159	音	ON / **sound**	立 (stand)[37] + 日 (sun)[17]	音
0160	昭	SHOO / **bright**	日 (sun)[17] + 召 (summon)[116]	昭
0161	冒	BOO / **risk**	日 (sun)[17] + 目 (eye)[62]	冒
0162	星	SEI / **star**	日 (sun)[17] + 生 (life)[142]	星
0163	香	KOO / **fragrance**	禾 (grain)[K33] + 日 (sun)[17]	香
0164	昧	MAI / **obscure**	日 (sun)[17] + 未 (not yet)[44]	昧
0165	止	SHI / **stop**	Someone standing before barrier	止
0166	正	SEI / **correct**	一 (one)[01] + 止 (stop)[165]	正
0167	是	ZE / **right, correct**	日 (sun)[17] + 正 (correct)[166]	是
0168	晶	SHOO / **crystal**	日 (three suns)[17]	晶

Day four: writing practice

旦	早	旨	昇	者	月	明
旦	早	旨	昇	者	月	明
王	旺	東	易	音	昭	冒
王	旺	東	易	音	昭	冒
星	香	味	止	正	是	晶
星	香	味	止	正	是	晶

Day five: story sketch

旦	dawn: 日 (sun) + 一 (one) + Twinkles After Nighttime
早	early: 日 (sun) + 十 (ten) + SOOn
旨	purport: 匕 (sitting) + 日 (sun) + Something Has Importance
昇	rise: 日 (sun) + 升 (measure) + Sun HOrizon Over
者	person: 耂 (old man) + 日 (sun) + Standard Human Attribute
月	moon: (crescent moon) + Globe Eclipses The SUn
明	bright: 日 (sun) + 月 (moon) + Moon Emits Illumination
王	king: (crown) + Orders Others
旺	flourishing: 日 (sun) + 王 (king) + Obvious Opulence
東	east: 日 (sun) + 木 (tree) + TOward Orient
易	divination: 日 (sun) + *knives* + Envision Koming Incidents
音	sound: 立 (stand) + 日 (sun) + One Noise
昭	bright: 日 (sun) + 召 (summon) + SHine Often On
冒	risk: 日 (sun) + 目 (eye) + Bravely Overcome Odds
星	star: 日 (sun) + 生 (life) + Sky Evening Illuminator
香	fragrance: 禾 (grain) + 日 (sun) + KOmforting Odor
昧	obscure: 日 (sun) + 未 (not yet) + Mostly Ambiguous Image
止	stop: (someone standing before barrier) + Surely Halt Individual
正	correct: 一 (one) + 止 (stop) + Set Exactly Into
是	right: 日 (sun) + 正 (correct) + Zero Errors
晶	crystal: 日 (three suns) + SHines Off Of

Day six: character clusters

I   Complete the characters using the clues.

1	日	Zero Errors (ZE)
2	未	Mostly Ambiguous Image (MAI)
3	目	Bravely Overcome Odds (BOO)
4	日	SHine Often On (SHOO)
5	日	Something Has Importance (SHI)

II   Compose the compounds using the clues.

1   (KOO) 公   +   (SEI) ____   =   _____ (fairness)
      public

2   (JO) 女   +   (OO) ____   =   _____ (queen)
      woman

3   (KOO) ____   +   (SUI) 水   =   _____ (perfume)
                         water

4   (I) 医   +   (SHA) ____   =   _____ (doctor)
      medicine

5   (SEI) ____   +   (ZA) 座   =   _____ (constellation)
                               seat

III   Complete the sentences using the clues.

1   去年ガソリンの値段が上___した。
     Kyonen gasorin no nedan ga jooSHOO shita.
     Last year the price of gasoline went up.

2   なぜ遅れたのか説___しなさい。
     Naze okureta no ka setsuMEI shinasai.
     Explain why you were late.

3   ___末までにはパリから帰ってきます。
     GETSUmatsu made ni wa pari kara kaette kimasu.
     I will return from Paris by the end of the month.

4   この単語の発___は難しいです。
     Kono tango no hatsuON wa muzukashii desu.
     The pronunciation of this word is difficult.

5   先週の会議は中___になりました。
     Senshuu no kaigi wa chuuSHI ni narimashita.
     Last week's meeting was called off.

9

DOWN TO EARTH

Day one: crossword puzzle

Across

3. Fasten Ultimate Union
8. Have One Orientation
9. Brother Oversees Order (P)
11. Sides Hugged Until Uniform
12. Kind Equal Individuals
14. KOal Outlet
17. Just Indicate
18. Sprint On Over
20. Zone All Inhabit
21. Jewish Institute

Down

1. SHared Alliance (A)
2. Bring Acres Increase (C)
4. Soon Here Indeed
5. KEep Incarcerated (P)
6. KOntentment Obvious
7. Rural Inhabitation (V)
10. Affects Tense SUrface (P)
13. Japanese Occupy Openly (P)
15. Domestic Orb
16. Hill ANgular
19. Shaft Enters Into

Day two: acrostics

1   Association: S H _ _ _ _   A _ _ _ _ _ _ _

2   Cultivate: B _ _ _ _   A _ _ _ _   I _ _ _ _ _ _ _

3   Seal: F _ _ _ _ _   U _ _ _ _ _ _ _   U _ _ _ _

4   Arrive: S _ _ _   H _ _ _   I _ _ _ _ _

5   Punishment: K E _ _   I _ _ _ _ _ _ _ _ _ _

6   Happiness: K O _ _ _ _ _ _ _ _ _   O _ _ _ _ _ _

7   Village: R _ _ _ _   I _ _ _ _ _ _ _ _ _ _

8   Direction: H _ _ _   O _ _   O _ _ _ _ _ _ _ _ _

9   Priest: B _ _ _ _ _ _   O _ _ _ _ _ _ _   O _ _ _ _

10   Pressure: A _ _ _ _ _ _   T _ _ _ _   S U _ _ _ _ _

11   Circumference: S _ _ _ _   H _ _ _ _ _   U _ _ _ _   U _ _ _ _ _ _

12   Type: K _ _ _   E _ _ _ _   I _ _ _ _ _ _ _ _ _

13   Place: J _ _ _ _ _ _ _   O _ _ _ _ _   O _ _ _ _ _

14   Mine: K O _ _   O _ _ _ _ _

15   Earth: D _ _ _ _ _ _ _   O _ _

16   Slope: H _ _ _   A N _ _ _ _ _

17   Show: J _ _ _   I _ _ _ _ _ _ _

18   Run: S _ _ _ _ _   O _   O _ _ _

19   Well: S _ _ _ _   E _ _ _ _ _   I _ _ _

20   Be: Z _ _ _   A _ _   I _ _ _ _ _ _

21   Temple: J _ _ _ _ _   I _ _ _ _ _ _ _ _

Day three: componental analysis

Course Number	Kanji	ON Reading(s) / Core Concept(s)	Primary Components	Kanji Canvas
0169	土	DO / **earth, ground**	Surface and growth	土
0170	圧	ATSU / **pressure**	厂 (cliff)[K14] + 土 (earth)[169]	圧
0171	寺	JI / **temple**	土 (earth)[169] + 寸 (measure)[11]	寺
0172	在	ZAI / **be, reside**	扌 (*hand*)[K21] + 土 (earth)[169]	在
0173	至	SHI / **arrive; extreme**	一 (one)[01] + 厶 (self)[K18] + 土 (earth)[169]	至
0174	方	HOO / **direction**	Boat tethered to dock	方
0175	坊	BOO / **priest; boy**	土 (earth)[169] + 方 (direction)[174]	坊
0176	示	JI, SHI / **show; altar**	Three legged altar and offering	示
0177	社	SHA / **association; shrine**	礻 (altar)[K34] + 土 (earth)[169]	社
0178	坂	HAN / **slope**	土 (earth)[169] + 反 (oppose)[58]	坂
0179	走	SOO / **run**	土 (earth)[169] + 止 (*stop*)[165]	走
0180	坑	KOO / **mine, pit**	土 (earth)[169] + 亢 (flat)[K22]	坑
0181	里	RI / **village; distance**	田 (field)[60] + 土 (earth)[169]	里
0182	周	SHUU / **circumference**	冂 (border)[K27] + 土 (earth)[169] + 口 (mouth)[106]	周
0183	幸	KOO / **happiness; luck**	土 (earth)[169] + ⺊ (split)[K35] + 干 (dry)[24]	幸
0184	井	SEI, SHOO / **well**	Well frame from above	井
0185	刑	KEI / **punishment**	井 (*well*)[184] + 刂 (cut)[K36]	刑
0186	型	KEI / **type**	刑 (punishment)[185] + 土 (earth)[169]	型
0187	封	FUU, HOO / **seal; fief**	圭 (raised)[K37] + 寸 (measure)[11]	封
0188	場	JOO / **place**	土 (earth)[169] + 易 (*easy*)[158]	場
0189	培	BAI / **cultivate**	土 (earth)[169] + 立 (stand)[37] + 口 (open)[106]	培

Day four: writing practice

土	圧	寺	在	至	方 坊
土	圧	寺	在	至	方 坊
示	社	坂	走	坑	里 周
示	社	坂	走	坑	里 周
幸	井	刑	型	封	場 培
幸	井	刑	型	封	場 培

Day five: story sketch

土	earth: (surface and growth) + Domestic Orb
圧	pressure: 厂 (cliff) + 土 (earth) + Affects Tense SUrface
寺	temple: 土 (earth) + 寸 (measure) + Jewish Institute
在	be: 扌 (*hand*) + 土 (earth) + Zone All Inhabit
至	arrive: 一 (one) + 厶 (self) + 土 (earth) + Soon Here Indeed
方	direction: (boat tethered to dock) + Have One Orientation
坊	priest: 土 (earth) + 方 (direction) + Brother Oversees Order
示	show: (three legged altar and offering) + Just Indicate
社	association: 礻 (altar) + 土 (earth) + SHared Alliance
坂	slope: 土 (earth) + 反 (oppose) + Hill ANgular
走	run: 土 (earth) + 止 (*stop*) + Sprint On Over
坑	mine: 土 (earth) + 亢 (flat) + KOal Outlet
里	village: 田 (field) + 土 (earth) + Rural Inhabitation
周	circumference: 冂 (border) + 土 (earth) + 口 (mouth) + Sides Hugged Until Uniform
幸	happiness: 土 (earth) + ⸌ (split) + 干 (dry) + KOntentment Obvious
井	well: (well frame from above) + Shaft Enters Into
刑	punishment: 井 (*well*) + 刂 (cut) + KEep Incarcerated
型	type: 刑 (punishment) + 土 (earth) + Kind Equal Individuals
封	seal: 圭 (raised) + 寸 (measure) + Fasten Ultimate Union
場	place: 土 (earth) + 易 (*easy*) + Japanese Occupy Openly
培	cultivate: 土 (earth) + 立 (stand) + 口 (open) + Bring Acres Increase

Day six: character clusters

I   Complete the characters using the clues.

1	寸	Fasten Ultimate Union (FUU)
2	土	Jewish Institute (JI)
3	冂	Sides Hugged Until Uniform (SHUU)
4	土	Kind Equal Individuals (KEI)
5	反	Hill ANgular (HAN)

II   Compose the compounds using the clues.

1   (AN) 暗   +   (JI) _____   =   _____ (hint)
    dark

2   (DO) _____   +   (TE) 手   =   _____ (embankment)
                         hand

3   (KYOO) 競   +   (SOO) _____   =   _____ (race)
    compete

4   (FU) 不   +   (KOO) _____   =   _____ (unhappiness)
    not

5   (SHI) _____   +   (KYUU) 急   =   _____ (urgent)
                         hurry

III Complete the sentences using the clues.

1   ジムは十年前に工___で働いていました。
    Jimu wa juunen mae ni kooJOO de hataraite imashita.
    Jim worked in a factory ten years ago.

2   このカメラは___庫がありますか。
    Kono kamera wa ZAIko ga arimasuka.
    Is this camera in stock?

3   親はよく子供に___力をかける。
    Oya wa yoku kodomo ni ATSUryoku o kakeru.
    Parents often put pressure on children.

4   母は日本語と英語を両___とも話せる。
    Haha wa nihongo to eigo o ryooHOO tomo hanaseru.
    My mother can speak both Japanese and English.

5   その会___は自転車を作っています。
    Sono kaiSHA wa jitensha o tsukutte imasu.
    That company makes bicycles.

10

PUT INTO WORDS

Day one: crossword puzzle

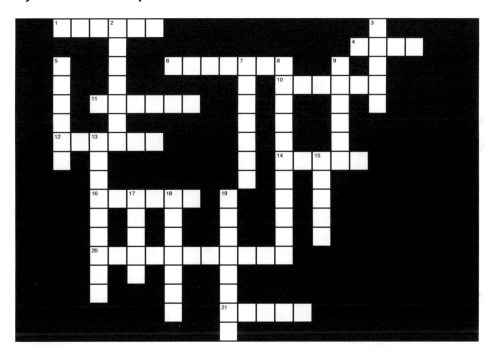

Across

1. Konsent Yes Official
4. Greatest O'clock
6. Have Your Objective Observation (C)
10. Keeps Information
11. KOmmunity Orbit (P)
12. Words Articulated
14. Horizontal Equal Is
16. Take Offense On
20. Kommunicates UNderstanding
21. Stream ENlarged

Down

2. Kount Every Interval (M)
3. Guide ENunciation (W)
5. SHOut Offense (A)
7. To Accord KUstody
8. Yields Alien Kultural Understanding (T)
9. ZEstfully Tastes SUrface
13. SET Something Up
15. Halt Often Overnight
17. Sincere Hope IN
18. To Eliminate Inaccuracy
19. Fatal Utterance (O)

Day two: acrostics

1 Permit: K _ _ _ _ _ _   Y _ _   O _ _ _ _ _ _

2 Measure: K _ _ _ _   E _ _ _ _   I _ _ _ _ _ _ _

3 Words: G _ _ _ _   E N _ _ _ _ _ _ _ _

4 Noon: G _ _ _ _ _ _ _   O _ _ _ _ _

5 Accuse: S H O _ _   O _ _ _ _ _ _

6 Comment: H _ _ _   Y _ _ _   O _ _ _ _ _ _ _ _   O _ _ _ _ _ _ _ _ _

7 Entrust: T _   A _ _ _ _ _   K U _ _ _ _ _

8 Translation: Y _ _ _ _ _   A _ _ _ _   K _ _ _ _ _ _ _   U _ _ _ _ _ _ _ _ _ _

9 Tongue: Z E _ _ _ _ _ _ _   T _ _ _ _ _   S U _ _ _ _ _

10 Record: K _ _ _ _   I _ _ _ _ _ _ _ _ _

11 Public: K O _ _ _ _ _ _ _   O _ _ _ _

12 Speech: W _ _ _ _   A _ _ _ _ _ _ _ _ _

13 Establish: S E T   S _ _ _ _ _ _ _ _   U _

14 Level: H _ _ _ _ _ _ _ _ _   E _ _ _ _   I _

15 Visit: H _ _ _   O _ _ _ _   O _ _ _ _ _ _ _

16 Attack: T _ _ _   O _ _ _ _ _ _   O _

17 Trust: S _ _ _ _ _ _   H _ _ _   I _

18 Correct: T _   E _ _ _ _ _ _ _ _   I _ _ _ _ _ _ _ _

19 Obituary: F _ _ _ _   U _ _ _ _ _ _ _

20 Instruction: K _ _ _ _ _ _ _ _ _ _ _   U N _ _ _ _ _ _ _ _ _ _ _

21 River: S _ _ _ _ _ _   E N _ _ _ _ _ _

Day three: componential analysis

Course Number	Kanji	ON Reading(s) / Core Concept(s)	Primary Components	Kanji Canvas
0190	言	GEN / words	Issuing from the mouth	言
0191	信	SHIN / trust	亻 (person)[K16] + 言 (words)[190]	信
0192	計	KEI / measure	言 (words)[190] + 十 (ten)[06]	計
0193	訂	TEI / correct, revise	言 (words)[190] + 丁 (exact)[87]	訂
0194	訃	FU / obituary	言 (words)[190] + 卜 (divination)[K10]	訃
0195	記	KI / record	言 (words)[190] + 己 (self)[132]	記
0196	討	TOO / attack	言 (words)[190] + 寸 (measure)[11]	討
0197	託	TAKU / entrust	言 (words)[190] + ノ (accent)[K2] + 七 (seven)[03]	託
0198	川	SEN / river	Water flowing	川
0199	訓	KUN / instruction	言 (words)[190] + 川 (river)[198]	訓
0200	訳	YAKU / translation	言 (words)[190] + 尺 (measure)[12]	訳
0201	訪	HOO / visit	言 (words)[190] + 方 (direction)[174]	訪
0202	設	SETSU / establish	言 (words)[190] + 殳 (club)[K23]	設
0203	午	GO / noon	ノ (accent)[K2] + 干 (dry)[24]	午
0204	許	KYO / permit	言 (words)[190] + 午 (noon)[203]	許
0205	公	KOO / public	八 (eight)[04] + 厶 (self)[K18]	公
0206	訟	SHOO / accuse	言 (words)[190] + 公 (public)[205]	訟
0207	平	HEI / level	干 (dry)[24] + 丷 (split)[K35]	平
0208	評	HYOO / comment	言 (words)[190] + 平 (level)[207]	評
0209	舌	ZETSU / tongue	Sticks out of mouth	舌
0210	話	WA / speech	言 (words)[190] + 舌 (tongue)[209]	話

Day four: writing practice

言 信 計 訂 訃 記 討

言 信 計 訂 訃 記 討

託 川 訓 訳 訪 設 午

託 川 訓 訳 訪 設 午

許 公 訟 平 評 舌 話

許 公 訟 平 評 舌 話

Day five: story sketch

言	words: (issuing from the mouth) + Guide ENunciation
信	trust: 亻 (person) + 言 (words) + Sincere Hope IN
計	measure: 言 (words) + 十 (ten) + Kount Every Interval
訂	correct: 言 (words) + 丁 (exact) + To Eliminate Inaccuracy
訃	obituary: 言 (words) + 卜 (divination) + Fatal Utterance
記	record: 言 (words) + 己 (self) + Keeps Information
討	attack: 言 (words) + 寸 (measure) + Take Offense On
託	entrust: 言 (words) + 丿 (accent) + 七 (seven) + To Accord KUstody
川	river: (water flowing) + Stream ENlarged
訓	instruction: 言 (words) + 川 (river) + Kommunicates UNderstanding
訳	translation: 言 (words) + 尺 (measure) + Yields Alien Kultural Understanding
訪	visit: 言 (words) + 方 (direction) + Halt Often Overnight
設	establish: 言 (words) + 殳 (club) + SET Something Up
午	noon: 丿 (accent) + 干 (dry) + Greatest O'clock
許	permit: 言 (words) + 午 (noon) + Konsent Yes Official
公	public: 八 (eight) + 厶 (self) + KOmmunity Orbit
訟	accuse: 言 (words) + 公 (public) + SHOut Offense
平	level: 干 (dry) + 丶丿 (split) + Horizontal Equal Is
評	comment: 言 (words) + 平 (level) + Have Your Objective Observation
舌	tongue: (sticks out of mouth) + ZEstfully Tastes SUrface
話	speech: 言 (words) + 舌 (tongue) + Words Articulated

Day six: character clusters

I   Complete the characters using the clues.

1	川	Kommunicates UNderstanding (KUN)
2	言	Have Your Objective Observation (HYOO)
3	寸	Take Offense On (TOO)
4	言	To Accord KUstody (TAKU)
5	尺	Yields Alien Kultural Understanding (YAKU)

II   Compose the compounds using the clues.

1   (SETSU) _____   +   (RITSU) 立   =   _____ (establishment)
                            stand

2   (KAI) 会   +   (WA) _____   =   _____ (conversation)
        meet

3   (KEI) _____   +   (SAN) 算   =   _____ (calculation)
                        calculation

4   (HOO) 方   +   (GEN) _____   =   _____ (dialect)
        direction

5   (TEI) _____   +   (SEI) 正   =   _____ (correction)
                        correct

III   Complete the sentences using the clues.

1   ポールは自分に自＿＿がある。
    Pooru wa jibun ni jiSHIN ga aru.
    Paul has confidence in himself.

2   木曜日の＿＿後にここで会いましょう。
    Mokuyoobi no GOgo ni koko de aimashoo.
    Let's meet here on Thursday afternoon.

3   このアパートの大きさはだいたい＿＿均です。
    Kono apaato no ookisa wa daitai HEIkin desu.
    The size of this apartment is about average.

4   きのう一人で＿＿園に行きました。
    Kinoo hitori de KOOen ni ikimashita.
    Yesterday I went to the park alone.

5   名前と住所を＿＿入してください。
    Namae to juusho o KInyuu shite kudasai.
    Please fill in your name and address.

REVIEW: LESSONS 6–10

I   Given the character and meaning, write the pronunciation.

1 右 right_____ 2 志 aim _____ 3 昇 rise _____

4 在 be _____ 5 討 attack_____ 6 品 goods_____

7 息 breath _____ 8 是 right_____ 9 場 place_____

10 話 speech _____ 11 加 add_____ 12 芯 core_____

13 東 east_____ 14 坊 priest _____ 15 訪 visit_____

16 刀 sword _____ 17 忙 busy_____ 18 昭 bright _____

19 坑 mine_____ 20 叱 scold _____ 21 今 now_____

22 音 sound _____ 23 坂 slope _____ 24 訟 accuse _____

25 味 taste_____ 26 思 think _____ 27 止 stop _____

28 型 type_____ 29 託 entrust _____ 30 同 same_____

II   Given the character and pronunciation, write the meaning.

1 召 SHOO _____ 2 必 HITSU _____ 3 旨 SHI _____

4 圧 ATSU _____ 5 訃 FU _____ 6 兄 KEI _____

7 忘 BOO_____ 8 旺 OO _____ 9 社 SHA _____

10 訓 KUN _____ 11 夕 SEKI _____ 12 許 KYO_____

13 周 SHUU _____ 14 評 HYOO _____ 15 可 KA _____

16 忠 CHUU _____ 17 易 EKI _____ 18 香 KOO _____

19 里 RI _____ 20 訳 YAKU _____ 21 応 OO _____

22 昧 MAI_____   23 封 FUU_____   24 刑 KEI _____

25 幸 KOO _____   26 忍 NIN_____   27 性 SEI _____

28 至 SHI _____   29 培 BAI_____   30 恒 KOO_____

III   Given the meaning and pronunciation, write the character.

1	mouth	KOO	_____	2 dead	BOO	_____
3	temple	JI	_____	4 correct	TEI	_____
5	old	KO	_____	6 heart	SHIN	_____
7	dawn	TAN	_____	8 show	JI	_____
9	river	SEN	_____	10 star	SEI	_____
11	tongue	ZETSU	_____	12 name	MEI	_____
13	risk	BOO	_____	14 each	KAKU	_____
15	blade	JIN	_____	16 abhor	KI	_____
17	well	SEI	_____	18 king	OO	_____
19	phrase	KU	_____	20 occupy	SEN	_____
21	early	SOO	_____	22 crystal	SHOO	_____
23	life	SEI	_____	24 moon	GETSU	_____
25	establish	SETSU	_____			

IV   Compose compounds using the following characters.

自 明 正 者 念 方 計 号 合 己 言 向 平 記 土 信 走 台 午 公

1 (JI) ____   +   (KO) ____   =   _____ (self)

2 (SOO) ____   +   (SHA) ____   =   _____ (runner)

3 (DO) ____   +   (DAI) ____   =   _____ (foundation)

4 (HOO) ____   +   (KOO) ____   =   _____ (direction)

5 (KOO) ____   +   (HEI) ____   =   _____ (fairness)

6 (GEN) ____   +   (MEI) ____   =   _____ (declaration)

7 (SHOO) ____   +   (GO) ____   =   _____ (noon)

8 (GOO) ____   +   (KEI) ____   =   _____ (total)

9 (KI) ____   +   (GOO) ____   =   _____ (symbol)

10 (SHIN) ____   +   (NEN) ____   =   _____ (belief)

11

A COMMON THREAD

Day one: crossword puzzle

Across
4. Reach Unified Increase (A)
7. Kurl Yarn Up Under
11. NArrow Interior
13. Spinning Hairs Into
14. Kommentary Important (C)
17. SHow Others Oneself
18. Substance Original
19. Bind Over Often
21. Books UNderscore

Down
1. Your Assurance KUstomarily
2. SHarply INtone (S)
3. Feel UNclear
5. Mark Ornaments Name
6. Troops Occupy Nightly (E)
8. Break Up Number
9. Suits HIm Nicely (G)
10. Slim And Intricate (S)
12. Just UNpolluted
15. Kin Evolve Intricately
16. KOchineal Object (C)
20. NOtable Offer

Day two: acrostics

1 Promise: Y _ _ _   A _ _ _ _ _ _ _ _   K U _ _ _ _ _ _ _ _

2 State: S H _ _ _ _ _   I N _ _ _ _

3 Confused: F _ _ _   U N _ _ _ _ _

4 Accumulate: R _ _ _ _   U _ _ _ _ _ _   I _ _ _ _ _ _ _

5 Crest: M _ _ _   O _ _ _ _ _ _ _ _   N _ _ _

6 Encampment: T _ _ _ _ _   O _ _ _ _ _   N _ _ _ _ _ _

7 Entwine: K _ _ _   Y _ _ _   U _   U _ _ _ _

8 Divide: B _ _ _ _   U _   N _ _ _ _ _

9 Gentleman: S _ _ _ _   H I _   N _ _ _ _ _

10 Slender: S _ _ _   A _ _   I _ _ _ _ _ _ _ _

11 Inside: N A _ _ _ _   I _ _ _ _ _ _ _

12 Pure: J _ _ _   U N _ _ _ _ _ _ _ _

13 Thread: S _ _ _ _ _ _ _   H _ _ _ _   I _ _ _

14 Chronicle: K _ _ _ _ _ _ _ _ _   I _ _ _ _ _ _ _

15 Lineage: K _ _   E _ _ _ _ _ _   I _ _ _ _ _ _ _ _ _

16 Crimson: K O _ _ _ _ _ _ _   O _ _ _ _ _

17 Introduce: S H _ _   O _ _ _ _ _ _   O _ _ _ _ _ _

18 Element: S _ _ _ _ _ _ _ _   O _ _ _ _ _ _ _

19 Spin: B _ _ _   O _ _ _   O _ _ _ _

20 Pay: N O _ _ _ _ _   O _ _ _ _

21 Writing: B _ _ _ _   U N _ _ _ _ _ _ _ _

Day three: componential analysis

Course Number	Kanji	ON Reading(s) / Core Concept(s)	Primary Components	Kanji Canvas
0211	糸	SHI / thread	Twisted silk threads	糸
0212	系	KEI / lineage; system	一 (*one*)[01] + 糸 (thread)[211]	系
0213	紅	KOO / crimson	糸 (thread)[211] + 工 (work)[26]	紅
0214	糾	KYUU / entwine; examine	糸 (thread)[211] + 丩 (fork)[K38]	糾
0215	紀	KI / chronicle	糸 (thread)[211] + 己 (self)[132]	紀
0216	約	YAKU / promise	糸 (thread)[211] + 勺 (measure)[K39]	約
0217	素	SO, SU / element; plain	生 (*life*)[142] + 糸 (thread)[211]	素
0218	紡	BOO / spin	糸 (thread)[211] + 方 (direction)[174]	紡
0219	分	BUN / divide	八 (eight)[04] + 刀 (sword)[115]	分
0220	紛	FUN / confused	糸 (thread)[211] + 分 (divide)[219]	紛
0221	文	BUN / writing	Intricate pattern	文
0222	紋	MON / crest; pattern	糸 (thread)[211] + 文 (writing)[221]	紋
0223	屯	TON / encampment	七 (seven)[03] + 山 (mountain)[71]	屯
0224	純	JUN / pure	糸 (thread)[211] + 屯 (encampment)[223]	純
0225	内	NAI / inside	冂 (border)[K27] + 人 (person)[64]	内
0226	納	NOO / pay; accept; store	糸 (thread)[211] + 内 (inside)[225]	納
0227	累	RUI / accumulate	田 (field)[60] + 糸 (thread)[211]	累
0228	細	SAI / slender; minute	糸 (thread)[211] + 田 (field)[60]	細
0229	紹	SHOO / introduce	糸 (thread)[211] + 召 (summon)[116]	紹
0230	申	SHIN / state	Bolt of lightning	申
0231	紳	SHIN / gentleman	糸 (thread)[211] + 申 (state)[230]	紳

Day four: writing practice

糸	系	紅	糾	紀	約	素
糸	系	紅	糾	紀	約	素
紡	分	紛	文	紋	屯	純
紡	分	紛	文	紋	屯	純
内	納	累	細	紹	申	紳
内	納	累	細	紹	申	紳

Day five: story sketch

糸	thread: (twisted silk threads) + Spinning Hairs Into
系	lineage: 一 (*one*) + 糸 (thread) + Kin Evolve Intricately
紅	crimson: 糸 (thread) + 工 (work) + KOchineal Object
糾	entwine: 糸 (thread) + 丩 (fork) + Kurl Yarn Up Under
紀	chronicle: 糸 (thread) + 己 (self) + Kommentary Important
約	promise: 糸 (thread) + 勺 (measure) + Your Assurance KUstomarily
素	element: 生 (*life*) + 糸 (thread) + Substance Original
紡	spin: 糸 (thread) + 方 (direction) + Bind Over Often
分	divide: 八 (eight) + 刀 (sword) + Break Up Number
紛	confused: 糸 (thread) + 分 (divide) + Feel UNclear
文	writing: (intricate pattern) + Books UNderscore
紋	crest: 糸 (thread) + 文 (writing) + Mark Ornaments Name
屯	encampment: 七 (seven) + 山 (mountain) + Troops Occupy Nightly
純	pure: 糸 (thread) + 屯 (encampment) + Just UNpolluted
内	inside: 冂 (border) + 人 (person) + NArrow Interior
納	pay: 糸 (thread) + 内 (inside) + NOtable Offer
累	accumulate: 田 (field) + 糸 (thread) + Reach Unified Increase
細	slender: 糸 (thread) + 田 (field) + Slim And Intricate
紹	introduce: 糸 (thread) + 召 (summon) + SHow Others Oneself
申	state: (bolt of lightning) + SHarply INtone
紳	gentleman: 糸 (thread) + 申 (state) + Suits HIm Nicely

Day six: character clusters

I Complete the characters using the clues.

1	田	Reach Unified Increase (RUI)
2	糸	Just UNpolluted (JUN)
3	方	Bind Over Often (BOO)
4	糸	Kin Evolve Intricately (KEI)
5	糸	Substance Original (SO)

II Compose the compounds using the clues.

1 (KOKU) 国   +   (NAI) ____   =   _____ (domestic)
   country

2 (SAI) ____   +   (KU) 工   =   _____ (workmanship)
                      work

3 (SHIN) ____   +   (SEI) 請   =   _____ (application)
                       request

4 (SHI) 指   +   (MON) ____   =   _____ (fingerprint)
   finger

5 (FUN) ____   +   (SOO) 争   =   _____ (dispute)
                      compete

III Complete the sentences using the clues.

1 私は日本___化に興味があります。
   Watashi wa nihon BUNka ni kyoomi ga arimasu.
   I am interested in Japanese culture.

2 イタリアレストランの予___をしましたか。
   Itaria resutoran no yoYAKU o shimashita ka.
   Did you make reservations at the Italian restaurant?

3 このホテルは19世___に建てられた。
   Kono hoteru wa juukyuu seiKI ni taterareta.
   This hotel was built in the nineteenth century.

4 山本さんをご___介いたします。
   Yamamoto-san o go-SHOOkai itashimasu.
   May I introduce you to Mr. Yamamoto?

5 火事の原因を___析してください。
   Kaji no gen'in o BUNseki shite kudasai.
   Please analyze the cause of the fire.

12

PLANT LIFE

Day one: crossword puzzle

Across

1. Massive Overgrowth (T)
5. Sod HIghlights BAckyard
7. Strength Over Others
10. Juvenile Attribute KUstomarily
12. Budding YOung Organism
14. Deltoid Ample Individual
15. Graphic Expressive Illustration
16. Signal Earlier Khronological Interval
17. Eminent Importance
19. HOnored Odor
21. Keenly Unpleasant (P)

Down

2. Opposes Opposites
3. Space Outdoors Opulent (V)
4. KAndy (C)
6. Grinder Acute (F)
8. Ingested Mashed Ordinarily
9. Krop Adornment (F)
11. KOmpletely Overgrown
13. SOd Occupant
18. Kontinually Afflict (T)
20. Growth Arising

Day two: acrostics

1 Thick: M _ _ _ _ _ _   O _ _ _ _ _ _ _ _

2 Center: O _ _ _ _ _ _   O _ _ _ _ _ _ _

3 Villa: S _ _ _ _   O _ _ _ _ _ _ _   O _ _ _ _ _

4 Confection: K A _ _ _

5 Lawn: S _ _   H I _ _ _ _ _ _ _ _   B A _ _ _ _ _ _

6 Fang: G _ _ _ _ _ _   A _ _ _ _

7 Powerful: S _ _ _ _ _ _ _   O _ _ _   O _ _ _ _ _

8 Potato: I _ _ _ _ _ _ _   M _ _ _ _ _   O _ _ _ _ _ _ _ _

9 Flower: K _ _ _   A _ _ _ _ _ _ _ _

10 Young: J _ _ _ _ _ _ _ _   A _ _ _ _ _ _ _ _   K U _ _ _ _ _ _ _ _ _

11 Wild: K O _ _ _ _ _ _ _   O _ _ _ _ _ _ _ _

12 Seedling: B _ _ _ _ _ _   Y O _ _ _   O _ _ _ _ _ _ _

13 Grass: S O _   O _ _ _ _ _ _ _

14 Big: D _ _ _ _ _ _   A _ _ _ _   I _ _ _ _ _ _ _ _

15 Art: G _ _ _ _ _ _   E _ _ _ _ _ _ _ _ _   I _ _ _ _ _ _ _ _ _ _

16 Past: S _ _ _ _ _   E _ _ _ _ _ _   K _ _ _ _ _ _ _ _ _ _ _   I _ _ _ _ _ _ _

17 Distinguished: E _ _ _ _ _ _   I _ _ _ _ _ _ _ _ _

18 Torment: K _ _ _ _ _ _ _ _ _ _   A _ _ _ _ _ _

19 Fragrant: H O _ _ _ _ _   O _ _ _

20 Bud: G _ _ _ _ _   A _ _ _ _ _ _

21 Painful: K _ _ _ _ _   U _ _ _ _ _ _ _ _ _

Day three: componential analysis

Course Number	Kanji	ON Reading(s) / Core Concept(s)	Primary Components	Kanji Canvas
0232	芋	imo / potato	艹 (plants)[K29] + 丁 (exact)[87] + 一 (one)[01]	芋
0233	大	DAI, TAI / big	Person standing with arms and legs spread	大
0234	央	OO / center	大 (big)[233] + 口 (mouth)[106]	央
0235	英	EI / distinguished	艹 (plants)[K29] + 央 (center)[234]	英
0236	花	KA / flower	艹 (plants)[K29] + 化 (change)[65]	花
0237	芸	GEI / art; skill	艹 (plants)[K29] + 二 (two)[02] + ム (self)[K18]	芸
0238	芳	HOO / fragrant	艹 (plants)[K29] + 方 (direction)[174]	芳
0239	芝	shiba / lawn	艹 (plants)[K29] + 亠 (top)[K1] + 人 (*person*)[64]	芝
0240	牙	GA, GE / fang	Large tooth protruding from open mouth	牙
0241	芽	GA / bud, sprout	艹 (plants)[K29] + 牙 (fang)[240]	芽
0242	苛	KA / torment	艹 (plants)[K29] + 可 (possible)[109]	苛
0243	苦	KU / painful; bitter	艹 (plants)[K29] + 古 (old)[108]	苦
0244	若	JAKU / young	艹 (plants)[K29] + 右 (right)[107]	若
0245	昔	SEKI / past	艹 (plants)[K29] + 一 (one)[01] + 日 (day)[17]	昔
0246	苗	BYOO / seedling	艹 (plants)[K29] + 田 (field)[60]	苗
0247	茂	MO / thick	艹 (plants)[K29] + 戈 (spear)[K20]	茂
0248	草	SOO / grass	艹 (plants)[K29] + 早 (early)[149]	草
0249	壮	SOO / powerful; grand	丬 (side)[K40] + 士 (samurai)[67]	壮
0250	荘	SOO / villa; solemn	艹 (plants)[K29] + 壮 (powerful)[249]	荘
0251	荒	KOO / wild	艹 (plants)[K29] + 亡 (dead)[134] + 川 (river)[198]	荒
0252	菓	KA / confection	艹 (plants)[K29] + 果 (fruit)[61]	菓

Day four: writing practice

芋	大	央	英	花	芸	芳
芋	大	央	英	花	芸	芳
芝	牙	芽	苛	苦	若	昔
芝	牙	芽	苛	苦	若	昔
苗	茂	草	壯	莊	荒	菓
苗	茂	草	壯	莊	荒	菓

Day five: story sketch

芋	potato: ⁺ (plants) + 丁 (exact) + 一 (one) + Ingested Mashed Ordinarily
大	big: (person standing with arms and legs spread) + Deltoid Ample Individual
央	center: 大 (big) + 口 (mouth) + Opposes Opposites
英	distinguished: ⁺ (plants) + 央 (center) + Eminent Importance
花	flower: ⁺ (plants) + 化 (change) + Krop Adornment
芸	art: ⁺ (plants) + 二 (two) + 厶 (self) + Graphic Expressive Illustration
芳	fragrant: ⁺ (plants) + 方 (direction) + HOnored Odor
芝	lawn: ⁺ (plants) + 亠 (top) + 人 (*person*) + Sod HIghlights BAckyard
牙	fang: (large tooth protruding from open mouth) + Grinder Acute
芽	bud: ⁺ (plants) + 牙 (fang) + Growth Arising
苛	torment: ⁺ (plants) + 可 (possible) + Kontinually Afflict
苦	painful: ⁺ (plants) + 古 (old) + Keenly Unpleasant
若	young: ⁺ (plants) + 右 (right) + Juvenile Attribute KUstomarily
昔	past: ⁺ (plants) + 一 (one) + 日 (day) + Signal Earlier Khronological Interval
苗	seedling: ⁺ (plants) + 田 (field) + Budding YOung Organism
茂	thick: ⁺ (plants) + 戈 (spear) + Massive Overgrowth
草	grass: ⁺ (plants) + 早 (early) + SOd Occupant
壮	powerful: 丬 (side) + 士 (samurai) + Strength Over Others
荘	villa: ⁺ (plants) + 壮 (powerful) + Space Outdoors Opulent
荒	wild: ⁺ (plants) + 亡 (dead) + 川 (river) + KOmpletely Overgrown
菓	confection: ⁺ (plants) + 果 (fruit) + KAndy

Day six: character clusters

I Complete the characters using the clues.

1	⺾	Budding YOung Organism (BYOO)
2	日	Signal Earlier Khronological Interval (SEKI)
3	扌	Strength Over Others (SOO)
4	可	Kontinually Afflict (KA)
5	⺾	Juvenile Attribute KUstomarily (JAKU)

II Compose the compounds using the clues.

1 (KAI) 開   +   (KA) ____   =   _____ (bloom)
   open

2 (KA) ____   +   (SHI) 子   =   _____ (sweets)
               child

3 (HOO) ____   +   (KOO) 香   =   _____ (fragrance)
                fragrance

4 (SHU) 手   +   (GEI) ____   =   _____ (handicraft)
   hand

5 (EI) ____   +   (SAI) 才   =   _____ (talent)
             talent

III Complete the sentences using the clues.

1 姉は＿＿学でフランス語を勉強しています。
Ane wa DAIgaku de furansu-go o benkyoo shite imasu.
My older sister is studying French at university.

2 書店は市の中＿＿にあります。
Shoten wa shi no chuuOO ni arimasu.
The bookstore is in the center of the city.

3 その村は強い地震で＿＿廃した。
Sono mura wa tsuyoi jishin de KOOhai shita.
That village was ruined by the large earthquake.

4 八月に沖さんの別＿＿に泊まります。
Hachigatsu ni Oki-san no besSOO ni tomarimasu.
I will stay at Mr. Oki's villa in August.

5 生け花を習うのに＿＿心しました。
Ikebana o narau no ni KUshin shimashita.
I made great effort to learn flower arrangement.

13

ON THE MOVE

Day one: crossword puzzle

Across

1. SHeds ITSelf Unnoticed (L)
4. Bent Ears Inundated
6. Theological ENtity
12. HAsten Keen Urge (P)
14. Take Each Turn SUccessively
15. Jolt INtense (F)
16. Now YUrt Underneath
18. Klose IN
19. Seven Habitual Unified Units
20. KOntain (two words: P/I)
21. Ship On Out

Down

2. JUst To Speak Up
3. Greet Each Invitee
5. MEntally Intermingled (P)
7. HEre Nearby (V)
8. Journey UNdulation (two words: G/A)
9. Heed ENcore
10. Trouble Out Of
11. Sprint On Kourse Urgently
13. Gives You A Konverse Universe
17. Some Objects Klosely United

Day two: acrostics

1 Lose: S H _ _ _   I T S _ _ _   U _ _ _ _ _ _ _

2 State: J U _ _   T _   S _ _ _ _   U _

3 Welcome: G _ _ _ _   E _ _ _   I _ _ _ _ _ _

4 Rice: B _ _ _   E _ _ _   I _ _ _ _ _ _ _ _

5 Perplexed: M E _ _ _ _ _ _   I _ _ _ _ _ _ _ _ _ _

6 Heaven: T _ _ _ _ _ _ _ _ _   E N _ _ _ _

7 Vicinity: H E _ _   N _ _ _ _ _

8 Go Around: J _ _ _ _ _ _   U N _ _ _ _ _ _ _ _

9 Return: H _ _ _   E N _ _ _ _

10 Escape: T _ _ _ _ _ _   O _ _   O _

11 Fast: S _ _ _ _ _   O _   K _ _ _ _ _   U _ _ _ _ _ _

12 Press: H A _ _ _ _   K _ _ _   U _ _ _

13 Reverse: G _ _ _ _   Y _ _   A   K _ _ _ _ _ _ _   U _ _ _ _ _ _ _

14 Alternate: T _ _ _   E _ _ _   T _ _ _   S U _ _ _ _ _ _ _ _ _

15 Fast: J _ _ _   I N _ _ _ _ _

16 Enter: N _ _   Y U _ _   U _ _ _ _ _ _ _ _

17 Bundle: S _ _ _   O _ _ _ _ _ _   K _ _ _ _ _ _   U _ _ _ _ _

18 Near: K _ _ _ _   I N

19 Week: S _ _ _ _   H _ _ _ _ _ _ _   U _ _ _ _ _ _   U _ _ _ _

20 Put Into: K O _ _ _ _ _ (MU)

21 Send: S _ _ _   O _   O _ _

Day three: componential analysis

Course Number	Kanji	ON Reading(s) / Core Concept(s)	Primary Components	Kanji Canvas
0253	辺	HEN / vicinity	辶 (move)[K41] + 刀 (sword)[115]	辺
0254	入	NYUU / enter	Entrance to dwelling	入
0255	込	ko(mu) / put into, include	辶 (move)[K41] + 入 (enter)[254]	込
0256	巡	JUN / go around	辶 (move)[K41] + 川 (*river*)[198]	巡
0257	迅	JIN / fast	辶 (move)[K41] + *broken leg of table*	迅
0258	近	KIN / near	辶 (move)[K41] + 斤 (ax)[55]	近
0259	返	HEN / return	辶 (move)[K41] + 反 (oppose)[58]	返
0260	迎	GEI / welcome	辶 (move)[K41] + 卬 (measured bow)[K42]	迎
0261	天	TEN / heaven	一 (one)[01] + 大 (big)[233]	天
0262	送	SOO / send	辶 (move)[K41] + ⸝⸜ (split)[K35] + 天 (heaven)[261]	送
0263	迫	HAKU / press	辶 (move)[K41] + 白 (white)[18]	迫
0264	述	JUTSU / state	辶 (move)[K41] + 木 (tree)[43] + 丶 (accent)[K2]	述
0265	失	SHITSU / lose	夫 (husband)[94] + ノ (accent)[K2]	失
0266	迭	TETSU / alternate	辶 (move)[K41] + 失 (lose)[265]	迭
0267	逆	GYAKU / reverse	辶 (move)[K41] + ⸝⸜ (away)[K35] + 一 (one)[01] + 山 (*mountain*)[71]	逆
0268	逃	TOO / escape	辶 (move)[K41] + 兆 (trillion)[21]	逃
0269	米	BEI, MAI / rice	Grain-laden ear of rice	米
0270	迷	MEI / perplexed	辶 (move)[K41] + 米 (rice)[269]	迷
0271	束	SOKU / bundle	木 (wood)[43] + 口 (mouth)[106]	束
0272	速	SOKU / fast	辶 (move)[K41] + 束 (bundle)[271]	速
0273	週	SHUU / week	辶 (move)[K41] + 周 (around)[182]	週

Day four: writing practice

辺	入	込	巡	迅	近	返
辺	入	込	巡	迅	近	返
迎	天	送	迫	述	失	迭
迎	天	送	迫	述	失	迭
逆	逃	米	迷	束	速	週
逆	逃	米	迷	束	速	週

Day five: story sketch

辺	vicinity: 辶 (move) + 刀 (sword) + HEre Nearby
入	enter: (entrance to dwelling) + Now YUrt Underneath
込	put into: 辶 (move) + 入 (enter) + KOntain
巡	go around: 辶 (move) + 川 (*river*) + Journey UNdulation
迅	fast: 辶 (move) + *broken leg of table* + Jolt INtense
近	near: 辶 (move) + 斤 (ax) + Klose IN
返	return: 辶 (move) + 反 (oppose) + Heed ENcore
迎	welcome: 辶 (move) + 卬 (measured bow) + Greet Each Invitee
天	heaven: 一 (one) + 大 (big) + Theological ENtity
送	send: 辶 (move) + 丷 (split) + 天 (heaven) + Ship On Out
迫	press: 辶 (move) + 白 (white) + HAsten Keen Urge
述	state: 辶 (move) + 木 (tree) + 丶 (accent) + JUst To Speak Up
失	lose: 夫 (husband) + 丿 (accent) + SHeds ITSelf Unnoticed
迭	alternate: 辶 (move) + 失 (lose) + Take Each Turn SUccessively
逆	reverse: 辶 (move) + 丷 (away) + 一 (one) + 屮 (mountain) + Gives You A Konverse Universe
逃	escape: 辶 (move) + 兆 (trillion) + Trouble Out Of
米	rice: (grain-laden ear of rice) + Bent Ears Inundated
迷	perplexed: 辶 (move) + 米 (rice) + MEntally Intermingled
束	bundle: 木 (wood) + 口 (mouth) + Some Objects Klosely United
速	fast: 辶 (move) + 束 (bundle) + Sprint On Kourse Urgently
週	week: 辶 (move) + 周 (around) + Seven Habitual Unified Units

Day six: character clusters

I   Complete the characters using the clues.

1	辶	Sprint On Kourse Urgently (SOKU)
2	白	HAsten Keen Urge (HAKU)
3	辶	Trouble Out Of (TOO)
4	刀	HEre Nearby (HEN)
5	辶	Greet Each Invitee (GEI)

II   Compose the compounds using the clues.

1   (SOO) ____   +   (KIN) 金   =   _____ (remittance)
                          money

2   (KI) 記   +   (JUTSU) ____   =   _____ (description)
       record

3   (MEI) ____   +   (SHIN) 信   =   _____ (superstition)
                          trust

5   (HAN) 反   +   (GYAKU) ____   =   _____ (rebellion)
       oppose

4   (SHITSU) ____   +   (REI) 礼   =   _____ (impoliteness)
                          propriety

III   Complete the sentences using the clues.

1   日本の___気は変わりやすいですね。
    Nihon no TENki wa kawari yasui desu ne.
    The weather in Japan changes easily.

2   高田さんはすぐに___事の電話をしてきた。
    Takada-san wa sugu ni HENji no denwa o shite kita.
    Mr. Takada returned my call immediately.

3   今度の___末はテニスをしましょうか。
    Kondo no SHUUmatsu wa tenisu o shimashoo ka.
    Let's play tennis this weekend.

4   データをコンピュータに___力してください。
    Deeta o conpyuuta ni NYUUryoku shite kudasai.
    Please input the data into the computer.

5   この___所に薬屋がありますか。
    Kono KINjo ni kusuriya ga arimasu ka.
    Is there a pharmacy in this neighborhood?

14

IN THE FLESH

Day one: crossword puzzle

Across

2. HInge Jostles Into (E)
4. Zone Enter Nearly
6. Similar Head Of Offspring
8. Hand Of Kompass Upward
9. BOdy Overweight
11. Keeps Epaulet Noticed (S)
13. Dispose All The SUrplus (R)
16. Hind Area Indicates
17. TAkes Nerve
18. Kover Interwoven
19. Konjunction Oblique (T)
20. KOnsent On
21. Soft Human Inside

Down

1. Tender Abode Impregnated
3. Kleans Arteries Naturally
5. Heavy Increase
7. Insides (S)
10. Dismembered Organism Outstanding
12. Knock On
14. Your Unyielding Urge (H)
15. Naked Inner KUt (M)

Day two: acrostics

1 Womb: T _ _ _ _ _ A _ _ _ _ I _ _ _ _ _ _ _ _ _

2 Elbow: H I _ _ _ J _ _ _ _ _ _ I _ _ _

3 Liver: K _ _ _ _ _ A _ _ _ _ _ _ _ N _ _ _ _ _ _ _

4 Before: Z _ _ _ E _ _ _ _ N _ _ _ _ _

5 Fatten: H _ _ _ _ I _ _ _ _ _ _ _

6 Resemble: S _ _ _ _ _ _ H _ _ _ O _ O _ _ _ _ _ _ _

7 Stomach: I _ _ _ _ _ _

8 North: H _ _ _ O _ K _ _ _ _ _ _ U _ _ _ _ _

9 Fat: B O _ _ O _ _ _ _ _ _ _ _

10 Trunk: D _ _ _ _ _ _ _ _ _ _ O _ _ _ _ _ _ _ O _ _ _ _ _ _ _ _ _

11 Shoulder: K _ _ _ _ E _ _ _ _ _ _ N _ _ _ _ _ _

12 Door: K _ _ _ _ O _

13 Remove: D _ _ _ _ _ _ A _ _ T _ _ S U _ _ _ _ _

14 Have: Y _ _ _ U _ _ _ _ _ _ _ _ U _ _ _

15 Meat: N _ _ _ _ I _ _ _ _ K U _

16 Back: H _ _ _ A _ _ _ I _ _ _ _ _ _ _ _

17 Courage: T A _ _ _ N _ _ _ _

18 Skin: K _ _ _ _ I _ _ _ _ _ _ _ _ _

19 Thigh: K _ _ _ _ _ _ _ _ _ _ O _ _ _ _ _ _

20 Agree: K O _ _ _ _ _ O _

21 Fat: S _ _ _ H _ _ _ _ I _ _ _ _ _

Day three: componential analysis

Course Number	Kanji	ON Reading(s) / Core Concept(s)	Primary Components	Kanji Canvas
0274	肉	NIKU / **meat, flesh, body**	Fillet	肉
0275	有	YUU / **have; exist**	手 (*hand*)[85] + 月 (flesh)[K43]	有
0276	肌	KI / **skin**	月 (body)[K43] + 几 (table)[K11]	肌
0277	肖	SHOO / **resemble**	⺌ (small)[K44] + 月 (body)[K43]	肖
0278	肝	KAN / **liver; vital**	月 (body)[K43] + 干 (dry)[24]	肝
0279	肘	hiji / **elbow**	月 (body)[K43] + 寸 (measure)[11]	肘
0280	肪	BOO / **fat**	月 (flesh)[K43] + 方 (direction)[174]	肪
0281	肯	KOO / **agree**	止 (stop)[165] + 月 (meat)[K43]	肯
0282	肥	HI / **fatten**	月 (flesh)[K43] + 巴 (spiral pattern)[K45]	巴
0283	股	KO / **thigh**	月 (flesh)[K43] + 殳 (club)[K23]	股
0284	戸	KO / **door**	Wood frame with opening	戸
0285	肩	KEN / **shoulder**	戸 (door)[284] + 月 (flesh)[K43]	肩
0286	胃	I / **stomach**	田 (field)[60] + 月 (flesh)[K43]	胃
0287	胎	TAI / **womb**	月 (flesh)[K43] + 台 (platform)[114]	胎
0288	胆	TAN / **courage; gall**	月 (body)[K43] + 旦 (dawn)[148]	胆
0289	前	ZEN / **before**	丶ソ (split)[K35] + 一 (one)[01] + 月 (flesh)[K43] + 刂 (cut)[K36]	前
0290	北	HOKU / **north**	Two persons sitting back to back	北
0291	背	HAI / **back**	北 (north)[290] + 月 (flesh)[K43]	背
0292	胴	DOO / **trunk**	月 (flesh)[K43] + 同 (same)[119]	胴
0293	脂	SHI / **fat**	月 (flesh)[K43] + 旨 (gist)[150]	脂
0294	脱	DATSU / **remove; escape**	月 (flesh)[K43] + 丶ソ (split)[K35] + 兄 (older brother)[117]	脱

Day four: writing practice

肉	有	肌	肖	肝	肘	肪
肉	有	肌	肖	肝	肘	肪
肯	肥	股	戶	肩	胃	胎
肯	肥	股	戶	肩	胃	胎
胆	前	北	背	胴	脂	脱
胆	前	北	背	胴	脂	脱

Day five: story sketch

肉	meat: (fillet) + Naked Inner KUt
有	have: 手 (*hand*) + 月 (flesh) + Your Unyielding Urge
肌	skin: 月 (body) + 几 (table) + Kover Interwoven
肖	resemble: ⺌ (small) + 月 (body) + Similar Head Of Offspring
肝	liver: 月 (body) + 干 (dry) + Kleans Arteries Naturally
肘	elbow: 月 (body) + 寸 (measure) + HInge Jostles Into
肪	fat: 月 (flesh) + 方 (direction) + BOdy Overweight
肯	agree: 止 (stop) + 月 (meat) + KOnsent On
肥	fatten: 月 (flesh) + 巴 (spiral pattern) + Heavy Increase
股	thigh: 月 (flesh) + 殳 (club) + Konjunction Oblique
戸	door: (wood frame with opening) + Knock On
肩	shoulder: 戸 (door) + 月 (flesh) + Keeps Epaulet Noticed
胃	stomach: 田 (field) + 月 (flesh) + Insides
胎	womb: 月 (flesh) + 台 (platform) + Tender Abode Impregnated
胆	courage: 月 (body) + 旦 (dawn) + TAkes Nerve
前	before: ⺍ (split) + 一 (one) + 月 (flesh) + 刂 (cut) + Zone Enter Nearly
北	north: (two persons sitting back to back) + Hand Of Kompass Upward
背	back: 北 (north) + 月 (flesh) + Hind Area Indicates
胴	trunk: 月 (flesh) + 同 (same) + Dismembered Organism Outstanding
脂	fat: 月 (flesh) + 旨 (gist) + Soft Human Inside
脱	remove: 月 (flesh) + ⺍ (split) + 兄 (older brother) + Dispose All The SUrplus

Day six: character clusters

I Complete the characters using the clues.

1	月	Kleans Arteries Naturally (KAN)
2	台	Tender Abode Impregnated (TAI)
3	毌	Insides (I)
4	兄	Dispose All The SUrplus (DATSU)
5	月	Konjunction Oblique (KO)

II Compose the compounds using the clues.

1 (DAI) 大   +   (TAN) ____   =   _____ (boldness)
     big

2 (DOO) ____   +   (TAI) 体   =   _____ (trunk/ torso)
                       body

3 (HOKU) ____   +   (TOO) 東   =   _____ (northeast)
                       east

4 (YU) 油   +   (SHI) ____   =   _____ (fat)
     oil

5 (KOO) ____   +   (TEI) 定   =   _____ (affirmation)
                       fix

III Complete the sentences using the clues.

1 私は以___にダブリンを訪れました。
Watashi wa iZEN ni daburin o otozuremashita.
I have visited Dublin before.

2 今夜のコンサートは___外で行われます。
Konya no konsaato wa KOgai de okonawaremasu.
Tonight's concert will be held outside.

3 その決定は女性に___利なものでした。
Sono kettei wa josei ni YUUri na mono deshita.
That decision was favorable to women.

4 時々夕食に牛___を食べる。
Tokidoki yuushoku ni gyuuNIKU o taberu.
Sometimes I eat beef for dinner.

5 ラストシーンの___景は富士山です。
Rasuto shiin no HAIkei wa fujisan desu.
In the background of the last scene is Mount Fuji.

15

STRIKE ZONE

Day one: crossword puzzle

Across

3. Kounty Unit (W)
7. Success AT SUicide
8. Sails HUll Underneath
10. KOercive Offense
11. Your AKtion Undertaken
14. State Exerts Influence (G)
17. Everyone Kontracts Infection
19. Kurrently Over
20. Karry Out Objective
21. Korrective Action Induces (R)

Down

1. BOvine KUisine (P)
2. Measures Attenuated Items (two words)
4. Hand One Over
5. Kall You Urgently Utter
6. Openhanded Offense (B)
9. Has Alike Nature (S)
12. Konvey Eternal Insight
13. Divide ANgular (S)
15. Kall Yet Upon Us
16. Become OTherwise SUbmerged
18. Convey Human Intent

Day two: acrostics

1 Pasture: B O _ _ _ _   K U _ _ _ _ _

2 Sheet Counter: M _ _ _ _ _ _ _   A _ _ _ _ _ _ _ _   I _ _ _ _

3 Ward: K _ _ _ _ _   U _ _ _

4 Release: H _ _ _   O _ _   O _ _ _

5 Rescue: K _ _ _   Y _ _   U _ _ _ _ _ _   U _ _ _ _

6 Beat: O _ _ _ _ _ _ _ _   O _ _ _ _ _ _

7 Kill: S _ _ _ _ _ _   A T S U _ _ _ _ _

8 Boat: S _ _ _ _   H U _ _   U _ _ _ _ _ _ _ _

9 Sort: H _ _   A _ _ _ _   N _ _ _ _ _

10 Attack: K O _ _ _ _ _ _   O _ _ _ _ _ _

11 Service: Y _ _ _   A K _ _ _ _   U _ _ _ _ _ _ _ _

12 Enlighten: K _ _ _ _ _   E _ _ _ _ _ _   I _ _ _ _ _ _

13 Step: D _ _ _ _ _   A N _ _ _ _ _

14 Government: S _ _ _ _   E _ _ _ _ _   I _ _ _ _ _ _ _ _

15 Request: K _ _ _   Y _ _   U _ _ _   U _

16 Sink: B _ _ _ _ _   O T _ _ _ _ _ _ _   S U _ _ _ _ _ _

17 Epidemic: E _ _ _ _ _ _ _   K _ _ _ _ _ _ _ _   I _ _ _ _ _ _ _ _

18 Do: C _ _ _ _ _   H _ _ _ _   I _ _ _ _ _

19 Past: K _ _ _ _ _ _ _ _   O _ _ _

20 Go: K _ _ _ _   O _ _   O _ _ _ _ _ _ _ _

21 Reform: K _ _ _ _ _ _ _ _ _   A _ _ _ _ _   I _ _ _ _ _ _

Day three: componential analysis

Course Number	Kanji	ON Reading(s) / Core Concept(s)	Primary Components	Kanji Canvas
0295	改	KAI / **reform, change**	己 (self)[132] + 攵 (strike)[K46]	改
0296	攻	KOO / **attack**	工 (work)[26] + 攵 (strike)[K46]	攻
0297	行	KOO, GYOO / **go**	Crossroads	行
0298	役	YAKU, EKI / **service; battle**	彳 (go)[K47] + 殳 (club)[K23]	役
0299	没	BOTSU / **sink**	氵 (water)[K6] + 殳 (club)[K23]	没
0300	放	HOO / **release**	方 (direction)[174] + 攵 (strike)[K46]	放
0301	牧	BOKU / **pasture**	牛 (cow)[75] + 攵 (strike)[K46]	牧
0302	枚	MAI / **sheet counter**	木 (wood)[43] + 攵 (strike)[K46]	枚
0303	区	KU / **ward**	匸 (container)[K48] + メ (mark)[K49]	区
0304	殴	OO / **beat**	区 (ward)[303] + 殳 (club)[K23]	殴
0305	疫	EKI / **epidemic**	疒 (illness)[K50] + 殳 (club)[K23]	疫
0306	段	DAN / **step**	*serrated cliff* + 殳 (club)[K23]	段
0307	政	SEI / **government**	正 (correct)[166] + 攵 (strike)[K46]	政
0308	故	KO / **past; reason**	古 (old)[108] + 攵 (strike)[K46]	故
0309	致	CHI / **do; cause**	至 (arrive)[173] + 攵 (strike)[K46]	致
0310	殺	SATSU / **kill**	メ (mark)[K49] + 木 (wood)[43] + 殳 (club)[K23]	殺
0311	舟	SHUU / **boat**	Hull and oars	舟
0312	般	HAN / **sort**	舟 (boat)[311] + 殳 (club)[K23]	般
0313	啓	KEI / **enlighten**	戸 (door)[284] + 攵 (strike)[K46] + 口 (open)[106]	啓
0314	求	KYUU / **request, seek**	一 (top)[K1] + 水 (*water*)[22] + 丶 (accent)[K2]	求
0315	救	KYUU / **rescue**	求 (request)[314] + 攵 (strike)[K46]	救

Day four: writing practice

改	攻	行	役	没	放	牧
改	攻	行	役	没	放	牧
枚	区	殴	疫	段	政	故
枚	区	殴	疫	段	政	故
致	殺	舟	般	啓	求	救
致	殺	舟	般	啓	求	救

Day five: story sketch

改	reform: 己 (self) + 攵 (strike) + Korrective Action Induces
攻	attack: 工 (work) + 攵 (strike) + KOercive Offense
行	go: (crossroads) + Karry Out Objective
役	service: 彳 (go) + 殳 (club) + Your AKtion Undertaken
没	sink: 氵 (water) + 殳 (club) + Become OTherwise SUbmerged
放	release: 方 (direction) + 攵 (strike) + Hand One Over
牧	pasture: 牛 (cow) + 攵 (strike) + BOvine KUisine
枚	sheet counter: 木 (wood) + 攵 (strike) + Measures Attenuated Items
区	ward: 匚 (container) + ✕ (mark) + Kounty Unit
殴	beat: 区 (ward) + 殳 (club) + Openhanded Offense
疫	epidemic: 疒 (illness) + 殳 (club) + Everyone Kontracts Infection
段	step: *serrated cliff* + 殳 (club) + Divide ANgular
政	government: 正 (correct) + 攵 (strike) + State Exerts Influence
故	past: 古 (old) + 攵 (strike) + Kurrently Over
致	do: 至 (arrive) + 攵 (strike) + Convey Human Intent
殺	kill: ✕ (mark) + 木 (wood) + 殳 (club) + Success AT SUicide
舟	boat: (hull and oars) + Sails HUll Underneath
般	sort: 舟 (boat) + 殳 (club) + Has Alike Nature
啓	enlighten: 戸 (door) + 攵 (strike) + 口 (open) + Konvey Eternal Insight
求	request: 亠 (top) + 水 (*water*) + 丶 (accent) + Kall Yet Upon Us
救	rescue: 求 (request) + 攵 (strike) + Kall You Urgently Utter

Day six: character clusters

I   Complete the characters using the clues.

1	殳	Has Alike Nature (HAN)
2	疒	Everyone Kontracts Infection (EKI)
3	求	Kall You Urgently Utter (KYUU)
4	口	Konvey Eternal Insight (KEI)
5	攵	Measures Attenuated Items (MAI)

II   Compose the compounds using the clues.

1   (NICHI) 日   +   (BOTSU) ____   =   _____ (sunset)
    sun

2   (KAI) ____   +   (SEI) 正   =   _____ (revision)
                          correct

3   (HOO) ____   +   (KA) 火   =   _____ (arson)
                          fire

4   (JI) 事   +   (KO) ____   =   _____ (accident)
    matter

5   (YAKU) ____   +   (WARI) 割   =   _____ (role/ part)
                          divide

III Complete the sentences using the clues.

1   京都への旅___はどうでしたか。
    Kyooto e no ryoKOO wa doo deshita ka.
    How was your trip to Kyoto?

2   多くの人は___治に興味がありません。
    Ooku no hito wa SEIji ni kyoomi ga arimasen.
    Many people are not interested in politics.

3   田中さんは自___したそうです。
    Tanaka-san wa jiSATSU shita soo desu.
    I heard that Mr. Tanaka committed suicide.

4   両チームの___別ができません。
    Ryoo chiiimu no KUbetsu ga dekimasen.
    It is difficult to distinguish between the teams.

5   魚の値___がずいぶん上がりました。
    Sakana no neDAN ga zuibun agarimashita.
    Fish prices have gone up a lot.

REVIEW: LESSONS 11–15

I   Given the character and meaning, write the pronunciation.

1 芸 art _____   2 迫 press _____   3 有 have _____

4 区 ward _____   5 純 pure _____   6 茂 thick _____

7 糸 thread _____   8 述 state _____   9 肯 agree _____

10 段 step _____   11 紅 crimson _____ 12 芝 lawn _____

13 週 week _____   14 胎 womb _____   15 救 rescue _____

16 紋 crest _____   17 牙 fang _____   18 逃 escape _____

19 肌 skin _____   20 殴 beat _____   21 紡 spin _____

22 荒 wild _____   23 逆 reverse _____ 24 肘 elbow _____

25 致 do _____   26 細 slender _____ 27 央 center _____

28 肥 fatten _____ 29 前 before _____   30 般 sort _____

II   Given the character and pronunciation, write the meaning.

1 迷 MEI _____   2 芋 imo _____   3 系 KEI _____

4 肝 KAN _____   5 枚 MAI _____   6 屯 TON _____

7 苛 KA _____   8 込 ko _____   9 肩 KEN _____

10 啓 KEI _____   11 累 RUI _____   12 芽 GA _____

13 巡 JUN _____   14 脱 DATSU _____   15 糾 KYUU _____

16 荘 SOO _____   17 迎 GEI _____   18 胆 TAN _____

19 改 KAI _____   20 素 SO _____   21 菓 KA _____

22 背 HAI _____   23 殺 SATSU _____   24 紳 SHIN _____

25 苦 KU _____   26 股 KO _____   27 役 YAKU _____

28 苗 BYOO _____   29 紹 SHOO _____   30 英 EI _____

III   Given the meaning and pronunciation, write the character.

1 return	HEN	_____	2 meat	NIKU	_____
3 chronicle	KI	_____	4 attack	KOO	_____
5 divide	BUN	_____	6 past	SEKI	_____
7 flower	KA	_____	8 heaven	TEN	_____
9 trunk	DOO	_____	10 request	KYUU	_____
11 writing	BUN	_____	12 fragrant	HOO	_____
13 alternate	TETSU	_____	14 resemble	SHOO	_____
15 past	KO	_____	16 inside	NAI	_____
17 young	JAKU	_____	18 rice	BEI	_____
19 stomach	I	_____	20 sink	BOTSU	_____
21 north	HOKU	_____	22 state	SHIN	_____
23 boat	SHUU	_____	24 door	KO	_____
25 epidemic	EKI	_____			

IV   Compose compounds using the following characters.

東 近 放 壮 肪 政 大 迅 約 失 脂 草 行 紛 速 送 辺 納 入 牧

1 (FUN) _____   +   (SHITSU) _____   =   _____ (loss)

2 (NOO) _____   +   (NYUU) _____   =   _____ (payment)

3 (SOO) _____   +   (DAI) _____   =   _____ (magnificence)

4 (HOO) _____   +   (SOO) _____   =   _____ (broadcasting)

5 (YAKU) _____   +   (SOKU) _____   =   _____ (promise)

6 (GYOO) _____   +   (SEI) _____   =   _____ (administration)

7 (SHI) _____   +   (BOO) _____   =   _____ (fat)

8 (BOKU) _____   +   (SOO) _____   =   _____ (grass)

9 (KIN) _____   +   (PEN) _____   =   _____ (vicinity)

10 (JIN) _____   +   (SOKU) _____   =   _____ (quickness)

16

UNDER THE SAME ROOF

Day one: crossword puzzle

Across

8. Kommands A Nation
9. Great Integrity
12. Space Has ITS Use
15. SHelter Under
18. Upward
19. To Eliminate Imprecision
20. Just ITs SUbstance (R)
21. Konsider Your Average KUstomer (G)

Down

1. Jagged Ideogram (C)
2. Surely ENunciate (A)
3. Something Has Other (M)
4. HOard Opulent
5. SHared Unworldly Understanding
6. Koncluded All Now (C)
7. Give An Injury
10. The Abiding Kin Unit
11. Kavernous Entry To Space Underneath
13. God's ENtry
14. Contains HUge Universe
16. SHort Individual
17. Green You Ornamentally Kan Use (J)

Day two: acrostics

1 Character: J _ _ _ _ _   I _ _ _ _ _ _ _

2 Announce: S _ _ _ _ _   E N _ _ _ _ _ _ _

3 Moreover: S _ _ _ _ _ _ _ _   H _ _   O _ _ _ _

4 Treasure: H O _ _ _   O _ _ _ _ _ _

5 Religion: S H _ _ _ _   U _ _ _ _ _ _ _ _   U _ _ _ _ _ _ _ _ _ _ _

6 Complete: K _ _ _ _ _ _ _ _   A _ _   N _ _

7 Harm: G _ _ _   A _   I _ _ _ _ _

8 Government: K _ _ _ _ _ _ _   A   N _ _ _ _ _

9 Right: G _ _ _ _   I _ _ _ _ _ _ _

10 Home: T _ _   A _ _ _ _ _ _   K _ _   U _ _ _

11 Hole: K _ _ _ _ _ _ _ _   E _ _ _ _   T _   S _ _ _ _   U _ _ _ _ _ _ _ _

12 Room: S _ _ _ _   H _ _   I T S   U _ _

13 Origin: G _ _ _   E N _ _ _

14 Space: C _ _ _ _ _ _ _   H U _ _   U _ _ _ _ _ _ _

15 Protect: S H _ _ _ _ _   U _ _ _ _

16 Child: S H _ _ _   I _ _ _ _ _ _ _ _

17 Jewel: G _ _ _ _   Y _ _   O _ _ _ _ _ _ _ _ _ _ _   K _ _   U _ _

18 Heavens: U _ _ _ _ _

19 Fix: T _   E _ _ _ _ _ _ _ _   I _ _ _ _ _ _ _ _ _

20 Real: J _ _ _   I T _   S U _ _ _ _ _ _

21 Guest: K _ _ _ _ _ _ _   Y _ _ _   A _ _ _ _ _ _   K U _ _ _ _ _ _

Day three: componential analysis

Course Number	Kanji	ON Reading(s) Core Concept(s)	Primary Components	Kanji Canvas
0316	穴	KETSU **hole**	宀 (roof)^{K51} + 八 (eight)^{04}	穴
0317	守	SHU **protect**	宀 (roof)^{K51} + 寸 (measure)^{11}	守
0318	宅	TAKU **home**	宀 (roof)^{K51} + ノ (accent)^{K2} + 七 (seven)^{03}	宅
0319	宇	U **heavens**	宀 (roof)^{K51} + 丁 (exact)^{87} + 一 (one)^{01}	宇
0320	子	SHI, SU **child**	Wrapped in clothes with arms outstretched	子
0321	字	JI **character**	宀 (roof)^{K51} + 子 (child)^{320}	字
0322	元	GEN, GAN **origin**	二 (two)^{02} + 儿 (boy)^{K5}	元
0323	完	KAN **complete**	宀 (roof)^{K51} + 元 (origin)^{322}	完
0324	定	TEI, JOO **fix; decide**	宀 (roof)^{K51} + 正 (correct)^{166}	定
0325	実	JITSU **real**	宀 (roof)^{K51} + 三 (three)^{09} + 人 (person)^{64}	実
0326	宗	SHUU **religion**	宀 (roof)^{K51} + 示 (altar)^{176}	宗
0327	官	KAN **government**	宀 (roof)^{K51} + 𠂤 (buttocks)^{K52}	官
0328	宙	CHUU **space**	宀 (roof)^{K51} + 由 (reason)^{39}	宙
0329	玉	GYOKU **jewel**	String of jade beads	玉
0330	宝	HOO **treasure**	宀 (roof)^{K51} + 玉 (jewel)^{329}	宝
0331	且	SHO **moreover**	Three blocks on a base	且
0332	宜	GI **right, appropriate**	宀 (roof)^{K51} + 且 (moreover)^{331}	宜
0333	宣	SEN **announce**	宀 (roof)^{K51} + 二 (two)^{02} + 日 (day)^{17}	宣
0334	室	SHITSU **room**	宀 (roof)^{K51} + 至 (arrive)^{173}	室
0335	客	KYAKU **guest, visitor**	宀 (roof)^{K51} + 各 (each)^{122}	客
0336	害	GAI **harm**	宀 (roof)^{K51} + 生 (*life*)^{142} + 口 (open)^{106}	害

Day four: writing practice

穴	守	宅	宇	子	字	元
穴	守	宅	宇	子	字	元
完	定	実	宗	官	宙	玉
完	定	実	宗	官	宙	玉
宝	且	宜	宣	室	客	害
宝	且	宜	宣	室	客	害

Day five: story sketch

穴	hole: 宀 (roof) + 八 (eight) + Kavernous Entry To Space Underneath
守	protect: 宀 (roof) + 寸 (measure) + SHelter Under
宅	home: 宀 (roof) + 丿 (accent) + 七 (seven) + The Abiding Kin Unit
宇	heavens: 宀 (roof) + 丁 (exact) + 一 (one) + Upward
子	child: (wrapped in clothes with arms outstretched) + SHort Individual
字	character: 宀 (roof) + 子 (child) + Jagged Ideogram
元	origin: 二 (two) + 儿 (boy) + God's ENtry
完	complete: 宀 (roof) + 元 (origin) + Koncluded All Now
定	fix: 宀 (roof) + 正 (correct) + To Eliminate Imprecision
実	real: 宀 (roof) + 三 (three) + 人 (person) + Just ITs SUbstance
宗	religion: 宀 (roof) + 示 (altar) + SHared Unworldly Understanding
官	government: 宀 (roof) + 𠂤 (buttocks) + Kommands A Nation
宙	space: 宀 (roof) + 由 (reason) + Contains HUge Universe
玉	jewel: (string of jade beads) + Green You Ornamentally Kan Use
宝	treasure: 宀 (roof) + 玉 (jewel) + HOard Opulent
且	moreover: (three blocks on a base) + Something Has Other
宜	right: 宀 (roof) + 且 (moreover) + Great Integrity
宣	announce: 宀 (roof) + 二 (two) + 日 (day) + Surely ENunciate
室	room: 宀 (roof) + 至 (arrive) + Space Has ITS Use
客	guest: 宀 (roof) + 各 (each) + Konsider Your Average KUstomer
害	harm: 宀 (roof) + 生 (*life*) + 口 (open) + Give An Injury

Day six: character clusters

I   Complete the characters using the clues.

1	宀	Kommands A Nation (KAN)
2	王	Green You Ornamentally Kan Use (GYOKU)
3	宀	Kavernous Entry To Space Underneath (KETSU)
4	儿	God's ENtry (GEN)
5	宀	SHelter Under (SHU)

II   Compose the compounds using the clues.

1   (GEN) 原   +   (SHI) ____   =   _____ (atom)
        original

2   (HOO) ____   +   (SEKI) 石   =   _____ (jewel)
                                stone

3   (KOO) 公   +   (GAI) ____   =   _____ (pollution)
        public

4   (JUU) 住   +   (TAKU) ____   =   _____ (residence)
        reside

5   (SHITSU) ____   +   (NAI) 内   =   _____ (interior)
                                inside

III   Complete the sentences using the clues.

1   プロジェクトはもうすぐ＿＿成します。
      Purojekuto wa moo sugu KANsei shimasu.
      The project will soon be complete.

2   明日は何か予＿＿がありますか。
      Ashita wa nani-ka yoTEI ga arimasu ka.
      Do you have any plans tomorrow?

3   バーバラが社長だというのは事＿＿です。
      Baabara ga shachoo da to iu no wa jiJITSU desu.
      It is a fact that Barbara is company president.

4   ラジオでその＿＿伝を聞きました。
      Rajio de sono SENden o kikimashita.
      I heard that advertisement on the radio.

5   このバスには50人乗＿＿を収容できます。
      Kono basu ni wa go-juu-nin jooKYAKU o shuuyoo dekimasu.
      This bus can hold fifty passengers.

17

WOMEN'S LIB

Day one: crossword puzzle

Across

4. Jump Outcomes (S)
7. Special Entitled Identity (S)
9. Makes YOu Outstanding (E)
11. Mindlessly Obeys Others (I)
14. Spouse Attracts Interest
15. Sun Exit Is
19. Initiates Nuptials
20. Nucleus INseminated
21. Herself Imperial

Down

1. Agitated Not (P)
2. INduce
3. Your Observation Overpowers
5. Maiden Alde (two words: Y/S)
6. Yes Observance Obligatory
8. Delicate Accord
10. Tips Snatch Unsuspecting MEal
12. KOngenial Origin (L)
13. Block Oncoming Object
16. Dominantly Owned
17. Jovial Ovaries
18. Start HIstory

Day two: acrostics

1 Peaceful: A _ _ _ _ _ _ _   N _ _

2 Cause: I N _ _ _ _

3 Bewitching: Y _ _ _   O _ _ _ _ _ _ _ _ _   O _ _ _ _ _ _ _ _

4 Similar: J _ _ _   O _ _ _ _ _ _ _

5 Younger Sister: M _ _ _ _ _ _   A I _ _

6 Necessary: Y _ _   O _ _ _ _ _ _ _ _   O _ _ _ _ _ _ _ _

7 Surname: S _ _ _ _ _ _   E _ _ _ _ _ _ _   I _ _ _ _ _ _ _

8 Agreement: D _ _ _ _ _ _ _   A _ _ _ _ _

9 Exquisite: M _ _ _ _   Y O _   O _ _ _ _ _ _ _ _ _

10 Claw: T _ _ _   S _ _ _ _ _ _   U _ _ _ _ _ _ _ _ _ _   M E _ _

11 Irrational: M _ _ _ _ _ _ _ _   O _ _ _ _   O _ _ _ _ _

12 Like: K O _ _ _ _ _ _ _   O _ _ _ _ _

13 Obstruct: B _ _ _ _   O _ _ _ _ _ _ _   O _ _ _ _ _

14 Wife: S _ _ _ _ _   A _ _ _ _ _ _ _   I _ _ _ _ _ _ _

15 West: S _ _   E _ _ _   I _

16 Slave: D _ _ _ _ _ _ _ _ _   O _ _ _ _

17 Woman: J _ _ _ _ _   O _ _ _ _ _ _

18 Begin: S _ _ _ _   H I _ _ _ _ _

19 Marriage: I _ _ _ _ _ _ _ _   N _ _ _ _ _ _ _

20 Pregnant: N _ _ _ _ _ _   I N _ _ _ _ _ _ _ _ _

21 Queen: H _ _ _ _ _ _   I _ _ _ _ _ _ _

Day three: componential analysis

Course Number	Kanji	ON Reading(s) / Core Concept(s)	Primary Components	Kanji Canvas
0337	女	JO / **woman**	Seated with legs crossed	女
0338	奴	DO / **slave**	女 (woman)[337] + 又 (hand)[K15]	奴
0339	妄	MOO, BOO / **irrational; rash**	亡 (dead)[134] + 女 (woman)[337]	妄
0340	安	AN / **peaceful; cheap**	宀 (roof)[K51] + 女 (woman)[337]	安
0341	好	KOO / **like; good**	女 (woman)[337] + 子 (child)[320]	好
0342	妃	HI / **queen; princess**	女 (woman)[337] + 己 (self)[132]	妃
0343	如	JO, NYO / **similar, like**	女 (woman)[337] + 口 (mouth)[106]	如
0344	妊	NIN / **pregnant**	女 (woman)[337] + ノ (accent)[K2] + 士 (samurai)[67]	妊
0345	妙	MYOO / **exquisite**	女 (woman)[337] + 少 (little)[32]	妙
0346	妨	BOO / **obstruct**	女 (woman)[337] + 方 (direction)[174]	妨
0347	妖	YOO / **bewitching**	女 (woman)[337] + 夭 (heaven)[261]	妖
0348	爪	tsume / **claw; fingernail**	Curved, pointed nails	爪
0349	妥	DA / **agreement**	爫 (claw)[K53] + 女 (woman)[337]	妥
0350	姓	SEI / **surname**	女 (woman)[337] + 生 (life)[142]	姓
0351	妹	MAI / **younger sister**	女 (woman)[337] + 未 (not yet)[44]	妹
0352	始	SHI / **begin**	女 (woman)[337] + 台 (platform)[114]	始
0353	妻	SAI / **wife**	十 (ten)[06] + ヨ (open hand)[K54] + 女 (woman)[337]	妻
0354	西	SEI / **west**	Sun sinking below horizon	西
0355	要	YOO / **necessary**	西 (west)[354] + 女 (woman)[337]	要
0356	因	IN / **cause**	囗 (enclosure)[K4] + 大 (big)[233]	因
0357	姻	IN / **marriage**	女 (woman)[337] + 因 (cause)[356]	姻

Day four: writing practice

女	奴	妄	安	好	妃	如
女	奴	妄	安	好	妃	如
妊	妙	妨	妖	爪	妥	姓
妊	妙	妨	妖	爪	妥	姓
妹	始	妻	西	要	因	姻
妹	始	妻	西	要	因	姻

Day five: story sketch

女	woman: (seated with legs crossed) + Jovial Ovaries
奴	slave: 女 (woman) + 又 (right hand) + Dominantly Owned
妄	irrational: 亡 (dead) + 女 (woman) + Mindlessly Obeys Others
安	peaceful: 宀 (roof) + 女 (woman) + Agitated Not
好	like: 女 (woman) + 子 (child) + KOngenial Origin
妃	queen: 女 (woman) + 己 (self) + Herself Imperial
如	similar: 女 (woman) + 口 (mouth) + Jump Outcomes
妊	pregnant: 女 (woman) + ノ (accent) + 士 (samurai) + Nucleus INseminated
妙	exquisite: 女 (woman) + 少 (little) + Makes YOu Outstanding
妨	obstruct: 女 (woman) + 方 (direction) + Block Oncoming Object
妖	bewitching: 女 (woman) + 夭 (heaven) + Your Observation Overpowers
爪	claw: (curved, pointed nails) + Tips Snatch Unsuspecting MEal
妥	agreement: ⺥ (claw) + 女 (woman) + Delicate Accord
姓	surname: 女 (woman) + 生 (life) + Special Entitled Identity
妹	younger sister: 女 (woman) + 未 (not yet) + Maiden AIde
始	begin: 女 (woman) + 台 (platform) + Start HIstory
妻	wife: 十 (ten) + ヨ (open hand) + 女 (woman) + Spouse Attracts Interest
西	west: (sun sinking below horizon) + Sun Exit Is
要	necessary: 西 (west) + 女 (woman) + Yes Observance Obligatory
因	cause: 口 (enclosure) + 大 (big) + INduce
姻	marriage: 女 (woman) + 因 (cause) + Initiates Nuptials

Day six: character clusters

I   Complete the characters using the clues.

1	女	Dominantly Owned (DO)
2	亡	Mindlessly Obeys Others (MOO)
3	女	Herself Imperial (HI)
4	未	Maiden AIde (MAI)
5	女	Spouse Attracts Interest (SAI)

II   Compose the compounds using the clues.

1   (KOO) 巧   +   (MYOO) ____   =   _____ (clever)
    skill

2   (FU) 不   +   (NIN) ____   =   _____ (sterility)
    not

3   (JO) ____   +   (SEI) 性   =   _____ (woman)
                    sex

4   (KAI) 開   +   (SHI) ____   =   _____ (beginning)
    open

5   (DA) ____   +   (KYOO) 協   =   _____ (compromise)
                    cooperation

III   Complete the sentences using the clues.

1   その事故の原＿＿はなんでしたか。
    Sono jiko no genIN wa nan deshita ka.
    What was the cause of the accident?

2   心配する必＿＿はないと思う。
    Shinpai suru hitsuYOO wa nai to omou.
    I think that there is no need to worry.

3   北＿＿には人口が少ないです。
    HokuSEI ni wa jinkoo ga sukunai desu.
    In the northwest there is a small population.

4   知らない人が私にとても＿＿意を示した。
    Shiranai hito ga watashi ni totemo KOOi o shimeshita.
    The stranger was very kind to me.

5   このビルにいれば＿＿全です。
    Kono biru ni ireba ANzen desu.
    If you stay in this building, it is safe.

18
MONEY MAKER

Day one: crossword puzzle

Across

2. Kommercial Assets (G)
4. Desire ONly
6. King Obtains Obeisance (T)
11. TEmperate Integrity
13. Standard Ordinary KUstom
15. Wealth Affords Influence
16. HArmfully Impede
19. SElf Kulpability Implies (R)
20. Have Auction Now
21. Individual Name (M)

Down

1. Brief Artful Inflection
3. Continuously HOld
5. Konsider Invaluable (P)
7. Fully Undertake
8. Closely HOld Onto (A)
9. BArgain Item
10. Temporarily Avail Item
12. Zillion Assets Indicate
14. KAlcium Item (S)
17. Buy Offer Other
18. Holdings INadequate

Day two: acrostics

1 Song: B _ _ _ _   A _ _ _ _ _   I _ _ _ _ _ _ _ _

2 Goods: K _ _ _ _ _ _ _ _   A _ _ _ _ _

3 Store: C _ _ _ _ _ _ _ _ _ _   H O _ _

4 Covet: D _ _ _ _ _   O N _ _

5 Precious: K _ _ _ _ _ _ _   I _ _ _ _ _ _ _ _

6 Tribute: K _ _ _   O _ _ _ _ _ _   O _ _ _ _ _ _ _

7 Bear: F _ _ _ _   U _ _ _ _ _ _ _ _

8 Affix: C _ _ _ _ _ _   H O _ _   O _ _ _

9 Buy: B A _ _ _ _ _   I _ _ _

10 Lend: T _ _ _ _ _ _ _ _ _   A _ _ _ _   I _ _ _

11 Chaste: T E _ _ _ _ _ _ _   I _ _ _ _ _ _ _ _

12 Wealth: Z _ _ _ _ _ _   A _ _ _ _ _   I _ _ _ _ _ _ _

13 Rule: S _ _ _ _ _ _ _   O _ _ _ _ _ _ _   K U _ _ _ _

14 Shell: K A _ _ _ _ _   I _ _ _

15 Bribe: W _ _ _ _ _ _   A _ _ _ _ _ _   I _ _ _ _ _ _ _ _

16 Defeat: H A _ _ _ _ _ _ _   I _ _ _ _ _

17 Trade: B _ _   O _ _ _ _   O _ _ _ _

18 Poor: H _ _ _ _ _ _ _   I N _ _ _ _ _ _ _ _

19 Responsibility: S E _ _   K _ _ _ _ _ _ _ _ _   I _ _ _ _ _ _

20 Sell: H _ _ _   A _ _ _ _ _ _   N _ _

21 Member: I _ _ _ _ _ _ _ _ _   N _ _ _

Day three: componential analysis

Course Number	Kanji	ON Reading(s) / Core Concept(s)	Primary Components	Kanji Canvas
0358	貝	kai / **shell (money)**	Shellfish	貝
0359	則	SOKU / **rule**	貝 (money)[358] + 刂 (cut)[K36]	則
0360	負	FU / **bear; defeat**	⺈ (bending)[K55] + 貝 (money)[358]	負
0361	貞	TEI / **chaste**	卜 (divination)[K10] + 貝 (money)[358]	貞
0362	財	ZAI / **wealth**	貝 (money)[358] + 才 (talent)[52]	財
0363	員	IN / **member**	口 (mouth)[106] + 貝 (money)[358]	員
0364	貢	KOO / **tribute**	工 (work)[26] + 貝 (money)[358]	貢
0365	唄	BAI / **song**	口 (mouth)[106] + 貝 (money)[358]	唄
0366	貨	KA / **goods**	化 (change)[65] + 貝 (money)[358]	貨
0367	責	SEKI / **responsibility**	生 (*life*)[142] + 貝 (money)[358]	責
0368	敗	HAI / **defeat**	貝 (money)[358] + 攵 (strike)[K46]	敗
0369	貧	HIN, BIN / **poor**	分 (divide)[219] + 貝 (money)[358]	貧
0370	販	HAN / **sell**	貝 (moncy)[358] + 反 (oppose)[58]	販
0371	貪	DON / **covet**	今 (now)[139] + 貝 (money)[358]	貪
0372	貼	CHOO / **affix**	貝 (money)[358] + 占 (occupy)[112]	貼
0373	買	BAI / **buy**	罒 (net)[K56] + 貝 (money)[358]	買
0374	貸	TAI / **lend**	代 (replace)[73] + 貝 (money)[358]	貸
0375	貴	KI / **precious; noble**	中 (middle)[77] + 一 (one)[01] + 貝 (money)[358]	貴
0376	貯	CHO / **store, save**	貝 (money)[358] + 宀 (roof)[K51] + 丁 (exact)[87]	貯
0377	貿	BOO / **trade**	*sharp* (cf. 489) + 貝 (money)[358]	貿
0378	賄	WAI / **bribe**	貝 (money)[358] + 有 (have)[275]	賄

Day four: writing practice

貝	則	負	貞	財	員	貢
貝	則	負	貞	財	員	貢
唄	貨	責	敗	貧	販	貪
唄	貨	責	敗	貧	販	貪
貼	買	貸	貴	貯	貿	賄
貼	買	貸	貴	貯	貿	賄

Day five: story sketch

貝	shell: (shellfish) + KAlcium Item
則	rule: 貝 (money) + 刂 (cut) + Standard Ordinary KUstom
負	bear: ⺈ (bending) + 貝 (money) + Fully Undertake
貞	chaste: 卜 (divination) + 貝 (money) + TEmperate Integrity
財	wealth: 貝 (money) + 才 (talent) + Zillion Assets Indicate
員	member: 口 (mouth) + 貝 (money) + Individual Name
貢	tribute: 工 (work) + 貝 (money) + King Obtains Obeisance
唄	song: 口 (mouth) + 貝 (money) + Brief Artful Inflection
貨	goods: 化 (change) + 貝 (money) + Kommercial Assets
責	responsibility: 生 (*life*) + 貝 (money) + SElf Kulpability Implies
敗	defeat: 貝 (money) + 攵 (strike) + HArmfully Impede
貧	poor: 分 (divide) + 貝 (money) + Holdings INadequate
販	sell: 貝 (money) + 反 (oppose) + Have Auction Now
貪	covet: 今 (now) + 貝 (money) + Desire ONly
貼	affix: 貝 (money) + 占 (occupy) + Closely HOld Onto
買	buy: 罒 (net) + 貝 (money) + BArgain Item
貸	lend: 代 (replace) + 貝 (money) + Temporarily Avail Item
貴	precious: 中 (middle) + 一 (one) + 貝 (money) + Konsider Invaluable
貯	store: 貝 (money) + 宀 (roof) + 丁 (exact) + Continuously HOld
貿	trade: *sharp* + 貝 (money) + Buy Offer Other
賄	bribe: 貝 (money) + 有 (have) + Wealth Affords Influence

Day six: character clusters

I Complete the characters using the clues.

1	貝	Kommercial Assets (KA)
2	口	Brief Artful Inflection (BAI)
3	工	King Obtains Obeisance (KOO)
4	貝	HArmfully Impede (HAI)
5	罒	BArgain Item (BAI)

II Compose the compounds using the clues.

1 (ZAI) _____ + (SAN) 産 = _____ (property)
                product

2 (FU) _____ + (TAN) 担 = _____ (burden)
                bear

3 (HIN) _____ + (KON) 困 = _____ (poverty)
                difficulty

4 (HAN) _____ + (BAI) 売 = _____ (sales)
                sell

5 (KI) _____ + (ZOKU) 族 = _____ (nobility)
                family, clan

III Complete the sentences using the clues.

1 いつも規＿＿を守らなければならない。
Itsumo kiSOKU o mamoranakereba naranai.
We must always obey the rules.

2 その仕事は自分の＿＿任です。
Sono shigoto wa jibun no SEKInin desu.
That job is my responsibility.

3 私は車を買うために＿＿金している。
Watashi wa kuruma o kau tame ni CHOkin shite iru.
I am saving money to buy a car.

4 日本はイタリアと多くの商品を＿＿易しています。
Nihon wa itaria to ooku no shoohin o BOOeki shite imasu.
Japan trades many goods with Italy.

5 矢野さんはスポーツクラブの会＿＿です。
Yano-san wa supootsu kurabu no kaiIN desu.
Mr. Yano is a member of the sports club.

19

UNDER COVER

Day one: crossword puzzle

Across

4. Right YOur Objective
5. Kotton INterwoven
8. REquisite Instruction
9. MErely Invisible (H)
13. Stocks Odd Objects
14. Zone ENtire
16. Break Out That's So Unexpected
17. Seek A Key Unseen
19. Interwoven (C)
20. SHocking INcursion (I)
21. The Empire Icon

Down

1. Savory Heart Of KUlture
2. Kourse Intent (P)
3. KIng's Nuggets
6. SHeltered Abode
7. Yield Offer
10. Yet Over (E)
11. Judgment On Opinion (S)
12. SHape Alike (C)
15. Initial CHarter Integer
18. Konference AIm

Day two: acrostics

1 Food: S _ _ _ _ _   H _ _ _ _   O _   K U _ _ _ _ _

2 Plan: K _ _ _ _ _   I _ _ _ _ _

3 Gold: K I _ _ _   N _ _ _ _ _ _

4 Good: R _ _ _ _   Y O _ _   O _ _ _ _ _ _ _

5 Cloth: K _ _ _ _ _   I N _ _ _ _ _ _ _

6 House: S H _ _ _ _ _ _ _   A _ _ _ _

7 Give: Y _ _ _ _   O _ _ _ _

8 Order: R E _ _ _ _ _ _ _   I _ _ _ _ _ _ _ _ _

9 Hidden: M E _ _ _ _   I _ _ _ _ _ _ _

10 Excess: Y _ _   O _ _ _

11 Superfluous: J _ _ _ _ _ _ _   O _   O _ _ _ _ _ _

12 Copy: S H _ _ _   A _ _ _ _

13 Storehouse: S _ _ _ _ _   O _ _   O _ _ _ _ _ _

14 Complete: Z _ _ _   E N _ _ _ _

15 One: I _ _ _ _ _ _   C H _ _ _ _ _   I _ _ _ _ _ _

16 Sudden: B _ _ _ _   O _ _   T _ _ _ _   S _   U _ _ _ _ _ _ _ _ _

17 Search: S _ _ _   A   K _ _   U _ _ _ _ _

18 Meet: K _ _ _ _ _ _ _ _ _   A I _

19 Clothes: I _ _ _ _ _ _ _ _ _

20 Invade: S H _ _ _ _ _ _   I N _ _ _ _ _ _ _

21 Emperor: T _ _   E _ _ _ _ _   I _ _ _

Day three: componential analysis

Course Number	Kanji	ON Reading(s) / Core Concept(s)	Primary Components	Kanji Canvas
0379	冗	JOO / superfluous	冖 (cover)[K26] + 几 (table)[K11]	冗
0380	令	REI / order, command	𠆢 (cover)[K26] + 一 (one)[01] + 卩 (bowing)[K57]	令
0381	与	YO / give	丂 (emerge)[K28] + 一 (one)[01]	与
0382	写	SHA / copy	冖 (cover)[K26] + 与 (give)[381]	写
0383	会	KAI / meet	𠆢 (cover)[K26] + 二 (two)[02] + 厶 (self)[K18]	会
0384	全	ZEN / complete	𠆢 (cover)[K26] + 王 (king)[155]	全
0385	企	KI / plan	𠆢 (cover)[K26] + 止 (stop)[165]	企
0386	余	YO / excess, remaining	𠆢 (cover)[K26] + 二 (two)[02] + 小 (small)[31]	余
0387	壱	ICHI / one	士 (samurai)[67] + 冖 (cover)[K26] + ヒ (sitting)[K17]	壱
0388	金	KIN / gold; money; metal	𠆢 (cover)[K26] + *nuggets* + 土 (ground)[169]	金
0389	舎	SHA / house	𠆢 (cover)[K26] + 土 (ground)[169] + 口 (open)[106]	舎
0390	侵	SHIN / invade, violate	亻 (person)[K16] + ヨ (open hand)[K54] + 冖 (cover)[K26] + 又 (hand)[K15]	侵
0391	勃	BOTSU / sudden	十 (ten)[06] + 冖 (cover)[K26] + 子 (child)[320] + 力 (power)[07]	勃
0392	倉	SOO / storehouse	𠆢 (cover)[K26] + 戸 (*door*)[284] + 口 (mouth)[106]	倉
0393	索	SAKU / search	十 (ten)[06] + 冖 (cover)[K26] + 糸 (thread)[211]	索
0394	冥	MEI, MYOO / hidden	冖 (cover)[K26] + 日 (sun)[17] + 六 (six)[14]	冥
0395	巾	KIN / cloth, towel	Towel hanging from pole	巾
0396	帝	TEI / emperor	立 (*stand*)[37] + 冖 (cover)[K26] + 巾 (cloth)[395]	帝
0397	衣	I / clothes	Robe folded over body	衣
0398	艮	RYOO / good	白 (white)[18] + 衣 (*clothes*)[397]	艮
0399	食	SHOKU / food; eat	𠆢 (cover)[K26] + 良 (good)[398]	食

Day four: writing practice

冗	令	与	写	会	全	企
冗	令	与	写	会	全	企
余	壱	金	舎	侵	勃	倉
余	壱	金	舎	侵	勃	倉
索	冥	巾	帝	衣	良	食
索	冥	巾	帝	衣	良	食

Day five: story sketch

冗	superfluous: 冖 (cover) + 几 (table) + Judgment On Opinion
令	order: 𠆢 (cover) + 一 (one) + 卩 (bowing) + REquisite Instruction
与	give: 丂 (emerge) + 一 (one) + Yield Offer
写	copy: 冖 (cover) + 与 (give) + SHape Alike
会	meet: 𠆢 (cover) + 二 (two) + 厶 (self) + Konference AIm
全	complete: 𠆢 (cover) + 王 (king) + Zone ENtire
企	plan: 𠆢 (cover) + 止 (stop) + Kourse Intent
余	excess: 𠆢 (cover) + 二 (two) + 小 (small) + Yet Over
壱	one: 士 (samurai) + 冖 (cover) + ヒ (sitting) + Initial CHarter Integer
金	gold: 𠆢 (cover) + *nuggets* + 土 (ground) + KIng's Nuggets
舎	house: 𠆢 (cover) + 土 (ground) + 口 (open) + SHeltered Abode
侵	invade: 亻 (person) + 彐 (open hand) + 冖 (cover) + 又 (hand) + SHocking INcursion
勃	sudden: 十 (ten) + 冖 (cover) + 子 (child) + 力 (power) + Break Out That's So Unexpected
倉	storehouse: 𠆢 (cover) + 戸 (*door*) + 口 (mouth) + Stocks Odd Objects
索	search: 十 (ten) + 冖 (cover) + 糸 (thread) + Seek A Key Unseen
冥	hidden: 冖 (cover) + 日 (sun) + 六 (six) + MErely Invisible
巾	cloth: (towel hanging from pole) + Kotton INterwoven
帝	emperor: 立 (*stand*) + 冖 (cover) + 巾 (cloth) + The Empire Icon
衣	clothes: (robe folded over body) + Interwoven
良	good: 白 (white) + 衣 (*clothes*) + Right YOur Objective
食	food: 𠆢 (cover) + 良 (good) + Savory Heart Of KUlture

Day six: character clusters

I   Complete the characters using the clues.

1	冂	Kourse Intent (KI)
2	亻	SHocking INcursion (SHIN)
3	士	Initial CHarter Integer (ICHI)
4	巾	The Empire Icon (TEI)
5	宀	MErely Invisible (MEI)

II   Compose the compounds using the clues.

1   (SHI) 思   +   (SAKU) _____   =   _____ (speculation)
        think

2   (YO) _____   +   (CHI) 地   =   _____ (room, space)
                                        ground

3   (RYOO) _____   +   (SHIN) 心   =   _____ (conscience)
                                        heart

4   (MEI) 命   +   (REI) _____   =   _____ (order)
        life

5   (JOO) _____   +   (DAN) 談   =   _____ (joke)
                                        talk

III   Complete the sentences using the clues.

1   クラス＿＿員がテストに合格しました。
    Kurasu ZENin ga tesuto ni gookaku shimashita.
    The whole class passed the test.

2   妹の＿＿真を撮るつもりです。
    Imooto no SHAshin o toru tsumori desu.
    I plan to take a photograph of my younger sister.

3   母から日本語の＿＿話を学んだ。
    Haha kara nihongo no KAIwa o mananda.
    I learned to speak Japanese from my mother.

4   このプレゼントは現＿＿で払ってもいいですか。
    Kono purezento wa genKIN de haratte mo ii desu ka.
    Can I pay for this present in cash?

5   今度の週末は外で＿＿事をしましょう。
    Kondo no shuumatsu wa soto de SHOKUji o shimashoo.
    Let's eat out this weekend.

20

CLOTHES LINE

Day one: crossword puzzle

Across

2. Ride YOnder (T)
5. Concealed Heart Utters Understanding (two words)
7. REnd This SUddenly
8. Kontinually You Occupy
11. Harmful Incident (U)
14. SHirt Underarm Unit (S)
16. Yields Utterly Unrestricted
17. Indispensable
18. HIde
20. KOncave Kleaves Uplands
21. Sewn Under Smoothed Out

Down

1. Totes Assorted Items
3. Honor Your Outward Order
4. SHow Opens (B)
6. Affliction Initiates (S)
9. To Exhibit Naked
10. Intimidates (F)
12. REpresents Things SUccessively
13. Continuous HOld On (L)
15. State Of Obliteration
19. Revealed All

Day two: acrostics

1 Bag: T _ _ _ _   A _ _ _ _ _ _ _   I _ _ _ _

2 Travel: R _ _ _   Y O _ _ _ _

3 Express: H _ _ _ _   Y _ _ _   O _ _ _ _ _ _   O _ _ _ _

4 Beginning: S H _ _   O _ _ _ _

5 Inner Feelings: C _ _ _ _ _ _ _ _   H _ _ _ _   U _ _ _ _ _   U _ _ _ _ _ _ _ _ _ _ _

6 Sorrow: A _ _ _ _ _ _ _ _   I _ _ _ _ _ _ _ _

7 Split: R E _ _   T _ _ _   S U _ _ _ _ _ _

8 Reside: K _ _ _ _ _ _ _ _ _ _   Y _ _   O _ _ _ _ _

9 Display: T _   E _ _ _ _ _ _   N _ _ _ _

10 Fear: I _ _ _ _ _ _ _ _ _ _

11 Undergo: H _ _ _ _ _ _   I _ _ _ _ _ _ _

12 Row: R E _ _ _ _ _ _ _ _   T _ _ _ _ _   S U _ _ _ _ _ _ _ _ _

13 Long: C _ _ _ _ _ _ _ _ _   H O _ _   O _

14 Sleeve: S H _ _ _   U _ _ _ _ _ _ _   U _ _ _

15 Loss: S _ _ _ _   O _   O _ _ _ _ _ _ _ _ _ _

16 Abundant: Y _ _ _ _ _ _   U _ _ _ _ _ _   U _ _ _ _ _ _ _ _ _ _

17 Depend: I _ _ _ _ _ _ _ _ _ _ _

18 Skin: H I _ _

19 Naked: R _ _ _ _ _ _ _   A _ _

20 Valley: K O _ _ _ _ _   K _ _ _ _ _ _   U _ _ _ _ _ _

21 Hem: S _ _ _   U _ _ _ _   S _ _ _ _ _ _ _   O _ _

Day three: componential analysis

Course Number	Kanji	ON Reading(s) / Core Concept(s)	Primary Components	Kanji Canvas
0400	初	SHO / **beginning, first**	衤 (clothes)[K58] + 刀 (knife)[115]	初
0401	表	HYOO / **express; surface**	生 (*life*)[142] + 衣 (clothes)[397]	表
0402	長	CHOO / **long; leader**	*hair* + 衣 (*clothes*)[397]	長
0403	依	I / **depend**	亻 (person)[K16] + 衣 (clothes)[397]	依
0404	畏	I / **fear**	田 (field)[60] + 衣 (*clothes*)[397]	畏
0405	衷	CHUU / **inner feelings**	衣 (clothes)[397] + 中 (middle)[77]	衷
0406	旅	RYO / **travel, journey**	方 (direction)[174] + 衣 (*clothes*)[397]	旅
0407	哀	AI / **sorrow, pity**	衣 (clothes)[397] + 口 (open)[106]	哀
0408	袖	SHUU / **sleeve**	衤 (clothes)[K58] + 由 (reason)[39]	袖
0409	皮	HI / **skin**	*animal skin* + 又 (hand)[K15]	皮
0410	被	HI / **undergo; cover**	衤 (clothes)[K58] + 皮 (skin)[409]	被
0411	展	TEN / **display**	尸 (bent body)[K59] + ⺾ (plants)[K29] + 衣 (*clothes*)[397]	展
0412	袋	TAI / **bag**	代 (replace)[73] + 衣 (clothes)[397]	袋
0413	谷	KOKU / **valley**	八 (*eight*)[04] + 𠆢 (cover)[K26] + 口 (open)[106]	谷
0414	裕	YUU / **abundant**	衤 (clothes)[K58] + 谷 (valley)[413]	裕
0415	列	RETSU / **row, line**	歹 (disintegrate)[K60] + 刂 (cut)[K36]	列
0416	裂	RETSU / **split, tear**	列 (row)[415] + 衣 (clothes)[397]	裂
0417	喪	SOO / **loss; mourn**	十 (ten)[06] + 口 (two mouths)[106] + 衣 (*clothes*)[397]	喪
0418	居	KYO / **reside, be**	尸 (bent body)[K59] + 古 (old)[108]	居
0419	裾	suso / **hem, cuff**	衤 (clothes)[K58] + 居 (reside)[418]	裾
0420	裸	RA / **naked**	衤 (clothes)[K58] + 果 (result)[61]	裸

Day four: writing practice

初	表	長	依	畏	衷	旅
初	表	長	依	畏	衷	旅
哀	袖	皮	被	展	袋	谷
哀	袖	皮	被	展	袋	谷
裕	列	裂	喪	居	裾	裸
裕	列	裂	喪	居	裾	裸

Day five: story sketch

初	beginning: 衤 (clothes) + 刀 (knife) + SHow Opens
表	express: 生 (*life*) + 衣 (clothes) + Honor Your Outward Order
長	long: *hair* + 衣 (*clothes*) + Continuous HOld On
依	depend: 亻 (person) + 衣 (clothes) + Indispensable
畏	fear: 田 (field) + 衣 (*clothes*) + Intimidates
衷	inner feelings: 衣 (clothes) + 中 (middle) + Concealed Heart Utters Understanding
旅	travel: 方 (direction) + 衣 (*clothes*) + Ride YOnder
哀	sorrow: 衣 (clothes) + 口 (open) + Affliction Initiates
袖	sleeve: 衤 (clothes) + 由 (reason) + SHirt Underarm Unit
皮	skin: *animal skin* + 又 (hand) + HIde
被	undergo: 衤 (clothes) + 皮 (skin) + Harmful Incident
展	display: 尸 (bent body) + 艹 (plants) + 衣 (*clothes*) + To Exhibit Naked
袋	bag: 代 (replace) + 衣 (clothes) + Totes Assorted Items
谷	valley: 八 (*eight*) + 𠆢 (cover) + 口 (open) + KOncave Kleaves Uplands
裕	abundant: 衤 (clothes) + 谷 (valley) + Yields Utterly Unrestricted
列	row: 歹 (disintegrate) + 刂 (cut) + REpresents Things SUccessively
裂	split: 列 (row) + 衣 (clothes) + REnd This SUddenly
喪	loss: 十 (ten) + 口 (two mouths) + 衣 (*clothes*) + State Of Obliteration
居	reside: 尸 (bent body) + 古 (old) + Kontinually You Occupy
裾	hem: 衤 (clothes) + 居 (reside) + Sewn Under Smoothed Out
裸	naked: 衤 (clothes) + 果 (result) + Revealed All

Day six: character clusters

I   Complete the characters using the clues.

1	代	Totes Assorted Items (TAI)
2	衣	Indispensable (I)
3	ネ	SHirt Underarm Unit (SHUU)
4	ヘ	KOncave Kleaves Uplands (KOKU)
5	口	Affliction Initiates (AI)

II   Compose the compounds using the clues.

1   (JUU) 住   +   (KYO) ____   =   _____ (dwelling)
    reside

2   (HYOO) ____   +   (GEN) 現   =   _____ (expression)
                                appear

3   (RA) ____   +   (TAI) 体   =   _____ (nude)
                                body

4   (GYOO) 行   +   (RETSU) ____   =   _____ (procession)
    go

5   (HI) ____   +   (KOKU) 告   =   _____ (defendant)
                                inform

III   Complete the sentences using the clues.

1   スイスには＿＿福な人々が多い。
    Suisu ni wa YUUfuku na hitobito ga ooi.
    There are many wealthy people in Switzerland.

2   さくらは成＿＿してプロの歌手になった。
    Sakura wa seiCHOO shite puro no kashu ni natta.
    Sakura grew up to be a professional singer.

3   そのグループは二つに分＿＿しました。
    Sono guruupu wa futatsu ni bunRETSU shimashita.
    That group was split into two.

4   最＿＿にタクシーで空港に行きます。
    SaiSHO ni takushii de kuukoo ni ikimasu.
    First I will go to the airport by taxi.

5   ピカソの絵がたくさん＿＿示されている。
    Pikaso no e ga takusan TENji sarete iru.
    Many of Picasso's paintings are being exhibited.

REVIEW: LESSONS 16–20

I   Given the character and meaning, write the pronunciation.

1 客 guest _____   2 妨 obstruct _____   3 貼 affix _____

4 索 search _____   5 展 display _____   6 穴 hole _____

7 奴 slave _____   8 貞 chaste _____   9 壱 one _____

10 畏 fear _____   11 元 origin _____   12 始 begin _____

13 唄 song _____   14 侵 invade _____   15 旅 travel _____

16 宜 right _____   17 妻 wife _____   18 貸 lend _____

19 衣 clothes _____   20 裾 hem _____   21 室 room _____

22 爪 claw _____   23 賄 bribe _____   24 企 plan _____

25 袖 sleeve _____   26 宅 home _____   27 妃 queen _____

28 則 rule _____   29 与 give _____   30 皮 skin _____

II   Given the character and pronunciation, write the meaning.

1 字 JI _____   2 妄 MOO _____   3 貢 KOO _____

4 倉 SOO _____   5 宣 SEN _____   6 衷 CHUU _____

7 妙 MYOO _____   8 責 SEKI _____   9 冗 JOO _____

10 喪 SOO _____   11 官 KAN _____   12 姻 IN _____

13 貧 HIN _____   14 勃 BOTSU _____   15 裂 RETSU _____

16 宝 HOO _____   17 妊 NIN _____   18 貴 KI _____

19 冥 MEI _____   20 初 SHO _____   21 妖 YOO _____

22 貿 BOO _____   23 金 KIN _____   24 妥 DA _____

25 哀 AI _____   26 袋 TAI _____   27 貪 DON _____

28 妹 MAI _____   29 且 SHO _____   30 貯 CHO _____

III Given the meaning and pronunciation, write the character.

1 protect	SHU	_____	2 similar	JO	_____
3 shell	kai	_____	4 order	REI	_____
5 express	HYOO	_____	6 jewel	GYOKU	_____
7 member	IN	_____	8 buy	BAI	_____
9 cloth	KIN	_____	10 depend	I	_____
11 child	SHI	_____	12 bear	FU	_____
13 row	RETSU	_____	14 sell	HAN	_____
15 valley	KOKU	_____	16 defeat	HAI	_____
17 west	SEI	_____	18 goods	KA	_____
19 house	SHA	_____	20 reside	KYO	_____
21 religion	SHUU	_____	22 food	SHOKU	_____
23 wealth	ZAI	_____	24 naked	RA	_____
25 surname	SEI	_____			

IV Compose compounds using the following characters.

実 要 被 良 宇 会 好 安 裕 定 長 写 帝 完 余 害 宙 全 女 因

1 (YO) _____   +   (YUU) _____   =   _____ (room, leeway)

2 (KAI) _____   +   (CHOO) _____   =   _____ (president)

3 (JO) _____   +   (TEI) _____   =   _____ (empress)

4 (KAN) _____   +   (ZEN) _____   =   _____ (perfection)

5 (U) _____   +   (CHUU) _____   =   _____ (universe)

6 (YOO) _____   +   (IN) _____   =   _____ (factor)

7 (RYOO) _____   +   (KOO) _____   =   _____ (good)

8 (SHA) _____   +   (JITSU) _____   =   _____ (realism)

9 (HI) _____   +   (GAI) _____   =   _____ (damage)

10 (AN) _____   +   (TEI) _____   =   _____ (stability)

21

FIRE DEPARTMENT

Day one: crossword puzzle

Across

3. Kindling Aflame
5. Enkindling Nature
7. Sear Hot On Oven
9. Stove Use Is
11. TOrch Offers
13. Sundry HOldings (M)
15. SHine On Others (I)
16. Reheats Oil (F)
17. Tapered ENd
19. Emission Noxious
20. HArd Tilled Area (two words: D/F)

Down

1. Steam Heat Applied
2. Zest ENlivens (L)
4. Scorch Once Over (P)
6. Season HUlls Undone
8. Made Unmade
10. Konstraint Essential To SUrvival (L)
12. RElentless Tense SUction
14. Serious Adverse Incident
18. Kreated After Incineration
21. KEnnel Native

Day two: acrostics

1 Boil: S _ _ _ _   H _ _ _   A _ _ _ _ _ _

2 Like: Z _ _ _   E N _ _ _ _ _ _

3 Fire: K _ _ _ _ _ _ _   A _ _ _ _ _

4 Parch: S _ _ _ _ _   O _ _ _   O _ _ _

5 Flame: E _ _ _ _ _ _ _ _ _   N _ _ _ _ _

6 Autumn: S _ _ _ _ _   H U _ _ _   U _ _ _ _ _

7 Burn: S _ _ _   H _ _   O _   O _ _ _

8 Not: M _ _ _   U _ _ _ _ _

9 Cook: S _ _ _ _   U _ _   I _

10 Lack: K _ _ _ _ _ _ _ _   E _ _ _ _ _ _ _ _   T _   S U _ _ _ _ _ _

11 Light: T O _ _ _   O _ _ _ _ _

12 Intense: R E _ _ _ _ _ _ _ _   T _ _ _ _   S U _ _ _ _ _

13 Manifold: S _ _ _ _ _   H O _ _ _ _ _ _

14 Disaster: S _ _ _ _ _ _   A _ _ _ _ _ _ _   I _ _ _ _ _ _ _

15 Illuminate: S H _ _ _   O _   O _ _ _ _ _

16 Furnace: R _ _ _ _ _ _   O _ _

17 Point: T _ _ _ _ _ _   E N _

18 Ash: K _ _ _ _ _ _   A _ _ _ _   I _ _ _ _ _ _ _ _ _ _

19 Smoke: E _ _ _ _ _ _ _   N _ _ _ _ _ _

20 Dry Field: H A _ _   T _ _ _ _ _   A _ _ _

21 Dog: K E _ _ _ _   N _ _ _ _ _

Day three: componential analysis

Course Number	Kanji	ON Reading(s) / Core Concept(s)	Primary Components	Kanji Canvas
0421	火	KA / fire	Flames	火
0422	灯	TOO / light; lamp	火 (fire)[421] + 丁 (exact)[87]	灯
0423	灰	KAI / ash	厂 (cliff)[K14] + 火 (fire)[421]	灰
0424	災	SAI / disaster	川 (*river*)[198] + 火 (fire)[421]	災
0425	炎	EN / flame	火 (fire)[421] + 火 (fire)[421]	炎
0426	炉	RO / furnace	火 (fire)[421] + 戸 (door)[284]	炉
0427	欠	KETSU / lack	Person yawning	欠
0428	炊	SUI / cook	火 (fire)[421] + 欠 (lack)[427]	炊
0429	秋	SHUU / autumn	禾 (grain)[K33] + 火 (fire)[421]	秋
0430	点	TEN / point	占 (occupy)[112] + 灬 (fire)[K61]	点
0431	畑	hata, hatake / dry field	火 (fire)[421] + 田 (field)[60]	畑
0432	烈	RETSU / intense	列 (row)[415] + 灬 (fire)[K61]	烈
0433	庶	SHO / manifold	广 (building)[K24] + 廿 (twenty)[K62] + 灬 (fire)[K61]	庶
0434	煮	SHA / boil	者 (person)[152] + 灬 (fire)[K61]	煮
0435	無	MU, BU / not; without	ノ (accent)[K2] + *floor beams* (cf. 1967) + 灬 (fire)[K61]	無
0436	焼	SHOO / burn	火 (fire)[421] + 十 (ten)[06] + 艹 (plants)[K29] + 一 (one)[01] + 儿 (boy)[K5]	焼
0437	照	SHOO / illuminate	昭 (bright)[160] + 灬 (fire)[K61]	照
0438	犬	KEN / dog	大 (big)[233] + 丶 (accent)[K2]	犬
0439	然	ZEN / like, so	月 (*flesh*)[K43] + 犬 (dog)[438] + 灬 (fire)[K61]	然
0440	煙	EN / smoke	火 (fire)[421] + 西 (west)[354] + 土 (ground)[169]	煙
0441	燥	SOO / parch	火 (fire)[421] + 品 (goods)[126] + 木 (wood)[43]	燥

Day four: writing practice

火	灯	灰	災	炎	炉	欠
火	灯	灰	災	炎	炉	欠
炊	秋	点	畑	烈	庶	煮
炊	秋	点	畑	烈	庶	煮
無	焼	照	犬	然	煙	燥
無	焼	照	犬	然	煙	燥

Day five: story sketch

火	fire: (flames) + Kindling Aflame
灯	light: 火 (fire) + 丁 (exact) + TOrch Offers
灰	ash: 厂 (cliff) + 火 (fire) + Kreated After Incineration
災	disaster: 川 (*river*) + 火 (fire) + Serious Adverse Incident
炎	flame: 火 (fire) + 火 (fire) + Enkindling Nature
炉	furnace: 火 (fire) + 戸 (door) + Reheats Oil
欠	lack: (person yawning) + Konstraint Essential To SUrvival
炊	cook: 火 (fire) + 欠 (lack) + Stove Use Is
秋	autumn: 禾 (grain) + 火 (fire) + Season HUlls Undone
点	point: 占 (occupy) + 灬 (fire) + Tapered ENd
畑	dry field: 火 (fire) + 田 (field) + HArd Tilled Area
烈	intense: 列 (row) + 灬 (fire) + RElentless Tense SUction
庶	manifold: 广 (building) + 廿 (twenty) + 灬 (fire) + Sundry HOldings
煮	boil: 者 (person) + 灬 (fire) + Steam Heat Applied
無	not: ╱ (accent) + *floor beams* + 灬 (fire) + Made Unmade
焼	burn: 火 (fire) + 十 (ten) + 艹 (plants) + 一 (one) + 儿 (boy) + Sear Hot On Oven
照	illuminate: 昭 (bright) + 灬 (fire) + SHine On Others
犬	dog: 大 (big) + 丶 (accent) + KEnnel Native
然	like: 月 (*flesh*) + 犬 (dog) + 灬 (fire) + Zest ENlivens
煙	smoke: 火 (fire) + 西 (west) + 土 (ground) + Emission Noxious
燥	parch: 火 (fire) + 品 (goods) + 木 (wood) + Scorch Once Over

Day six: character clusters

I   Complete the characters using the clues.

1	广	Sundry HOldings (SHO)
2	禾	Season HUlls Undone (SHUU)
3	厂	Kreated After Incineration (KAI)
4	灬	Steam Heat Applied (SHA)
5	戸	Reheats Oil (RO)

II Compose the compounds using the clues.

1   (KA) _____   +   (ZAN) 山   =   _____ (volcano)
                              mountain

2   (KAN) 乾   +   (SOO) _____   =   _____ (dryness)
       dry

3   (TOO) _____   +   (DAI) 台   =   _____ (lighthouse)
                              platform

4   (HAI) 肺   +   (EN) _____   =   _____ (pneumonia)
       lungs

5   (SAI) _____   +   (GAI) 害   =   _____ (disaster)
                              harm

III Complete the sentences using the clues.

1   二年ごとに車を＿検してもらいます。
    Ni-nen goto ni kuruma o TENken shite moraimasu.
    The car is inspected once every two years.

2   猛＿＿なハリケーンがフロリダを襲いました。
    Mooretsu na harikeen ga furorida o osoimashita.
    A violent hurricane hit Florida.

3   小林さんはスペイン語を自＿＿に話せる。
    Kobayashi-san wa supeingo o shiZEN ni hanaseru.
    Mr. Kobayashi can speak Spanish naturally.

4   この本の地図を参＿＿してください。
    Kono hon no chizu o sanSHOO shite kudasai.
    Please refer to the map in this book.

5   音楽会の切符は＿料です。
    Ongakukai no kippu wa MUryoo desu.
    The concert tickets are free.

22

HEAVY METAL

Day one: crossword puzzle

Across
2. KOre Ore (M)
4. Glowing INgot (S)
7. Cast HOoks Offshore
9. Family Umbrella (F)
10. Some Amalgam KUrrently
12. Makes Emblematic Impression (I)
14. Rarify ENtirely
15. Ductile Ocherous Ore (C)
16. Dim ONe
19. Register Occurrences KUrsively
20. KOnsolidated
21. Jammed Utterly Up

Down
1. Jolts Until Unloaded
3. KOnstrain
5. Extremely Incisive
6. Kooks A Meal Accordingly (K)
8. TEnsile Tested SUbstance
11. Ring Emitting Instrument
13. SHarp INdicator (N)
17. Element Neurotoxic
18. HArd Container Holding Items

Day two: acrostics

1 Gun: J _ _ _ _   U _ _ _ _   U _ _ _ _ _ _ _

2 Mineral: K O _ _   O _ _

3 Restrain: K O _ _ _ _ _ _ _

4 Silver: G _ _ _ _ _ _   I N _ _ _

5 Sharp: E _ _ _ _ _ _ _ _   I _ _ _ _ _ _ _

6 Kettle: K _ _ _ _   A M _ _ _   A _ _ _ _ _ _ _ _ _

7 Fish: C _ _ _   H O _ _ _   O _ _ _ _ _ _ _

8 Iron: T E _ _ _ _ _   T _ _ _ _ _   S U _ _ _ _ _ _ _

9 Father: F _ _ _ _ _ _   U _ _ _ _ _ _ _

10 Mixed: S _ _ _   A _ _ _ _ _ _   K U _ _ _ _ _ _ _

11 Bell: R _ _ _   E _ _ _ _ _ _ _   I _ _ _ _ _ _ _ _

12 Inscription: M _ _ _ _   E _ _ _ _ _ _ _ _ _   I _ _ _ _ _ _ _ _

13 Needle: S H _ _ _   I N _ _ _ _ _ _ _

14 Refine: R _ _ _ _ _   E N _ _ _ _ _ _

15 Copper: D _ _ _ _ _ _   O _ _ _ _ _ _ _   O _ _

16 Dull: D _ _   O N _

17 Lead: E _ _ _ _ _ _   N _ _ _ _ _ _ _ _ _

18 Bowl: H A _ _   C _ _ _ _ _ _ _ _   H _ _ _ _ _ _   I _ _ _ _

19 Record: R _ _ _ _ _ _ _   O _ _ _ _ _ _ _ _ _ _   K U _ _ _ _ _ _

20 Hard: K O _ _ _ _ _ _ _ _ _

21 Full: J _ _ _ _ _ _   U _ _ _ _ _ _   U _

Day three: componential analysis

Course Number	Kanji	ON Reading(s) / Core Concept(s)	Primary Components	Kanji Canvas
0442	針	SHIN / needle	金 (metal)[388] + 十 (ten)[06]	針
0443	釣	CHOO / fish	金 (metal)[388] + 寸 (*measure*)[11]	釣
0444	鈍	DON / dull	金 (metal)[388] + 屯 (encampment)[223]	鈍
0445	父	FU / father	Hand holding stick	父
0446	釜	kama / kettle, pot	父 (father)[445] + 金 (metal)[388]	釜
0447	鉄	TETSU / iron	金 (metal)[388] + 失 (lose)[265]	鉄
0448	鉱	KOO / mineral, ore	金 (metal)[388] + 広 (wide)[101]	鉱
0449	鉛	EN / lead	金 (metal)[388] + 八 (eight)[04] + 口 (mouth)[106]	鉛
0450	鈴	REI, RIN / bell	金 (metal)[388] + 令 (order)[380]	鈴
0451	鉢	HACHI / bowl	金 (metal)[388] + 本 (basis)[83]	鉢
0452	銘	MEI / inscription	金 (metal)[388] + 名 (name)[124]	銘
0453	録	ROKU / record	金 (metal)[388] + ヨ (open hand)[K54] + 水 (water)[22]	録
0454	銅	DOO / copper	金 (metal)[388] + 同 (same)[119]	銅
0455	充	JUU / full, fill	亠 (top)[K1] + ム (self)[K18] + 儿 (boy)[K5]	充
0456	銃	JUU / gun	金 (metal)[388] + 充 (full)[455]	銃
0457	鋭	EI / sharp	金 (metal)[388] + ´` (split)[K35] + 兄 (older brother)[117]	鋭
0458	銀	GIN / silver	金 (metal)[388] + 良 (*good*)[398]	銀
0459	錯	SAKU / mixed	金 (metal)[388] + 昔 (past)[245]	錯
0460	錬	REN / refine	金 (metal)[388] + 東 (east)[157]	錬
0461	固	KO / hard, solid	囗 (enclosure)[K4] + 古 (old)[108]	固
0462	錮	KO / restrain	金 (metal)[388] + 固 (hard)[461]	錮

Day four: writing practice

針	釣	鈍	父	釜	鉄	鉱

| 針 | 釣 | 鈍 | 父 | 釜 | 鉄 | 鉱 |

| 鉛 | 鈴 | 鉢 | 銘 | 録 | 銅 | 充 |

| 鉛 | 鈴 | 鉢 | 銘 | 録 | 銅 | 充 |

| 銃 | 鋭 | 銀 | 錯 | 錬 | 固 | 錮 |

| 銃 | 鋭 | 銀 | 錯 | 錬 | 固 | 錮 |

Day five: story sketch

針	needle: 金 (metal) + 十 (ten) + SHarp INdicator
釣	fish: 金 (metal) + 寸 (*measure*) + Cast HOoks Offshore
鈍	dull: 金 (metal) + 屯 (encampment) + Dim ONe
父	father: (hand holding stick) + Family Umbrella
釜	kettle: 父 (father) + 金 (metal) + Kooks A Meal Accordingly
鉄	iron: 金 (metal) + 失 (lose) + TEnsile Tested SUbstance
鉱	mineral: 金 (metal) + 広 (wide) + KOre Ore
鉛	lead: 金 (metal) + 八 (eight) + 口 (mouth) + Element Neurotoxic
鈴	bell: 金 (metal) + 令 (order) + Ring Emitting Instrument
鉢	bowl: 金 (metal) + 本 (basis) + HArd Container Holding Items
銘	inscription: 金 (metal) + 名 (name) + Makes Emblematic Impression
録	record: 金 (metal) + ヨ (open hand) + 水 (water) + Register Occurrences KUrsively
銅	copper: 金 (metal) + 同 (same) + Ductile Ocherous Ore
充	full: 亠 (top) + ム (self) + 儿 (boy) + Jammed Utterly Up
銃	gun: 金 (metal) + 充 (full) + Jolts Until Unloaded
鋭	sharp: 金 (metal) + 丷 (split) + 兄 (older brother) + Extremely Incisive
銀	silver: 金 (metal) + 艮 (*good*) + Glowing INgot
錯	mixed: 金 (metal) + 昔 (past) + Some Amalgam KUrrently
錬	refine: 金 (metal) + 東 (east) + Rarify ENtirely
固	hard: 囗 (enclosure) + 古 (old) + KOnsolidated
錮	restrain: 金 (metal) + 固 (hard) + KOnstrain

Day six: character clusters

I Complete the characters using the clues.

1	金	Ring Emitting Instrument (REI)
2	兄	Extremely Incisive (EI)
3	父	Kooks A Meal Accordingly (KAMA)
4	本	HArd Container Holding Items (HACHI)
5	金	Rarify ENtirely (REN)

II Compose the compounds using the clues.

1 (KEN) 挙   + (JUU) ____   = _____ (pistol)
   perform

2 (TETSU) ____   + (DOO) 道   = _____ (railroad)
                    way, road

3 (KO) ____   + (TEI) 定   = _____ (fixed)
               fix

4 (SEI) 青   + (DOO) ____   = _____ (bronze)
   blue

5 (JUU) ____   + (DEN) 電   = _____ (charge)
               electricity

III Complete the sentences using the clues.

1 きのう＿＿行からお金を引き出した。
Kinoo GINkoo kara o-kane o hikidashita.
Yesterday I withdrew money from the bank.

2 私の祖＿＿はアルゼンチンに住んでいます。
Watashi no soFU wa aruzenchin ni sunde imasu.
My grandfather lives in Argentina.

3 ジェーンは＿＿筆で名前を書いた。
Jeen wa ENpitsu de namae o kaita.
Jane wrote her name in pencil.

4 大学は新しい方＿＿を立てました。
Daigaku wa atarashii hooSHIN o tatemashita.
The university made a new policy.

5 次の会議の記＿＿を取る。
Tsugi no kaigi no kiROKU o toru.
I will keep a record of the next meeting.

23

LEND A HAND

Day one: crossword puzzle

Across

5. Just Undergo
7. Koncrete ENtity
10. Kompletely Enter Into (two words)
13. Seek One Out
15. Sacred Annual Incident
16. Set Hands Ultimately Upon
17. Konduit Extends Incrementally
18. Kourse Entirely Intended
20. Sapling Ovaries Overripe (M)
21. Senior HUsband KUstomarily

Down

1. Set One Other
2. Jingle Inlet
3. Youthful Usual Union (F)
4. Determined Order (D)
6. FUrs Kover Up (C)
8. Kondition Arouses Incomprehension (M)
9. Just Over One
11. Serves HIs Nobleman (R)
12. Journalistic Outlines (D)
14. Komplete Your Uppermost Urge
19. Set Hold Upon

Day two: acrostics

1 Pair: S _ _   O _ _   O _ _ _ _

2 Ear: J _ _ _ _ _   I _ _ _ _

3 Friend: Y _ _ _ _ _ _ _   U _ _ _ _   U _ _ _ _

4 Degree: D _ _ _ _ _ _ _ _   O _ _ _ _

5 Receive: J _ _ _   U _ _ _ _ _ _

6 Clothes: F U _ _   K _ _ _ _   U _

7 Firm: K _ _ _ _ _ _ _   E N _ _ _ _

8 Mysterious: K _ _ _ _ _ _ _ _   A _ _ _ _ _ _   I _ _ _ _ _ _ _ _ _ _ _ _ _

9 Up: J _ _ _   O _ _ _   O _ _

10 Pass Through: K _ _ _ _ _ _ _ _ _   E _ _ _ _   I _ _ _

11 Retainer: S _ _ _ _ _ _   H I _   N _ _ _ _ _ _

12 Describe: J _ _ _ _ _ _ _ _ _ _   O _ _ _ _ _ _

13 Search: S _ _ _   O _ _   O _ _

14 Reach: K _ _ _ _ _ _ _   Y _ _ _   U _ _ _ _ _ _ _   U _ _ _

15 Festival: S _ _ _ _ _   A _ _ _ _ _   I _ _ _ _ _ _ _

16 Obtain: S _ _   H _ _ _ _   U _ _ _ _ _ _ _ _   U _ _ _

17 Stem: K _ _ _ _ _   E _ _ _ _ _ _   I _ _ _ _ _ _ _ _ _ _

18 Path: K _ _ _ _ _   E _ _ _ _ _ _ _   I _ _ _ _ _ _

19 Take: S _ _   H _ _ _   U _ _ _

20 Mulberry: S _ _ _ _ _ _   O _ _ _ _ _ _   O _ _ _ _ _ _

21 Uncle: S _ _ _ _ _   H U _ _ _ _ _   K U _ _ _ _ _ _ _ _

Day three: componential analysis

Course Number	Kanji	ON Reading(s) / Core Concept(s)	Primary Components	Kanji Canvas
0463	及	KYUU reach	人 (person)[64] + 又 (*hand*)[K15]	及
0464	双	SOO pair	又 (*hand*)[K15] + 又 (hand)[K15]	双
0465	友	YUU friend	手 (*hand*)[85] + 又 (hand)[K15]	友
0466	収	SHUU obtain, collect	丩 (fork)[K38] + 又 (hand)[K15]	収
0467	受	JU receive	⺥ (claw)[K53] + ⼍ (cover)[K26] + 又 (hand)[K15]	受
0468	怪	KAI mysterious	忄 (heart)[K31] + 又 (hand)[K15] + 土 (ground)[169]	怪
0469	茎	KEI stem	⺾ (plants)[K29] + 又 (hand)[K15] + 土 (ground)[169]	茎
0470	服	FUKU clothes; obey	月 (flesh)[K43] + ⺆ (bowing)[K57] + 又 (hand)[K15]	服
0471	径	KEI path	彳 (go)[K47] + 又 (hand)[K15] + 土 (ground)[169]	径
0472	耳	JI ear	Outline of outer ear	耳
0473	取	SHU take	耳 (ear)[472] + 又 (hand)[K15]	取
0474	上	JOO up	Area above a line	上
0475	叔	SHUKU uncle	上 (up)[474] + 小 (small)[31] + 又 (hand)[K15]	叔
0476	度	DO degree; time	广 (building)[K24] + 廿 (twenty)[K62] + 又 (hand)[K15]	度
0477	叙	JO describe	余 (excess)[386] + 又 (hand)[K15]	叙
0478	捜	SOO search	扌 (hand)[K21] + 由 (reason)[39] + 又 (hand)[K15]	捜
0479	桑	SOO mulberry	又 (three hands)[K15] + 木 (tree)[43]	桑
0480	経	KEI pass through	糸 (thread)[211] + 又 (hand)[K15] + 土 (earth)[169]	経
0481	祭	SAI festival; worship	月 (*flesh*)[K43] + 又 (hand)[K15] + 示 (show)[176]	祭
0482	臣	SHIN retainer	Large pupil looking both ways	臣
0483	堅	KEN firm	臣 (retainer)[482] + 又 (hand)[K15] + 土 (earth)[169]	堅

Day four: writing practice

及	双	友	収	受	怪	茎
及	双	友	収	受	怪	茎
服	径	耳	取	上	叔	度
服	径	耳	取	上	叔	度
叙	捜	桑	経	祭	臣	堅
叙	捜	桑	経	祭	臣	堅

Day five: story sketch

及	reach: 人 (person) + 又 (*hand*) + Komplete Your Uppermost Urge
双	pair: 又 (*hand*) + 又 (hand) + Set One Other
友	friend: 手 (*hand*) + 又 (hand) + Youthful Usual Union
収	obtain: 丩 (fork) + 又 (hand) + Set Hands Ultimately Upon
受	receive: ⍦ (claw) + 冖 (cover) + 又 (hand) + Just Undergo
怪	mysterious: 忄 (heart) + 又 (hand) + 土 (ground) + Kondition Arouses Incomprehension
茎	stem: 艹 (plants) + 又 (hand) + 土 (ground) + Konduit Extends Incrementally
服	clothes: 月 (flesh) + 卩 (bowing) + 又 (hand) + FUrs Kover Up
径	path: 彳 (go) + 又 (hand) + 土 (ground) + Kourse Entirely Intended
耳	ear: (outline of outer ear) + Jingle Inlet
取	take: 耳 (ear) + 又 (hand) + Set Hold Upon
上	up: (area above a line) + Just Over One
叔	uncle: 上 (up) + 小 (small) + 又 (hand) + Senior HUsband KUstomarily
度	degree: 广 (building) + 廿 (twenty) + 又 (hand) + Determined Order
叙	describe: 余 (excess) + 又 (hand) + Journalistic Outlines
捜	search: 扌 (hand) + 由 (reason) + 又 (hand) + Seek One Out
桑	mulberry: 又 (three hands) + 木 (tree) + Sapling Ovaries Overripe
経	pass through: 糸 (thread) + 又 (hand) + 土 (earth) + Kompletely Enter Into
祭	festival: 月 (*flesh*) + 又 (hand) + 示 (show) + Sacred Annual Incident
臣	retainer: (large pupil looking both ways) + Serves HIs Nobleman
堅	firm: 臣 (retainer) + 又 (hand) + 土 (earth) + Koncrete ENtity

Day six: character clusters

I Complete the characters using the clues.

1	木	Sapling Ovaries Overripe (SOO)
2	上	Senior HUsband KUstomarily (SHUKU)
3	土	Koncrete ENtity (KEN)
4	示	Sacred Annual Incident (SAI)
5	艹	Konduit Extends Incrementally (KEI)

II Compose the compounds using the clues.

1 (JU) _____ + (SHIN) 信 = _____ (reception)
           trust

2 (YUU) _____ + (JIN) 人 = _____ (friend)
          person

3 (KAI) _____ + (BUTSU) 物 = _____ (monster)
          thing

4 (FU) 普 + (KYUU) _____ = _____ (spread)
  generally

5 (SOO) _____ + (SAKU) 索 = _____ (search)
          search

III Complete the sentences using the clues.

1 メアリーのお母さんは___品な方です。
Mearii no okaasan wa JOOhin na kata desu.
Mary's mother is a refined person.

2 今___の土曜日はスキーをしましょう。
KonDO no doyoobi wa sukii o shimashoo.
Let's go skiing this coming Saturday.

3 ジェフは英語を教えた___験がある。
Jefu wa eigo o oshieta KEIken ga aru.
Jeff has experience teaching English.

4 小学生の時に制___を着ました。
Shoogakusei no toki ni seiFUKU o kimashita.
I wore a uniform when I was an elementary school student.

5 お手伝いの___入は少ないだと思います。
O-tetsudai no SHUUnyuu wa sukunai da to omoimasu.
I think that a maid's income is small.

24
FIELD OF VISION

Day one: crossword puzzle

Across

3. Joint Overlapping Object (T)
5. Reconnect Yoke Until United
8. Kommon Area Interest (W)
10. Behind ANother
13. Incompatible
15. Rumbling Atmospheric Intensity
16. Kontinually You Use Until (two words)
17. UNdulated Earth
18. CHickens In KUltivation
21. Underwater

Down

1. Kind Earnest Inclination (F)
2. Heart Acts Neutrally
4. Tally Alone Number
6. Render Your Answers KUrtailed (A)
7. Koncurrent YOur Occurrence
9. Gloomily ENigmatic
11. KAlmly Intervene (B)
12. SOoner Occured (F)
14. Hard And Narrow (E)
19. Community HOmes Occupy
20. Displays ANdrogen

Day two: acrostics

1 Favor: K _ _ _ E _ _ _ _ _ _ _ I _ _ _ _ _ _ _ _ _

2 Half: H _ _ _ _ A _ _ _ N _ _ _ _ _ _ _

3 Tatami: J _ _ _ _ O _ _ _ _ _ _ _ _ _ O _ _ _ _ _

4 Single: T _ _ _ _ A _ _ _ _ N _ _ _ _ _

5 Fasten: R _ _ _ _ _ _ _ Y _ _ _ U _ _ _ _ U _ _ _ _ _

6 Abbreviate: R _ _ _ _ _ Y _ _ _ A _ _ _ _ _ _ K U _ _ _ _ _ _ _

7 Together: K _ _ _ _ _ _ _ _ Y O _ _ O _ _ _ _ _ _ _ _

8 World: K _ _ _ _ _ A _ _ _ I _ _ _ _ _ _ _

9 Obscure: G _ _ _ _ _ _ _ E N _ _ _ _ _ _ _

10 Turn: B _ _ _ _ _ A N _ _ _ _ _

11 Between: K A _ _ _ _ I _ _ _ _ _ _ _ _

12 Formerly: S O _ _ _ _ O _ _ _ _ _ _

13 Different: I _ _ _ _ _ _ _ _ _ _

14 Edge: H _ _ _ A _ _ N _ _ _ _ _

15 Thunder: R _ _ _ _ _ _ _ A _ _ _ _ _ _ _ _ _ _ I _ _ _ _ _ _ _ _

16 Long Time: K _ _ _ _ _ _ _ _ _ _ Y _ _ U _ _ U _ _ _ _

17 Ridge: U N _ _ _ _ _ _ _ E _ _ _ _

18 Livestock: C H _ _ _ _ _ _ I _ K U _ _ _ _ _ _ _ _

19 Town: C _ _ _ _ _ _ _ _ H O _ _ _ O _ _ _ _ _

20 Man: D _ _ _ _ _ _ _ A N _ _ _ _ _ _

21 Rain: U _ _ _ _ _ _ _ _ _

Day three: componential analysis

Course Number	Kanji	ON Reading(s) / Core Concept(s)	Primary Components	Kanji Canvas
0484	男	DAN / man	田 (field)[60] + 力 (power)[07]	男
0485	町	CHOO / town	田 (field)[60] + 丁 (exact)[87]	町
0486	単	TAN / single	⺍ (ornate)[K63] + 田 (field)[60] + 十 (ten)[06]	単
0487	介	KAI / between	Person with arms and legs spread	介
0488	界	KAI / world; boundary	田 (field)[60] + 介 (between)[487]	界
0489	留	RYUU, RU / fasten; stop	*sharp* (cf. 377) + 田 (field)[60]	留
0490	恵	KEI, E / favor	十 (ten)[06] + 田 (field)[60] + 心 (heart)[127]	恵
0491	久	KYUU / long time	Bending person	久
0492	畝	une / ridge	亠 (top)[K1] + 田 (field)[60] + 久 (long time)[491]	畝
0493	半	HAN / half	⧄ (split)[K35] + 牛 (*cow*)[75]	半
0494	畔	HAN / edge, side	田 (field)[60] + 半 (half)[493]	畔
0495	玄	GEN / obscure, dark	亠 (lid)[K1] + 幺 (short thread)[K64]	玄
0496	畜	CHIKU / livestock	玄 (dark)[495] + 田 (field)[60]	畜
0497	略	RYAKU / abbreviate	田 (field)[60] + 各 (each)[122]	略
0498	曽	SOO / formerly, before	⧄ (split)[K35] + 田 (field)[60] + 日 (day)[17]	曽
0499	共	KYOO / together	⺾ (plants)[K29] + ⼌ (platform)[K65]	共
0500	異	I / different	田 (field)[60] + 共 (together)[499]	異
0501	番	BAN / turn; number; watch	一 (*one*)[01] + 米 (rice)[269] + 田 (field)[60]	番
0502	畳	JOO / tatami; fold	田 (field)[60] + 冖 (cover)[K26] + 且 (moreover)[331]	畳
0503	雨	U / rain	Raindrops falling from clouds	雨
0504	雷	RAI / thunder	雨 (rain)[503] + 田 (field)[60]	雷

Day four: writing practice

男	町	単	介	界	留	恵
男	町	単	介	界	留	恵
久	畝	半	畔	玄	畜	略
久	畝	半	畔	玄	畜	略
曽	共	異	番	畳	雨	雷
曽	共	異	番	畳	雨	雷

Day five: story sketch

男	man: 田 (field) + 力 (power) + Displays ANdrogen
町	town: 田 (field) + 丁 (exact) + Community HOmes Occupy
単	single: ⅍ (ornate) + 田 (field) + 十 (ten) + Tally Alone Number
介	between: (person with arms and legs spread) + KAlmly Intervene
界	world: 田 (field) + 介 (between) + Kommon Area Interest
留	fasten: *sharp* + 田 (field) + Reconnect Yoke Until United
恵	favor: 十 (ten) + 田 (field) + 心 (heart) + Kind Earnest Inclination
久	long time: (bending person) + Kontinually You Use Until
畝	ridge: 亠 (top) + 田 (field) + 久 (long time) + UNdulated Earth
半	half: ⅍ (split) + 牛 (*cow*) + Heart Acts Neutrally
畔	edge: 田 (field) + 半 (half) + Hard And Narrow
玄	obscure: 亠 (lid) + 幺 (short thread) + Gloomily ENigmatic
畜	livestock: 玄 (dark) + 田 (field) + CHickens In KUltivation
略	abbreviate: 田 (field) + 各 (each) + Render Your Answers KUrtailed
曽	formerly: ⅍ (split) + 田 (field) + 日 (day) + SOoner Occured
共	together: ⺾ (plants) + ㆒ (platform) + Koncurrent YOur Occurrence
異	different: 田 (field) + 共 (together) + Incompatible
番	turn: 一 (*one*) + 米 (rice) + 田 (field) + Behind ANother
畳	tatami: 田 (field) + 冖 (cover) + 且 (moreover) + Joint Overlapping Object
雨	rain: (raindrops falling from clouds) + Underwater
雷	thunder: 雨 (rain) + 田 (field) + Rumbling Atmospheric Intensity

Day six: character clusters

I   Complete the characters using the clues.

1	田	Joint Overlapping Object (JOO)
2	丁	Community HOmes Occupy (CHOO)
3	田	SOoner Occured (SOO)
4	久	UNdulated Earth (UNE)
5	田	Rumbling Atmospheric Intensity (RAI)

II   Compose the compounds using the clues.

1   (CHI) 知   +   (E) ____   =   _____ (wisdom)
         know

2   (KYOO) ____   +   (DOO) 同   =   _____ (cooperation)
                                     same

3   (DAN) ____   +   (SEI) 性   =   _____ (man, male)
                                     nature

4   (SHOO) 紹   +   (KAI) ____   =   _____ (introduction)
         introduce

5   (RYAKU) ____   +   (GO) 語   =   _____ (abbreviation)
                                     word

III   Complete the sentences using the clues.

1   私のポロシャツの＿＿分は白いです。
    Watashi no poroshatsu no HANbun wa shiroi desu.
    Half of my polo shirts are white.

2   その質問は簡＿＿すぎる。
    Sono shitsumon wa kanTAN sugiru.
    That question is too easy.

3   季節の中で秋が一＿＿好きです。
    Kisetsu no naka de aki ga ichiBAN suki desu.
    Among the seasons I like autumn the best.

4   ＿＿関で靴を脱ぐべきだ。
    GENkan de kutsu o nugu beki da.
    You should take off your shoes in the entrance.

5   ロンドンは世＿＿で最も物価が高い都市の一つです。
    Rondon wa seKAI de mottomo bukka ga takai toshi no hitotsu desu.
    London is one of the world's most expensive cities.

25

A PERFECT TEN

Day one: crossword puzzle

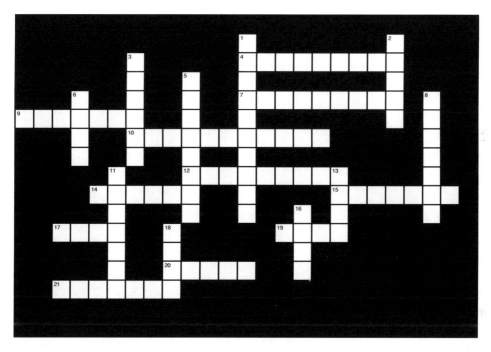

Across

4. Select ENtity
7. Huge Area KUltivated
9. Standard HAuler
10. Kollaboration YOu Others
12. Gear Useful
14. ZOnal Kriminal Usually
15. Simple Unpolluted Identity
17. Hostile Intent (M)
19. Reckons Interest To SUm
20. North ANtithesis
21. Supply An Imprint (P)

Down

1. SEt Interval (G)
2. Joint UNiformity (L)
3. Course Hasn't One KUrve
5. Settle On Total SUm (C)
6. Forest Upland
8. KOntrol Kontrary Urge (C)
11. SHarp INcision (P)
13. Sincere Heart INherent
16. Glimmering YOlky Onset
18. Hurry ONward

Day two: acrostics

1 Generation: S E _ I _ _ _ _ _ _ _

2 Level: J _ _ _ _ U N _ _ _ _ _ _ _

3 Direct: C _ _ _ _ _ _ H _ _ _ _ O _ _ K U _ _ _

4 Exclusive: S _ _ _ _ _ _ E N _ _ _ _

5 Complete: S _ _ _ _ _ O _ T _ _ _ _ S U _

6 Hill: F _ _ _ _ _ U _ _ _ _ _

7 Extensive: H _ _ _ A _ _ _ K U _ _ _ _ _ _ _

8 Conquer: K O _ _ _ _ _ K _ _ _ _ _ _ _ U _ _ _

9 Vehicle: S _ _ _ _ _ _ _ H A _ _ _ _

10 Cooperation: K _ _ _ _ _ _ _ _ _ _ _ Y O _ O _ _ _ _ _

11 Painful: S H _ _ _ I N _ _ _ _ _ _

12 Equipment: G _ _ _ U _ _ _ _ _

13 True: S _ _ _ _ _ _ H _ _ _ _ I N _ _ _ _ _ _

14 Bandit: Z O _ _ _ K _ _ _ _ _ _ _ U _ _ _ _ _ _

15 Refined: S _ _ _ _ _ U _ _ _ _ _ _ _ _ I _ _ _ _ _ _ _

16 Dawn: G _ _ _ _ _ _ _ _ _ Y O _ _ _ O _ _ _ _

17 Mean: H _ _ _ _ _ _ I _ _ _ _ _

18 Rush: H _ _ _ _ O N _ _ _ _

19 Rate: R _ _ _ _ _ _ I _ _ _ _ _ _ _ T _ S U _

20 South: N _ _ _ _ A N _ _ _ _ _ _ _ _

21 Publish: S _ _ _ _ _ _ A _ I _ _ _ _ _ _

Day three: componential analysis

Course Number	Kanji	ON Reading(s) / Core Concept(s)	Primary Components	Kanji Canvas
0505	世	SEI, SE **generation; world**	十 (ten)[06] + 廿 (twenty)[K62] + 一 (one)[01]	世
0506	辛	SHIN **painful**	立 (stand)[37] + 十 (ten)[06]	辛
0507	克	KOKU **conquer**	十 (ten)[06] + 兄 (older brother)[117]	克
0508	協	KYOO **cooperation**	十 (ten)[06] + 力 (three powers)[07]	協
0509	卒	SOTSU **complete**	亠 (top)[K1] + 人 (two persons)[64] + 十 (ten)[06]	卒
0510	奔	HON **rush**	大 (big)[233] + 十 (ten)[06] + 廾 (two hands)[K3]	奔
0511	阜	FU **hill**	自 (buttocks)[K52] + 十 (ten)[06]	阜
0512	直	CHOKU **direct, straight**	十 (ten)[06] + 目 (eye)[62] + ∟ (corner)[K30]	直
0513	南	NAN **south**	十 (ten)[06] + 冂 (border)[K27] + 丷 (split)[K35] + 干 (dry)[24]	南
0514	卑	HI **mean; humble**	*mask* (cf. 1287) + ノ (accent)[K2] + 十 (ten)[06]	卑
0515	具	GU **equipment, tool**	目 (eye)[62] + 丌 (platform)[K65]	具
0516	真	SHIN **true**	十 (ten)[06] + 具 (equipment)[515]	真
0517	粋	SUI **refined**	米 (rice)[269] + 九 (nine)[05] + 十 (ten)[06]	粋
0518	率	RITSU, SOTSU **rate; command**	亠 (top)[K1] + ⅈ⟨ (pieces)[K66] + 幺 (short thread)[K64] + 十 (ten)[06]	率
0519	暁	GYOO **dawn**	日 (sun)[17] + 十 (ten)[06] + 艹 (plants)[K29] + 一 (one)[01] + 儿 (boy)[K5]	暁
0520	専	SEN **exclusive**	十 (ten)[06] + 田 (field)[60] + 寸 (measure)[11]	専
0521	博	HAKU **extensive**	十 (ten)[06] + 専 (*exclusive*)[520]	博
0522	準	JUN **level; semi**	氵 (water)[K6] + 隹 (bird)[K67] + 十 (ten)[06]	準
0523	賊	ZOKU **bandit**	貝 (money)[358] + 十 (ten)[06] + 戈 (spear)[K20]	賊
0524	車	SHA **vehicle**	Chassis schematic	車
0525	載	SAI **publish; load**	十 (ten)[06] + 戈 (spear)[K20] + 車 (vehicle)[524]	載

Day four: writing practice

世	辛	克	協	卒	奔	阜
世	辛	克	協	卒	奔	阜
直	南	卑	具	真	粹	率
直	南	卑	具	真	粹	率
曉	專	博	準	賊	車	載
曉	專	博	準	賊	車	載

Day five: story sketch

世	generation: 十 (ten) + 廿 (twenty) + 一 (one) + SEt Interval
辛	painful: 立 (stand) + 十 (ten) + SHarp INcision
克	conquer: 十 (ten) + 兄 (older brother) + KOntrol Kontrary Urge
協	cooperation: 十 (ten) + 力 (three powers) + Kollaboration YOu Others
卒	complete: 亠 (top) + 人 (two persons) + 十 (ten) + Settle On Total SUm
奔	rush: 大 (big) + 十 (ten) + 廾 (two hands) + Hurry ONward
阜	hill: 白 (buttocks) + 十 (ten) + Forest Upland
直	direct: 十 (ten) + 目 (eye) + ∟ (corner) + Course Hasn't One KUrve
南	south: 十 (ten) + 冂 (border) + ⺀ (split) + 干 (dry) + North ANtithesis
卑	mean: *mask* + ノ (accent) + 十 (ten) + Hostile Intent
具	equipment: 目 (eye) + 𠆢 (platform) + Gear Useful
真	true: 十 (ten) + 具 (equipment) + Sincere Heart INherent
粹	refined: 米 (rice) + 九 (nine) + 十 (ten) + Simple Unpolluted Identity
率	rate: 亠 (top) + ⅺ (pieces) + 幺 (short thread) + 十 (ten) + Reckons Interest To SUm
曉	dawn: 日 (sun) + 十 (ten) + 艹 (plants) + 一 (one) + 儿 (boy) + Glimmering YOlky Onset
専	exclusive: 十 (ten) + 田 (field) + 寸 (measure) + Select ENtity
博	extensive: 十 (ten) + 専 (*exclusive*) + Huge Area KUltivated
準	level: 氵 (water) + 隹 (bird) + 十 (ten) + Joint UNiformity
賊	bandit: 貝 (money) + 十 (ten) + 戈 (spear) + ZOnal Kriminal Usually
車	vehicle: (chassis schematic) + Standard HAuler
載	publish: 十 (ten) + 戈 (spear) + 車 (vehicle) + Supply An Imprint

Day six: character clusters

I   Complete the characters using the clues.

1	立	SHarp INcision (SHIN)
2	十	Forest Upland (FU)
3	日	Glimmering YOlky Onset (GYOO)
4	大	Hurry ONward (HON)
5	寸	Select ENtity (SEN)

II   Compose the compounds using the clues.

1   (JUN) 純　　　+　　(SUI) ____　　　=　　_____ (purity)
    pure

2   (KYOO) ____　+　　(KAI) 会　　　=　　_____ (association)
                    meet

3   (NAN) ____　　+　　(TOO) 東　　　=　　_____ (southeast)
                   east

4   (HI) 比　　　　+　　(RITSU) ____　=　　_____ (ratio)
    compare

5   (KAI) 海　　　+　　(ZOKU) ____　=　　_____ (pirate)
   sea

III   Complete the sentences using the clues.

1   両親がその家___を買ってくれた。
　　Ryooshin ga sono kaGU o katte kureta.
　　My parents bought that furniture for me.

2   この件について___接話しましょう。
　　Kono ken ni tsuite CHOKUsetsu hanashimashoo.
　　Let's speak directly about this matter.

3   兄は去年大学を___業した。
　　Ani wa kyonen daigaku o SOTSUgyoo shita.
　　My older brother graduated from college last year.

4   私は電___で東京へ行くつもりです。
　　Watashi wa denSHA de tookyoo e iku tsumori desu.
　　I plan to go to Tokyo by train.

5   サリーは外国旅行の___備をしています。
　　Sarii wa gaikoku ryokoo no JUNbi o shite imasu.
　　Sally is making preparations for a trip overseas.

REVIEW: LESSONS 21–25

I   Given the character and meaning, write the pronunciation.

1 灯 light _____   2 釣 fish _____   3 双 pair _____

4 町 town _____   5 奔 rush _____   6 燥 parch _____

7 固 hard _____   8 堅 firm _____   9 畔 edge _____

10 留 fasten _____   11 炎 flame _____   12 鈍 dull _____

13 茎 stem _____   14 恵 favor _____   15 阜 hill _____

16 炊 cook _____   17 銃 gun _____   18 叔 uncle _____

19 畝 ridge _____   20 煮 boil _____   21 賊 bandit _____

22 及 reach _____   23 釜 kettle _____   24 界 world _____

25 暁 dawn _____   26 然 like _____   27 錯 mixed _____

28 捜 search _____   29 玄 obscure _____   30 準 level _____

II   Given the character and pronunciation, write the meaning.

1 炉 RO _____   2 針 SHIN _____   3 載 SAI _____

4 世 SEI _____   5 協 KYOO _____   6 畑 hata _____

7 取 SHU _____   8 鉱 KOO _____   9 久 KYUU _____

10 南 NAN _____   11 庶 SHO _____   12 鉛 EN _____

13 叙 JO _____   14 畜 CHIKU _____   15 卑 HI _____

16 焼 SHOO _____   17 錮 KO _____   18 異 I _____

19 桑 SOO _____   20 博 HAKU _____   21 無 MU _____

22 銀 GIN _____   23 祭 SAI _____   24 怪 KAI _____

25 略 RYAKU _____   26 烈 RETSU _____   27 鈴 REI _____

28 畳 JOO _____   29 専 SEN _____   30 鋭 EI _____

III Given the meaning and pronunciation, write the character.

1	inscription	MEI	_____	2	father	FU	_____
3	friend	YUU	_____	4	painful	SHIN	_____
5	man	DAN	_____	6	smoke	EN	_____
7	equipment	GU	_____	8	illuminate	SHOO	_____
9	together	KYOO	_____	10	refined	SUI	_____
11	disaster	SAI	_____	12	bowl	HACHI	_____
13	true	SHIN	_____	14	between	KAI	_____
15	complete	SOTSU	_____	16	lack	KETSU	_____
17	ash	KAI	_____	18	up	JOO	_____
19	autumn	SHUU	_____	20	full	JUU	_____
21	copper	DOO	_____	22	retainer	SHIN	_____
23	formerly	SOO	_____	24	ear	JI	_____
25	receive	JU	_____				

IV Compose compounds using the following characters.

点 車 錬 番 度 単 直 克 収 鉄 半 雨 犬 服 雷 径 経 率 録 火

1 (TAN) _____ + (SHA) _____ = _____ (motorcycle)

2 (BAN) _____ + (KEN) _____ = _____ (watchdog)

3 (TEN) _____ + (KA) _____ = _____ (ignition)

4 (RAI) _____ + (U) _____ = _____ (thunderstorm)

5 (KOKU) _____ + (FUKU) _____ = _____ (conquest)

6 (HAN) _____ + (KEI) _____ = _____ (radius)

7 (SHUU) _____ + (ROKU) _____ = _____ (recording)

8 (SOT) _____ + (CHOKU) _____ = _____ (frankness)

9 (KEI) _____ + (DO) _____ = _____ (longitude)

10 (REN) _____ + (TETSU) _____ = _____ (wrought iron)

26

OVER THE HILL

Day one: crossword puzzle

Across

2. Homogeneous Individuals (C)
6. Beside Another Individual
8. Fasten Underneath
11. Clarification Has INtention
12. Kompletely Years Used Up
14. Just Omit
15. Klosely Aligned Interval
18. Remains YOur Overlord (two words)
19. Set Obstacle
20. Barrier Only Objective (P)
21. Hill ANgle

Down

1. Riches Yield Ultimate Upgrade (P)
3. Rock Is KUltivated
4. Krumples ANatomically
5. Instruction Nurturer (I)
7. HEight Imperial (M)
9. Illumination Nebulous (S)
10. Komplete Amount Includes
13. Kome Off Of
16. Given ENd
17. Killer ENtails (D)

Day two: acrostics

1 Prosper: R _ _ _ _ _   Y _ _ _ _   U _ _ _ _ _ _ _   U _ _ _ _ _ _

2 Compare: H _ _ _ _ _ _ _ _ _   I _ _ _ _ _ _ _ _ _

3 Land: R _ _ _   I _   K U _ _ _ _ _ _ _ _

4 Collapse: K _ _ _ _ _ _ _   A N _ _ _ _ _ _ _ _ _ _

5 Institute: I _ _ _ _ _ _ _ _ _ _   N _ _ _ _ _ _ _

6 Accompany: B _ _ _ _ _   A _ _ _ _ _ _ _   I _ _ _ _ _ _ _ _ _

7 Majesty: H E _ _ _ _   I _ _ _ _ _ _ _

8 Attach: F _ _ _ _ _   U _ _ _ _ _ _ _ _ _

9 Shadow: I _ _ _ _ _ _ _ _ _ _   N _ _ _ _ _ _ _

10 All: K _ _ _ _ _ _ _   A _ _ _ _ _   I _ _ _ _ _ _ _

11 State: C _ _ _ _ _ _ _ _ _ _ _   H _ _   I N _ _ _ _ _ _ _

12 Old: K _ _ _ _ _ _ _ _ _   Y _ _ _ _   U _ _ _   U _

13 Descend: K _ _ _   O _ _   O _

14 Remove: J _ _ _   O _ _ _

15 Level: K _ _ _ _ _ _   A _ _ _ _ _ _ _   I _ _ _ _ _ _ _

16 Limit: G _ _ _ _   E N _

17 Danger: K _ _ _ _ _ _   E N _ _ _ _ _

18 Imperial Tomb: R _ _ _ _ _ _   Y O _ _   O _ _ _ _ _ _ _

19 Obstruct: S _ _   O _ _ _ _ _ _ _

20 Prevent: B _ _ _ _ _ _   O _ _ _   O _ _ _ _ _ _ _ _

21 Slope: H _ _ _   A N _ _ _

Day three: componential analysis

Course Number	Kanji	ON Reading(s) / Core Concept(s)	Primary Components	Kanji Canvas
0526	防	BOO **prevent; defend**	阝 (hill)[K68] + 方 (direction)[174]	防
0527	阪	HAN **slope**	阝 (hill)[K68] + 反 (oppose)[58]	阪
0528	阻	SO **obstruct**	阝 (hill)[K68] + 且 (moreover)[331]	阻
0529	附	FU **attach**	阝 (hill)[K68] + 付 (attach)[69]	附
0530	降	KOO **descend**	阝 (hill)[K68] + 夂 (step)[K13] + *one foot* (cf. 1973)	降
0531	限	GEN **limit**	阝 (hill)[K68] + 良 (*good*)[398]	限
0532	比	HI **compare**	匕 (sitting)[K17] + 匕 (sitting)[K17]	比
0533	陛	HEI **majesty**	阝 (hill)[K68] + 比 (compare)[532] + 土 (ground)[169]	陛
0534	除	JO, JI **remove; exclude**	阝 (hill)[K68] + 余 (excess)[386]	除
0535	院	IN **institute**	阝 (hill)[K68] + 完 (complete)[323]	院
0536	旧	KYUU **old**	｜ (string)[K69] + 日 (day)[17]	旧
0537	陥	KAN **collapse**	阝 (hill)[K68] + ⺈ (bending)[K55] + 旧 (old)[536]	陥
0538	陸	RIKU **land**	阝 (hill)[K68] + 土 (ground)[169] + 儿 (boy)[K5] + 土 (ground)[169]	陸
0539	陵	RYOO **imperial tomb**	阝 (hill)[K68] + 土 (ground)[169] + 儿 (boy)[K5] + 夂 (step)[K13]	陵
0540	険	KEN **danger; steep**	阝 (hill)[K68] + 僉 (discreet)[K70]	険
0541	陰	IN **shadow; negative**	阝 (hill)[K68] + 今 (now)[139] + 二 (two)[02] + ム (self)[K18]	陰
0542	隆	RYUU **prosper; high**	阝 (hill)[K68] + 夂 (step)[K13] + 生 (life)[142]	隆
0543	陳	CHIN **state**	阝 (hill)[K68] + 東 (east)[157]	陳
0544	陪	BAI **accompany**	阝 (hill)[K68] + 立 (stand)[37] + 口 (open)[106]	陪
0545	皆	KAI **all**	比 (compare)[532] + 白 (white)[18]	皆
0546	階	KAI **level, story**	阝 (hill)[K68] + 皆 (all)[545]	階

Day four: writing practice

防	阪	阻	附	降	限	比
防	阪	阻	附	降	限	比

陛	除	院	旧	陥	陸	陵
陛	除	院	旧	陥	陸	陵

険	陰	隆	陳	陪	皆	階
険	陰	隆	陳	陪	皆	階

Day five: story sketch

防	prevent: 阝 (hill) + 方 (direction) + Barrier Only Objective
阪	slope: 阝 (hill) + 反 (oppose) + Hill ANgle
阻	obstruct: 阝 (hill) + 且 (moreover) + Set Obstacle
附	attach: 阝 (hill) + 付 (attach) + Fasten Underneath
降	descend: 阝 (hill) + 夂 (step) + *one foot* + Kome Off Of
限	limit: 阝 (hill) + 良 (*good*) + Given ENd
比	compare: 匕 (sitting) + 匕 (sitting) + Homogeneous Individuals
陛	majesty: 阝 (hill) + 比 (compare) + 土 (ground) + HEight Imperial
除	remove: 阝 (hill) + 余 (excess) + Just Omit
院	institute: 阝 (hill) + 完 (complete) + Instruction Nurturer
旧	old:	(string) + 日 (day) + Kompletely Years Used Up
陥	collapse: 阝 (hill) + ⺈ (bending) + 旧 (old) + Krumples ANatomically
陸	land: 阝 (hill) + 土 (ground) + 儿 (boy) + 土 (ground) + Rock Is KUltivated
陵	imperial tomb: 阝 (hill) + 土 (ground) + 儿 (boy) + 夂 (step) + Remains YOur Overlord
険	danger: 阝 (hill) + 僉 (discreet) + Killer ENtails
陰	shadow: 阝 (hill) + 今 (now) + 二 (two) + ム (self) + Illumination Nebulous
隆	prosper: 阝 (hill) + 夂 (step) + 生 (life) + Riches Yield Ultimate Upgrade
陳	state: 阝 (hill) + 東 (east) + Clarification Has INtention
陪	accompany: 阝 (hill) + 立 (stand) + 口 (open) + Beside Another Individual
皆	all: 比 (compare) + 白 (white) + Komplete Amount Includes
階	level: 阝 (hill) + 皆 (all) + Klosely Aligned Interval

Day six: character clusters

I   Complete the characters using the clues.

1	阝	Hill ANgle (HAN)
2	日	Kompletely Years Used Up (KYUU)
3	且	Set Obstacle (SO)
4	白	Komplete Amount Includes (KAI)
5	阝	Clarification Has INtention (CHIN)

II   Compose the compounds using the clues.

1   (BYOO) 病   +   (IN) ____   =   _____ (hospital)
        illness

2   (KAI) ____   +   (DAN) 段   =   _____ (stairs)
                                     step

3   (BAI) ____   +   (SHIN) 審   =   _____ (jury)
                                     investigate

4   (MU) 無   +   (GEN) ____   =   _____ (infinity)
        without

5   (BOO) ____   +   (SUI) 水   =   _____ (waterproof)
                                     water

III   Complete the sentences using the clues.

1   学校の男女の＿＿率は2対1です。
    Gakkoo no danjo no HIritsu wa ni tai ichi desu.
    The ratio of boys to girls in school is two to one.

2   中国はアジア大＿＿にある。
    Chuugoku wa ajia taiRIKU ni aru.
    China is on the Asian continent.

3   不要な言葉をエッセーから削＿＿しなさい。
    Fuyoona kotoba o essee kara sakuJO shinasai.
    Eliminate unnecessary words from the essay.

4   この車には欠＿＿があります。
    Kono kuruma ni wa kekKAN ga arimasu.
    There is a defect in this car.

5   川で泳ぐのは危＿＿です。
    Kawa de oyogu no wa kiKEN desu.
    It is dangerous to swim in the river.

27
CUTTING EDGE

Day one: crossword puzzle

Across
8. Humans Assembled Now
10. Kut Amount To Split Up
11. Systematic Exact Influence
12. Kommercial ANnouncement
13. Short Amount KUt
14. Klip Atop
18. Follow Under KUstomarily (S)
19. Kills ENemy (S)
21. Body Open One

Down
1. Honorably ANalyze (J)
2. Same Each Item (E)
3. To Obtain Objective
4. Stamp And Type SUrface
5. JOurney On (R)
6. Judged One Over (S)
7. Zealously Alleviates Illness
9. Start On Original
15. SAnctuary To SUpplicate
16. KOnvincingly KUt (C)
17. Reaping Income
20. SHarply Impale

Day two: acrostics

1 Judge: H _ _ _ _ _ _ _ _   A N _ _ _ _ _

2 Equal: S _ _ _   E _ _ _   I _ _ _

3 Reach: T _   O _ _ _ _ _   O _ _ _ _ _ _ _

4 Print: S _ _ _ _   A _ _   T _ _ _   S U _ _ _ _ _

5 Ride: J O _ _ _ _ _   O _

6 Surplus: J _ _ _ _ _   O _ _   O _ _ _

7 Medicine: Z _ _ _ _ _ _ _ _   A _ _ _ _ _ _ _ _   I _ _ _ _ _ _

8 Group: H _ _ _ _ _ _   A _ _ _ _ _ _ _ _   N _ _

9 Create: S _ _ _ _   O _   O _ _ _ _ _ _

10 Divide: K _ _   A _ _ _ _ _   T _   S _ _ _ _   U _

11 Control: S _ _ _ _ _ _ _ _ _   E _ _ _ _   I _ _ _ _ _ _ _ _

12 Publish: K _ _ _ _ _ _ _ _ _   A N _ _ _ _ _ _ _ _ _

13 Pare: S _ _ _ _   A _ _ _ _ _   K U _

14 Cut: K _ _ _   A _ _ _ (RU)

15 Temple: S A _ _ _ _ _ _ _   T _   S U _ _ _ _ _ _ _ _

16 Carve: K O _ _ _ _ _ _ _ _ _ _   K U _

17 Profit: R _ _ _ _ _ _   I _ _ _ _ _

18 Secondary: F _ _ _ _ _   U _ _ _ _   K U _ _ _ _ _ _ _ _

19 Sword: K _ _ _ _   E N _ _ _

20 Stab: S H _ _ _ _ _ _   I _ _ _ _ _

21 Dissect: B _ _ _   O _ _ _   O _ _

Day three: componential analysis

Course Number	Kanji	ON Reading(s) / Core Concept(s)	Primary Components	Kanji Canvas
0547	刈	ka(ru) / **cut, crop**	メ (mark)[K49] + 刂 (cut)[K36]	刈
0548	刊	KAN / **publish**	干 (dry)[24] + 刂 (cut)[K36]	刊
0549	利	RI / **profit, benefit**	禾 (grain)[K33] + 刂 (cut)[K36]	利
0550	判	HAN / **judge; seal**	半 (half)[493] + 刂 (cut) [K36]	判
0551	刹	SATSU / **temple**	メ (mark)[K49] + 木 (tree)[43] + 刂 (cut)[K36]	刹
0552	制	SEI / **control; system**	止 (*stop*)[165] + 巾 (cloth)[395] + 刂 (cut)[K36]	制
0553	刷	SATSU / **print**	尸 (bent body)[K59] + 巾 (cloth)[395] + 刂 (cut)[K36]	刷
0554	到	TOO / **reach, arrive**	至 (arrive)[173] + 刂 (cut)[K36]	到
0555	刺	SHI / **stab, pierce**	*tree with broken branches* (cf. 952) + 刂 (cut)[K36]	刺
0556	刻	KOKU / **carve; time**	亥 (pig)[K71] + 刂 (cut)[K36]	刻
0557	削	SAKU / **pare**	肖 (resemble)[277] + 刂 (cut)[K36]	削
0558	班	HAN / **group**	玉 (jewel)[329] + 刂 (*cut*)[K36] + 王 (king)[155]	班
0559	剖	BOO / **dissect**	立 (stand)[37] + 口 (mouth)[106] + 刂 (cut)[K36]	剖
0560	剣	KEN / **sword**	僉 (discreet)[K70] + 刂 (cut)[K36]	剣
0561	斉	SEI / **equal**	文 (writing)[221] + 月 (*half-moon*)[153]	斉
0562	剤	ZAI / **medicine**	斉 (equal)[561] + 刂 (cut)[K36]	剤
0563	乗	JOO / **ride**	禾 (grain)[K33] + 田 (*field*)[60]	乗
0564	剰	JOO / **surplus**	乗 (ride)[563] + 刂 (cut)[K36]	剰
0565	副	FUKU / **secondary**	畐 (full)[K72] + 刂 (cut)[K36]	副
0566	割	KATSU / **divide**	害 (harm)[336] + 刂 (cut)[K36]	割
0567	創	SOO / **create**	倉 (storehouse)[392] + 刂 (cut)[K36]	創

Day four: writing practice

刈	刊	利	判	殺	制	刷
刈	刊	利	判	殺	制	刷

到	刺	刻	削	班	剖	劍
到	刺	刻	削	班	剖	劍

齊	劑	乗	剩	副	割	創
齊	劑	乗	剩	副	割	創

Day five: story sketch

刈	cut: ✕ (mark) + 刂 (cut) + Klip Atop
刊	publish: 干 (dry) + 刂 (cut) + Kommercial ANnouncement
利	profit: 禾 (grain) + 刂 (cut) + Reaping Income
判	judge: 半 (half) + 刂 (cut) + Honorably ANalyze
刹	temple: ✕ (mark) + 木 (tree) + 刂 (cut) + SAnctuary To SUpplicate
制	control: 止 (*stop*) + 巾 (cloth) + 刂 (cut) + Systematic Exact Influence
刷	print: 尸 (bent body) + 巾 (cloth) + 刂 (cut) + Stamp And Type SUrface
到	reach: 至 (arrive) + 刂 (cut) + To Obtain Objective
刺	stab: *tree with broken branches* + 刂 (cut) + SHarply Impale
刻	carve: 亥 (pig) + 刂 (cut) + KOnvincingly KUt
削	pare: 肖 (resemble) + 刂 (cut) + Short Amount KUt
班	group: 玉 (jewel) + 刂 (*cut*) + 王 (king) + Humans Assembled Now
剖	dissect: 立 (stand) + 口 (mouth) + 刂 (cut) + Body Open One
剣	sword: 僉 (discreet) + 刂 (cut) + Kills ENemy
斉	equal: 文 (writing) + 月 (*half-moon*) + Same Each Item
剤	medicine: 斉 (equal) + 刂 (cut) + Zealously Alleviates Illness
乗	ride: 禾 (grain) + 田 (*field*) + JOurney On
剰	surplus: 乗 (ride) + 刂 (cut) + Judged One Over
副	secondary: 畐 (full) + 刂 (cut) + Follow Under KUstomarily
割	divide: 害 (harm) + 刂 (cut) + Kut Amount To Split Up
創	create: 倉 (storehouse) + 刂 (cut) + Start On Original

Day six: character clusters

I   Complete the characters using the clues.

1	文	Same Each Item (SEI)
2	刂	Kommercial ANnouncement (KAN)
3	亥	KOnvincingly KUt (KOKU)
4	刂	Follow Under KUstomarily (FUKU)
5	立	Body Open One (BOO)

II   Compose the compounds using the clues.

1   (MEI) 名   +   (SHI) _____   =   _____ (business card)
    name

2   (JOO) _____   +   (KYAKU) 客   =   _____ (passenger)
                          guest

3   (HAN) _____   +   (DAN) 断   =   _____ (judgment)
                          decision

4   (SEN) 洗   +   (ZAI) _____   =   _____ (detergent)
    wash

5   (SAKU) _____   +   (GEN) 減   =   _____ (reduction)
                          decrease

III   Complete the sentences using the clues.

1   自転車で行くのが便＿＿です。
    Jitensha de iku no ga benRI desu.
    Going by bicycle is convenient.

2   その小説は五千部印＿＿された。
    Sono shoosetsu wa go-sen-bu inSATSU sareta.
    Five thousand copies of that novel were printed.

3   明日この便はトルコに＿＿着します。
    Ashita kono bin wa toruko ni TOOchaku shimasu.
    This flight arrives in Turkey tomorrow.

4   父は真＿＿な顔をしています。
    Chichi wa shinKEN na kao o shite imasu.
    My father has a serious look on his face.

5   私たちの会社は去年＿＿立されました。
    Watashi-tachi no kaisha wa kyonen SOOritsu saremashita.
    Our company was established last year.

28

A GRAIN OF TRUTH

Day one: crossword puzzle

Across

4. Tilled Oriental Organism
6. Sign HOnors One
10. Sphere Human Intimacy
13. Surcharge Obligatory
14. Klimate Interval
16. HIdden
18. Impel
19. Kause INfection
21. Zone Excise Imposed

Down

1. Teeming Amount (M)
2. KOnstructed Overhead (H)
3. Komponent Apart (S)
5. Invest
7. Success HUgely Unusual (E)
8. Warm Agreement (P)
9. TEnder Introduction (P)
11. Brief Yet Often Occurs
12. KOmposition Original (M)
15. Classification Has ITs SUccession
17. Tract Estimate Indicates
20. Seeds Upheld Inside

Day two: acrostics

1   Many: T _ _ _ _ _ _   A _ _ _ _ _

2   High: K O _ _ _ _ _ _ _ _   O _ _ _ _ _ _

3   Section: K _ _ _ _ _ _ _   A _ _ _ _

4   Rice: T _ _ _ _ _   O _ _ _ _ _ _   O _ _ _ _ _ _

5   Entrust: I _ _ _ _ _

6   Name: S _ _ _   H O _ _ _ _   O _ _

7   Excel: S _ _ _ _ _ _   H U _ _ _ _   U _ _ _ _ _ _

8   Peace: W _ _ _   A _ _ _ _ _ _ _ _

9   Present: T E _ _ _ _   I _ _ _ _ _ _ _ _ _ _

10 Private: S _ _ _ _ _   H _ _ _ _   I _ _ _ _ _ _ _

11 Second: B _ _ _ _   Y _ _   O _ _ _ _   O _ _ _ _ _

12 Manuscript: K O _ _ _ _ _ _ _ _   O _ _ _ _ _ _

13 Levy: S _ _ _ _ _ _ _ _   O _ _ _ _ _ _ _ _

14 Season: K _ _ _ _ _ _   I _ _ _ _ _ _ _

15 Order: C _ _ _ _ _ _ _ _ _ _ _ _   H _ _   I T _   S U _ _ _ _ _ _ _ _

16 Secret: H I _ _ _ _

17 Extent: T _ _ _ _   E _ _ _ _ _ _ _   I _ _ _ _ _ _ _ _

18 Move: I _ _ _ _

19 Bacteria: K _ _ _ _   I N _ _ _ _ _ _ _

20 Ear: S _ _ _ _   U _ _ _ _ _   I _ _ _ _ _

21 Tax: Z _ _ _   E _ _ _ _ _   I _ _ _ _ _ _

Day three: componential analysis

Course Number	Kanji	ON Reading(s) / Core Concept(s)	Primary Components	Kanji Canvas
0568	私	SHI / private; I	禾 (grain)K33 + ム (self)K18	私
0569	秀	SHUU / excel, excellent	禾 (grain)K33 + 及 (*reach*)463	秀
0570	和	WA / peace; Japan	禾 (grain)K33 + 口 (mouth)106	和
0571	季	KI / season	禾 (grain)K33 + 子 (child)320	季
0572	委	I / entrust	禾 (grain)K33 + 女 (woman)337	委
0573	科	KA / section; course	禾 (grain)K33 + 斗 (measure)15	科
0574	秒	BYOO / second	禾 (grain)K33 + 少 (little)32	秒
0575	称	SHOO / name	禾 (grain)K33 + ノ (accent)K2 + 丁 (exact)87 + 八 (*eight*)04	称
0576	秘	HI / secret	禾 (grain)K33 + 必 (inevitably)128	秘
0577	租	SO / levy	禾 (grain)K33 + 且 (moreover)331	租
0578	秩	CHITSU / order	禾 (grain)K33 + 失 (lose)265	秩
0579	菌	KIN / bacteria, germs	⺿ (plants)K29 + 囗 (enclosure)K4 + 禾 (grain)K33	菌
0580	多	TA / many	夕 (two evenings)123	多
0581	移	I / move, transfer	禾 (grain)K33 + 多 (many)580	移
0582	税	ZEI / tax	禾 (grain)K33 + ㇑ (split)K35 + 兄 (older brother)117	税
0583	呈	TEI / present	口 (mouth)106 + 王 (king)155	呈
0584	程	TEI / extent	禾 (grain)K33 + 呈 (present)583	程
0585	稲	TOO / rice	禾 (grain)K33 + ⺥ (claw)K53 + 臼 (old)536	稲
0586	高	KOO / high, tall	Tall building	高
0587	稿	KOO / manuscript	禾 (grain)K33 + 高 (high)586	稿
0588	穂	SUI / ear	禾 (grain)K33 + 恵 (favor)490	穂

Day four: writing practice

私	秀	和	季	委	科	秒
私	秀	和	季	委	科	秒

称	秘	租	秩	菌	多	移
称	秘	租	秩	菌	多	移

税	呈	程	稻	高	稿	穗
税	呈	程	稻	高	稿	穗

Day five: story sketch

私	private: 禾 (grain) + ム (self) + Sphere Human Intimacy
秀	excel: 禾 (grain) + 及 (*reach*) + Success HUgely Unusual
和	peace: 禾 (grain) + 口 (mouth) + Warm Agreement
季	season: 禾 (grain) + 子 (child) + Klimate Interval
委	entrust: 禾 (grain) + 女 (woman) + Invest
科	section: 禾 (grain) + 斗 (measure) + Komponent Apart
秒	second: 禾 (grain) + 少 (little) + Brief Yet Often Occurs
称	name: 禾 (grain) + ノ (accent) + 丁 (exact) + 八 (*eight*) + Sign HOnors One
秘	secret: 禾 (grain) + 必 (inevitably) + HIdden
租	levy: 禾 (grain) + 且 (moreover) + Surcharge Obligatory
秩	order: 禾 (grain) + 失 (lose) + Classification Has ITs SUccession
菌	bacteria: ⺾ (plants) + 囗 (enclosure) + 禾 (grain) + Kause INfection
多	many: 夕 (two evenings) + Teeming Amount
移	move: 禾 (grain) + 多 (many) + Impel
税	tax: 禾 (grain) + ヽノ (split) + 兄 (older brother) + Zone Excise Imposed
呈	present: 口 (mouth) + 王 (king) + TEnder Introduction
程	extent: 禾 (grain) + 呈 (present) + Tract Estimate Indicates
稲	rice: 禾 (grain) + ⺥ (claw) + 旧 (old) + Tilled Oriental Organism
高	high: (tall building) + KOnstructed Overhead
稿	manuscript: 禾 (grain) + 高 (high) + KOmposition Original
穂	ear: 禾 (grain) + 恵 (favor) + Seeds Upheld Inside

Day six: character clusters

I   Complete the characters using the clues.

1	禾	Invest (I)
2	禾	Brief Yet Often Occurs (BYOO)
3	王	TEnder Introduction (TEI)
4	禾	Seeds Upheld Inside (SUI)
5	⧾⧾	Kause INfection (KIN)

II   Compose the compounds using the clues.

1   (HEI) 平   +   (WA) ____   =   _____ (peace)
       level

2   (GEN) 原   +   (KOO) ____   =   _____ (manuscript)
       original

3   (KI) ____   +   (SETSU) 節   =   _____ (season)
                              season

4   (TAI) 対   +   (SHOO) ____   =   _____ (symmetry)
       oppose, pair

5   (KOO) ____   +   (DO) 度   =   _____ (altitude)
                              degree

III   Complete the sentences using the clues.

1   タバコには高い＿＿金がかけられている。
      Tabako ni wa takai ZEIkin ga kakerarete iru.
      There is a high tax on tobacco.

2   次の学期はどんな＿＿目がありますか。
      Tsugi no gakki wa donna KAmoku ga arimasu ka.
      What subjects do you have next semester?

3   社長には＿＿書が二人います。
      Shachoo ni wa HIsho ga futari imasu.
      The company president has two secretaries.

4   息子は＿＿立学校に通っている。
      Musuko wa SHIritsu gakkoo ni kayotte iru.
      My son attends a private school.

5   机を左へ＿＿動してくれました。
      Tsukue o hidari e Idoo shite kuremashita.
      The desk was moved to the left for me.

29

AT FULL STRENGTH

Day one: crossword puzzle

Across

1. REduced To SUbordinate (I)
5. Joint Offer (H)
6. Climbing High In KUlms
8. Begets ENergy (E)
10. Must Evade Now
12. KOmmercial Outcome
14. REally Inspire
18. YOung Offspring
19. Kompels YOu Ominously (T)
20. Drive One Onward
21. KOmmendable Outcome (M)

Down

2. Command HOnors King's Understanding (two words)
3. Keen INdustry
4. Crowned Head's Inclusive Name (two words: R/W)
7. Kontracts INtensely
9. KOmmon Outcome
11. Drive Oneself (E)
13. Dutifully Occupy Oneself
15. SHarply Overcome Opposition
16. RObust Occupation
17. JUdged Unwieldy

Day two: acrostics

1 Inferior: R E _ _ _ _ _   T _   S U _ _ _ _ _ _ _ _

2 Imperial Edict: C _ _ _ _ _ _   H O _ _ _ _   K _ _ _ _   U _ _ _ _ _ _ _ _ _ _

3 Work: K _ _ _   I N _ _ _ _ _ _

4 Royal We: C _ _ _ _ _ _   H _ _ _ _   I _ _ _ _ _ _ _ _   N _ _ _

5 Help: J _ _ _ _   O _ _ _ _

6 Bamboo: C _ _ _ _ _ _ _   H _ _ _   I _   K U _ _ _

7 Muscle: K _ _ _ _ _ _ _ _   I N _ _ _ _ _ _ _

8 Endeavor: B _ _ _ _ _ _   E N _ _ _ _

9 Effect: K O _ _ _ _   O _ _ _ _ _ _

10 Escape: M _ _ _   E _ _ _ _   N _ _

11 Exert: D _ _ _ _   O _ _ _ _ _ _

12 Exchange: K O _ _ _ _ _ _ _ _   O _ _ _ _ _ _

13 Work: D _ _ _ _ _ _ _ _   O _ _ _ _ _   O _ _ _ _ _ _

14 Encourage: R E _ _ _ _   I _ _ _ _ _ _

15 Win: S H _ _ _ _ _   O _ _ _ _ _ _ _   O _ _ _ _ _ _ _ _

16 Labor: R O _ _ _ _   O _ _ _ _ _ _ _ _ _

17 Heavy: J U _ _ _ _   U _ _ _ _ _ _ _

18 Infant: Y O _ _ _   O _ _ _ _ _ _ _ _

19 Threaten: K _ _ _ _ _ _   Y O _   O _ _ _ _ _ _ _ _

20 Move: D _ _ _ _   O _ _   O _ _ _ _ _

21 Merit: K O _ _ _ _ _ _ _ _   O _ _ _ _ _ _

Day three: componential analysis

Course Number	Kanji	ON Reading(s) / Core Concept(s)	Primary Components	Kanji Canvas
0589	功	KOO / **merit**	工 (work)[26] + 力 (strength)[07]	功
0590	幼	YOO / **infant**	幺 (short thread)[K64] + 力 (strength)[07]	幼
0591	劣	RETSU / **inferior**	少 (little)[32] + 力 (strength)[07]	劣
0592	労	ROO / **labor**	龸 (ornate roof)[K73] + 力 (strength)[07]	労
0593	助	JO / **help**	且 (moreover)[331] + 力 (strength)[07]	助
0594	努	DO / **exert**	奴 (slave)[338] + 力 (power)[07]	努
0595	励	REI / **encourage; strive**	厂 (cliff)[K14] + 万 (ten thousand)[08] + 力 (power)[07]	励
0596	交	KOO / **exchange**	亠 (top)[K1] + 父 (father)[445]	交
0597	効	KOO / **effect**	交 (exchange)[596] + 力 (power)[07]	効
0598	勅	CHOKU / **imperial edict**	束 (bundle)[271] + 力 (power)[07]	勅
0599	脅	KYOO / **threaten**	力 (three powers)[07] + 月 (flesh)[K43]	脅
0600	免	MEN / **escape**	Rabbit's ears, body and short legs	免
0601	勉	BEN / **endeavor**	免 (escape)[600] + 力 (power)[07]	勉
0602	勤	KIN / **work**	⺿ (plants)[K29] + 口 (mouth)[106] + 生 (*life*)[142] + 力 (power)[07]	勤
0603	朕	CHIN / **royal we**	月 (body)[K43] + 丶 (out)[K35] + 天 (heaven)[261]	朕
0604	勝	SHOO / **win**	朕 (*royal we*)[603] + 力 (power)[07]	勝
0605	竹	CHIKU / **bamboo**	Stems and spiky leaves	竹
0606	筋	KIN / **muscle; thread**	⺮ (bamboo)[K74] + 月 (flesh)[K43] + 力 (strength)[07]	筋
0607	重	JUU / **heavy**	千 (thousand)[10] + 里 (village)[181]	重
0608	動	DOO / **move**	重 (heavy)[607] + 力 (power)[07]	動
0609	働	DOO / **work**	亻 (person)[K16] + 動 (move)[608]	働

Day four: writing practice

功	幼	劣	労	助	努	励
功	幼	劣	労	助	努	励

交	効	勅	脅	免	勉	勤
交	効	勅	脅	免	勉	勤

朕	勝	竹	筋	重	動	働
朕	勝	竹	筋	重	動	働

Day five: story sketch

功	merit: 工 (work) + 力 (strength) + KOmmendable Outcome
幼	infant: 幺 (short thread) + 力 (strength) + YOung Offspring
劣	inferior: 少 (little) + 力 (strength) + REduced To SUbordinate
労	labor: ⺌ (ornate roof) + 力 (strength) + RObust Occupation
助	help: 且 (moreover) + 力 (strength) + Joint Offer
努	exert: 奴 (slave) + 力 (power) + Drive Oneself
励	encourage: 厂 (cliff) + 万 (ten thousand) + 力 (power) + REally Inspire
交	exchange: 亠 (top) + 父 (father) + KOmmercial Outcome
効	effect: 交 (exchange) + 力 (power) + KOmmon Outcome
勅	imperial edict: 束 (bundle) + 力 (power) + Command HOnors King's Understanding
脅	threaten: 力 (three powers) + 月 (flesh) + Kompels YOu Ominously
免	escape: (rabbit's ears, body and short legs) + Must Evade Now
勉	endeavor: 免 (escape) + 力 (power) + Begets ENergy
勤	work: ⺾ (plants) + 口 (mouth) + 生 (*life*) + 力 (power) + Keen INdustry
朕	royal we: 月 (body) + 丷 (out) + 天 (heaven) + Crowned Head's Inclusive Name
勝	win: 朕 (*royal we*) + 力 (power) + SHarply Overcome Opposition
竹	bamboo: (stems and spiky leaves) + Climbing High In KUlms
筋	muscle: ⺮ (bamboo) + 月 (flesh) + 力 (strength) + Kontracts INtensely
重	heavy: 千 (thousand) + 里 (village) + JUdged Unwieldy
動	move: 重 (heavy) + 力 (power) + Drive One Onward
働	work: 亻 (person) + 動 (move) + Dutifully Occupy Oneself

Day six: character clusters

I   Complete the characters using the clues.

1	月	Crowned Head's Inclusive Name (CHIN)
2	厂	REally Inspire (REI)
3	月	Kompels YOu Ominously (KYOO)
4	亻	Dutifully Occupy Oneself (DOO)
5	少	REduced To SUbordinate (RETSU)

II   Compose the compounds using the clues.

1 (JI) 白   +   (DOO) ____   =   _____ (automatic)
      self

2 (MEN) ____   +   (KYO) 許   =   _____ (license)
                         permit

3 (JO) ____   +   (SHU) 手   =   _____ (assistant)
                         hand

4 (KU) 苦   +   (ROO) ____   =   _____ (trouble)
      painful

5 (JUU) ____   +   (YOO) 要   =   _____ (importance)
                         necessary

III   Complete the sentences using the clues.

1   飛行機のチケットは二週間有＿＿です。
    Hikooki no chiketto wa nishuukan yuuKOO desu.
    The plane ticket is valid for two weeks.

2   ピアノを弾くには＿＿力がいる。
    Piano o hiku ni wa DOryoku ga iru.
    Playing the piano requires effort.

3   毎日一時間漢字を＿＿強します。
    Mainichi ichijikan kanji o BENkyoo shimasu.
    I study kanji for one hour every day.

4   スミスさんの計画は成＿＿だった。
    Sumisu-san no keikaku wa seiKOO datta.
    Mr. Smith's plan was a success.

5   このジャケットをもっと小さいのと＿＿換したい。
    Kono jaketto o motto chiisai no to KOOkan shitai.
    I want to exchange this jacket for a smaller one.

30

MOUNTAIN RANGE

Day one: crossword puzzle

Across
- 2. KOunt One
- 6. SAlient Kape Imposing (P)
- 7. Kite Alights
- 10. Regard YOked Oxen
- 12. See Utterly Upstanding
- 14. Krevice Yawns Over Opening
- 15. Ground ANgled
- 17. Koast Overlooks Ocean
- 19. Kourse Interrupts (F)
- 20. TOwering Opening Grants Entry (P)
- 21. Klimb Yet Upland Upon

Down
- 1. Yet Unseen Unknown (H)
- 3. Kurious Instance
- 4. Highlight Of Obliteration (C)
- 5. MInutely Tight SUbstance
- 8. Highest Overall Outlook
- 9. SEver Kliff Into (S)
- 11. Ordinary Kind Ascent (H)
- 13. Ground ANchor
- 16. Trees ANcient
- 18. Great Ascent Krests Upward

Day two: acrostics

1 Hidden: Y _ _   U _ _ _ _ _   U _ _ _ _ _ _

2 First: K O _ _ _   O _ _

3 Strange: K _ _ _ _ _ _   I _ _ _ _ _ _ _

4 Crumble: H _ _ _ _ _ _ _ _   O _   O _ _ _ _ _ _ _ _ _ _

5 Dense: M I _ _ _ _ _ _   T _ _ _ _   S U _ _ _ _ _ _ _

6 Promontory: S A _ _ _ _ _   K _ _ _   I _ _ _ _ _ _ _

7 Down: K _ _ _   A _ _ _ _ _ _

8 Peak: H _ _ _ _ _ _   O _ _ _ _ _   O _ _ _ _ _

9 Stone: S E _ _ _   K _ _ _ _   I _ _ _

10 Both: R _ _ _ _ _   Y O _ _ _   O _ _ _

11 Hill: O _ _ _ _ _ _ _   K _ _ _   A _ _ _ _ _

12 Revere: S _ _   U _ _ _ _ _ _   U _ _ _ _ _ _ _ _

13 Rock: G _ _ _ _ _   A N _ _ _ _

14 Gorge: K _ _ _ _ _ _   Y _ _ _ _   O _ _ _   O _ _ _ _ _ _

15 Bank: G _ _ _ _ _   A N _ _ _ _

16 Coal: T _ _ _ _   A N _ _ _ _ _

17 Cape: K _ _ _ _   O _ _ _ _ _ _ _ _   O _ _ _ _

18 Peak: G _ _ _ _   A _ _ _ _ _   K _ _ _ _ _   U _ _ _ _ _

19 Fork: K _ _ _ _ _   I _ _ _ _ _ _ _ _

20 Pass: T O _ _ _ _ _ _   O _ _ _ _ _ _   G _ _ _ _ _   E _ _ _ _

21 Hill: K _ _ _ _   Y _ _   U _ _ _ _ _   U _ _ _

Day three: componential analysis

Course Number	Kanji	ON Reading(s) / Core Concept(s)	Primary Components	Kanji Canvas
0610	両	RYOO / both	一 (one)[01] + 冂 (border)[K27] + 山 (mountain)[71]	両
0611	岸	GAN / bank, shore	山 (mountain)[71] + 厂 (cliff)[K14] + 干 (dry)[24]	岸
0612	岐	KI / fork	山 (mountain)[71] + 支 (branch)[79]	岐
0613	岡	oka / hill	冂 (border)[K27] + 丶丶 (away)[K35] + 一 (one)[01] + 山 (mountain)[71]	岡
0614	石	SEKI / stone	厂 (*cliff*)[K14] + 口 (open)[106]	石
0615	岩	GAN / rock	山 (mountain)[71] + 石 (stone)[614]	岩
0616	丘	KYUU / hill	斤 (ax)[55] + 一 (one)[01]	丘
0617	岳	GAKU / peak	丘 (hill)[616] + 山 (mountain)[71]	岳
0618	甲	KOO / first; shell	Suit of armor	甲
0619	岬	KOO / cape	山 (mountain)[71] + 甲 (first)[618]	岬
0620	幽	YUU / hidden	幺 (short threads)[K64] + 山 (mountain)[71]	幽
0621	炭	TAN / coal	山 (mountain)[71] + 灰 (ash)[423]	炭
0622	峡	KYOO / gorge	山 (mountain)[71] + 来 (between)[K75]	峡
0623	下	KA, GE / down	Area below a line	下
0624	峠	tooge / pass	山 (mountain)[71] + 上 (up)[474] + 下 (down)[623]	峠
0625	峰	HOO / peak	山 (mountain)[71] + 夂 (step)[K13] + 十 (ten)[06] + 二 (two)[02]	峰
0626	崩	HOO / crumble	山 (mountain)[71] + 月 (two bodies)[K43]	崩
0627	奇	KI / strange, odd	大 (big)[233] + 可 (possible)[109]	奇
0628	崎	saki / promontory	山 (mountain)[71] + 奇 (strange)[627]	崎
0629	密	MITSU / dense; secret	宀 (roof)[K51] + 必 (inevitably)[128] + 山 (mountain)[71]	密
0630	崇	SUU / revere	山 (mountain)[71] + 宗 (religion)[326]	崇

Day four: writing practice

両	岸	岐	岡	石	岩	丘
両	岸	岐	岡	石	岩	丘

岳	甲	岬	幽	炭	峡	下
岳	甲	岬	幽	炭	峡	下

峠	峰	崩	奇	崎	密	崇
峠	峰	崩	奇	崎	密	崇

Day five: story sketch

両	both: 一 (one) + 冂 (border) + 山 (mountain) + Regard YOked Oxen
岸	bank: 山 (mountain) + 厂 (cliff) + 干 (dry) + Ground ANgled
岐	fork: 山 (mountain) + 支 (branch) + Kourse Interrupts
岡	hill: 冂 (border) + 丷 (away) + 一 (one) + 山 (mountain) + Ordinary Kind Ascent
石	stone: 厂 (*cliff*) + 口 (open) + SEver Kliff Into
岩	rock: 山 (mountain) + 石 (stone) + Ground ANchor
丘	hill: 斤 (ax) + 一 (one) + Klimb Yet Upland Upon
岳	peak: 丘 (hill) + 山 (mountain) + Great Ascent Krests Upward
甲	first: (suit of armor) + KOunt One
岬	cape: 山 (mountain) + 甲 (first) + Koast Overlooks Ocean
幽	hidden: 幺 (short threads) + 山 (mountain) + Yet Unseen Unknown
炭	coal: 山 (mountain) + 灰 (ash) + Trees ANcient
峡	gorge: 山 (mountain) + 来 (between) + Krevice Yawns Over Opening
下	down: (area below a line) + Kite Alights
峠	pass: 山 (mountain) + 上 (up) + 下 (down) + TOwering Opening Grants Entry
峰	peak: 山 (mountain) + 夂 (step) + 十 (ten) + 二 (two) + Highest Overall Outlook
崩	crumble: 山 (mountain) + 月 (two bodies) + Highlight Of Obliteration
奇	strange: 大 (big) + 可 (possible) + Kurious Instance
崎	promontory: 山 (mountain) + 奇 (strange) + SAlient Kape Imposing
密	dense: 宀 (roof) + 必 (inevitably) + 山 (mountain) + MInutely Tight SUbstance
崇	revere: 山 (mountain) + 宗 (religion) + See Utterly Upstanding

Day six: character clusters

I   Complete the characters using the clues.

1	甲	Koast Overlooks Ocean (KOO)
2	山	See Utterly Upstanding (SUU)
3	门	Ordinary Kind Ascent (OKA)
4	山	Ground ANchor (GAN)
5	奇	SAlient Kape Imposing (SAKI)

II   Compose the compounds using the clues.

1   (SA) 砂   +   (KYUU) ____   =   _____ (dune)
    sand

2   (MITSU) ____   +   (RIN) 林   =   _____ (jungle)
                         forest

3   (SEKI) ____   +   (YU) 油   =   _____ (petroleum)
                         oil

4   (MOKU) 木   +   (TAN) ____   =   _____ (charcoal)
    wood

5   (YUU) ____   +   (REI) 霊   =   _____ (ghost)
                         spirit

III   Complete the sentences using the clues.

1   昨夜11時に___妙な電話があった。
    Sakuya juuichi-ji ni KImyoo na denwa ga atta.
    I received a mysterious phone call at 11:00 last night.

2   地震の後多くの建物が___壊した。
    Jishin no ato ooku no tatemono ga HOOkai shita.
    After the earthquake many buildings collapsed.

3   サラは夏休みに海___へ行きます。
    Sara wa natsu-yasumi ni kaiGAN e ikimasu.
    Sara will go to the seaside for summer vacation.

4   私の___親はふたりとも医者です。
    Watashi no RYOOshin wa futari tomo isha desu.
    Both of my parents are doctors.

5   ここから東京まで地___鉄で行けるよ。
    Koko kara tookyoo made chiKAtetsu de ikeru yo.
    You can take the subway to Tokyo from here.

REVIEW: LESSONS 26–30

I   Given the character and meaning, write the pronunciation.

1 阪 slope _____   2 判 judge _____   3 秀 excel _____

4 幼 infant _____   5 岐 fork _____   6 陳 state _____

7 乗 ride _____   8 穂 ear _____   9 重 heavy _____

10 峠 pass _____   11 附 attach _____   12 刈 cut _____

13 称 name _____   14 努 exert _____   15 岸 bank _____

16 階 level _____   17 斉 equal _____   18 稲 rice _____

19 効 effect _____   20 崇 revere _____   21 陸 land _____

22 刹 temple _____   23 季 season _____   24 削 pare _____

25 岡 hill _____   26 移 move _____   27 刷 print _____

28 秩 order _____   29 筋 muscle _____   30 岳 peak _____

II   Given the character and pronunciation, write the meaning.

1 陛 HEI _____   2 甲 KOO _____   3 剖 BOO _____

4 幽 YUU _____   5 励 REI _____   6 阻 SO _____

7 剤 ZAI _____   8 委 I _____   9 朕 CHIN _____

10 峰 HOO _____   11 陥 KAN _____   12 刺 SHI _____

13 菌 KIN _____   14 劣 RETSU _____   15 峡 KYOO _____

16 陵 RYOO _____   17 班 HAN _____   18 稿 KOO _____

19 勅 CHOKU _____   20 崎 saki _____   21 隆 RYUU _____

22 創 SOO _____ 　　23 科 KA _____ 　　24 竹 CHIKU _____

25 岬 KOO _____ 　　26 院 IN _____ 　　27 副 FUKU _____

28 程 TEI _____ 　　29 陪 BAI _____ 　　30 刻 KOKU_____

III　Given the meaning and pronunciation, write the character.

1 prevent	BOO	_____		2 publish	KAN	_____
3 second	BYOO	_____		4 help	JO	_____
5 hill	KYUU	_____		6 all	KAI	_____
7 surplus	JOO	_____		8 exchange	KOO	_____
9 both	RYOO	_____		10 crumble	HOO	_____
11 compare	HI	_____		12 reach	TOO	_____
13 peace	WA	_____		14 threaten	KYOO	_____
15 rock	GAN	_____		16 move	DOO	_____
17 divide	KATSU	_____		18 merit	KOO	_____
19 strange	KI	_____		20 old	KYUU	_____
21 many	TA	_____		22 high	KOO	_____
23 sword	KEN	_____		24 present	TEI	_____
25 private	SHI	_____				

IV　Compose compounds using the following characters.

密 利 降 免 労 税 陰 働 炭 制 下 勝 秘 租 除 勉 限 勤 険 石

1 (IN) _____ 　+　 (KEN) _____ 　=　 _____ (cunning)

2 (SEI) _____ 　+　 (GEN) _____ 　=　 _____ (restriction)

3 (SHOO) _____ 　+　 (RI) _____ 　=　 _____ (victory)

4 (MEN) _____ 　+　 (JO) _____ 　=　 _____ (exemption)

5 (SO) _____ 　+　 (ZEI) _____ 　=　 _____ (taxes)

6 (HI) _____ 　+　 (MITSU) _____ 　=　 _____ (secret)

7 (KA) _____ 　+　 (KOO) _____ 　=　 _____ (descent)

8 (ROO) _____ 　+　 (DOO) _____ 　=　 _____ (labor)

9 (SEKI) _____ 　+　 (TAN) _____ 　=　 _____ (coal)

10 (KIN) _____ 　+　 (BEN) _____ 　=　 _____ (diligence)

31

WATERMARK

Day one: crossword puzzle

Across

1. Deep Opaque Opening
5. Sooner ENter
7. Nunnery Inhabitant
8. Just Influence (G)
14. Hesitant Advance
15. KOnsiderable Overflow
16. Soggy Hissing Outlying Overgrowth (S)
19. Kondition YOu Occupy
21. KEen To Settle Upon

Down

2. Ensues Nearby
3. Stain ENtirely
4. Klear Yourself Out
6. Center Human Understanding Upon (C)
9. HOlds Order (L)
10. Damp Earth Impressible
11. Sponge ENergetically
12. Humans Issue Typical SUbstance (S)
13. Coast Has Unimpeded Undulations (O)
17. KATalytic SUbstance
18. Superior HUman (M)
20. Obscene

Day two: acrostics

1 Cave: D _ _ _   O _ _ _ _ _   O _ _ _ _ _ _

2 Along: E _ _ _ _ _ _   N _ _ _ _ _

3 Dye: S _ _ _ _   E N _ _ _ _ _ _

4 Leave: K _ _ _ _ _   Y _ _ _ _ _ _ _ _   O _ _

5 Precede: S _ _ _ _ _ _   E N _ _ _

6 Concentrate: C _ _ _ _ _ _   H _ _ _ _   U _ _ _ _ _ _ _ _ _ _ _   U _ _ _

7 Nun: N _ _ _ _ _ _ _   I _ _ _ _ _ _ _ _ _

8 Govern: J _ _ _   I _ _ _ _ _ _ _ _

9 Law: H O _ _ _   O _ _ _ _

10 Mud: D _ _ _   E _ _ _ _   I _ _ _ _ _ _ _ _ _

11 Wash: S _ _ _ _ _ _   E N _ _ _ _ _ _ _ _ _ _

12 Secrete: H _ _ _ _ _ _   I _ _ _ _   T _ _ _ _ _ _   S U _ _ _ _ _ _ _

13 Offshore: C _ _ _ _   H _ _   U _ _ _ _ _ _ _ _   U _ _ _ _ _ _ _ _ _ _

14 Wave: H _ _ _ _ _ _ _ _   A _ _ _ _ _ _

15 Flood: K O _ _ _ _ _ _ _ _ _ _   O _ _ _ _ _ _ _

16 Swamp: S _ _ _ _   H _ _ _ _ _ _   O _ _ _ _ _ _ _   O _ _ _ _ _ _ _ _ _

17 Active: K A T _ _ _ _ _ _   S U _ _ _ _ _ _ _

18 Master: S _ _ _ _ _ _ _ _   H U _ _ _

19 Situation: K _ _ _ _ _ _ _ _   Y O _   O _ _ _ _ _

20 Dirty: O _ _ _ _ _ _

21 Decide: K E _ _   T _   S _ _ _ _ _   U _ _ _

Day three: componential analysis

Course Number	Kanji	ON Reading(s) / Core Concept(s)	Primary Components	Kanji Canvas
0631	汚	O / dirty	氵 (water)[K6] + 丂 (emerge)[K28] + 一 (one)[01]	汚
0632	沖	CHUU / offshore	氵 (water)[K6] + 中 (middle)[77]	沖
0633	治	JI, CHI / govern; cure	氵 (water)[K6] + 台 (platform)[114]	治
0634	決	KETSU / decide	氵 (water)[K6] + 央 (center)[234]	決
0635	泌	HITSU, HI / secrete	氵 (water)[K6] + 必 (inevitably)[128]	泌
0636	波	HA / wave	氵 (water)[K6] + 皮 (skin)[409]	波
0637	沿	EN / along	氵 (water)[K6] + 八 (eight)[04] + 口 (mouth)[106]	沿
0638	況	KYOO / situation	氵 (water)[K6] + 兄 (older brother)[117]	況
0639	沼	SHOO / swamp	氵 (water)[K6] + 召 (summon)[116]	沼
0640	去	KYO, KO / leave; past	土 (ground)[169] + ム (self)[K18]	去
0641	法	HOO / law; method	氵 (water)[K6] + 去 (leave)[640]	法
0642	主	SHU / master	丶 (accent)[K2] + 王 (king)[155]	主
0643	注	CHUU / concentrate; pour	氵 (water)[K6] + 主 (master)[642]	注
0644	尼	NI / nun	尸 (bent body)[K59] + 匕 (sitting)[K17]	尼
0645	泥	DEI / mud	氵 (water)[K6] + 尼 (nun)[644]	泥
0646	洞	DOO / cave	氵 (water)[K6] + 同 (same)[119]	洞
0647	洪	KOO / flood	氵 (water)[K6] + 共 (together)[499]	洪
0648	活	KATSU / active, alive	氵 (water)[K6] + 舌 (tongue)[209]	活
0649	染	SEN / dye	氵 (water)[K6] + 九 (nine)[05] + 木 (tree)[43]	染
0650	先	SEN / precede	止 (stop)[165] + 儿 (boy)[K5]	先
0651	洗	SEN / wash	氵 (water)[K6] + 先 (precede)[650]	洗

Day four: writing practice

污	冲	治	决	泌	波	沿
污	冲	治	决	泌	波	沿
况	沼	去	法	主	注	尼
况	沼	去	法	主	注	尼
泥	洞	洪	活	染	先	洗
泥	洞	洪	活	染	先	洗

Day five: story sketch

污	dirty: 氵 (water) + 丂 (emerge) + 一 (one) + Obscene
冲	offshore: 氵 (water) + 中 (middle) + Coast Has Unimpeded Undulations
治	govern: 氵 (water) + 台 (platform) + Just Influence
决	decide: 氵 (water) + 央 (center) + KEen To Settle Upon
泌	secrete: 氵 (water) + 必 (inevitably) + Humans Issue Typical SUbstance
波	wave: 氵 (water) + 皮 (skin) + Hesitant Advance
沿	along: 氵 (water) + 八 (eight) + 口 (mouth) + Ensues Nearby
况	situation: 氵 (water) + 兄 (older brother) + Kondition YOu Occupy
沼	swamp: 氵 (water) + 召 (summon) + Soggy Hissing Outlying Overgrowth
去	leave: 土 (ground) + 厶 (self) + Klear Yourself Out
法	law: 氵 (water) + 去 (leave) + HOlds Order
主	master: 丶 (accent) + 王 (king) + Superior HUman
注	concentrate: 氵 (water) + 主 (master) + Center Human Understanding Upon
尼	nun: 尸 (bent body) + 匕 (sitting) + Nunnery Inhabitant
泥	mud: 氵 (water) + 尼 (nun) + Damp Earth Impressible
洞	cave: 氵 (water) + 同 (same) + Deep Opaque Opening
洪	flood: 氵 (water) + 共 (together) + KOnsiderable Overflow
活	active: 氵 (water) + 舌 (tongue) + KATalytic SUbstance
染	dye: 氵 (water) + 九 (nine) + 木 (tree) + Stain ENtirely
先	precede: 止 (*stop*) + 儿 (boy) + Sooner ENter
洗	wash: 氵 (water) + 先 (precede) + Sponge ENergetically

Day six: character clusters

I   Complete the characters using the clues.

1	召	Soggy Hissing Outlying Overgrowth (SHOO)
2	氵	Ensues Nearby (EN)
3	木	Stain ENtirely (SEN)
4	氵	Hesitant Advance (HA)
5	尸	Nunnery Inhabitant (NI)

II   Compose the compounds using the clues.

1   (JOO) 状   +   (KYOO) ____   =   _____ (condition)
     condition

2   (SEN) ____   +   (SEI) 生   =   _____ (teacher)
                                          life

3   (HOO) ____   +   (RITSU) 律   =   _____ (law)
                                          law

4   (SEI) 政   +   (JI) ____   =   _____ (politics)
     government

5   (SHU) ____   +   (FU) 婦   =   _____ (housewife)
                                          woman

III   Complete the sentences using the clues.

1   この時間を十分に＿＿用しなさい。
    Kono jikan o juubun ni KATSUyoo shinasai.
    Make good use of this time.

2   過＿＿五年間外国へ行ったことがない。
    KaKO go-nen-kan gaikoku e itta koto ga nai.
    I have not been to a foreign country in the past five years.

3   ブラウンさんはいつも土曜日に＿＿濯します。
    Buraun-san wa itsumo doyoobi ni SENtaku shimasu.
    Mr. Brown always washes clothes on Saturday.

4   夕食にピザを＿＿文しました。
    Yuushoku ni pizza o CHUUmon shimashita.
    I ordered pizza for dinner.

5   その問題は解＿＿できるよ。
    Sono mondai wa kaiKETSU dekiru yo.
    That problem is solvable.

32

TREE RINGS

Day one: crossword puzzle

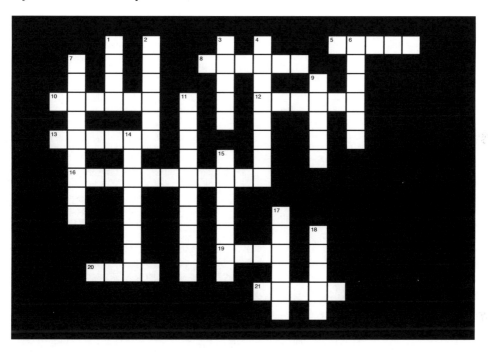

Across

5. KANdy
8. Off-white Offspring
10. Stem Has Increment
12. Kourses On Offer
13. Column HUge Upright
16. Study Assiduously
19. Kause ONe (R)
20. Source HOusehold Oils
21. Tender Oriental Orb

Down

1. Aim Necessitates
2. Slowly Accumulate Items
3. Hierarchy Enumerates Inferior
4. HOld (P)
6. Readily Yield Until Undulating
7. Scarlet HUe (V)
9. SHaded INterior (W)
11. KONfusing (D)
14. Believe One Observable (two words: A/C)
15. Has Exemplary Impression
17. Kontract Organically (W)
18. KApital Buyer Unit

Day two: acrostics

1 Plan: A _ _   N _ _ _ _ _ _ _ _ _ _ _

2 Gather: S _ _ _ _ _   A _ _ _ _ _ _ _ _ _   I _ _ _ _

3 Third: H _ _ _ _ _ _ _ _   E _ _ _ _ _ _ _ _ _   I _ _ _ _ _ _ _

4 Preserve: H O _ _

5 Sweet: K A N _ _

6 Willow: R _ _ _ _ _ _   Y _ _ _ _   U _ _ _ _   U _ _ _ _ _ _ _ _

7 Vermilion: S _ _ _ _ _ _   H U _

8 Cherry: O _ _ _ _ _ _ _   O _ _ _ _ _ _ _

9 Woods: S H _ _ _ _   I N _ _ _ _ _ _

10 Branch: S _ _ _   H _ _   I _ _ _ _ _ _ _ _

11 Difficulty: K O N _ _ _ _ _ _

12 School: K _ _ _ _ _ _   O _   O _ _ _ _

13 Pillar: C _ _ _ _ _   H U _ _   U _ _ _ _ _ _

14 A Certain: B _ _ _ _ _ _   O _ _   O _ _ _ _ _ _ _ _

15 Pattern: H _ _   E _ _ _ _ _ _ _ _   I _ _ _ _ _ _ _ _

16 Investigate: S _ _ _ _   A _ _ _ _ _ _ _ _ _ _

17 Wither: K _ _ _ _ _ _ _   O _ _ _ _ _ _ _ _ _

18 Stock: K A _ _ _ _ _   B _ _ _ _   U _ _ _

19 Root: K _ _ _ _   O N _

20 Pine: S _ _ _ _ _   H O _ _ _ _ _ _ _   O _ _ _

21 Peach: T _ _ _ _ _   O _ _ _ _ _ _ _   O _ _

Day three: componential analysis

Course Number	Kanji	ON Reading(s) / Core Concept(s)	Primary Components	Kanji Canvas
0652	困	KON / **difficulty**	囗 (enclosure)[K4] + 木 (tree)[43]	困
0653	松	SHOO / **pine**	木 (tree)[43] + 公 (public)[205]	松
0654	枝	SHI / **branch**	木 (tree)[43] + 支 (branch)[79]	枝
0655	采	SAI / **gather**	⚊ (claw)[K53] + 木 (tree)[43]	采
0656	柳	RYUU / **willow**	木 (tree)[43] + *supple branches*	柳
0657	枯	KO / **wither**	木 (tree)[43] + 古 (old)[108]	枯
0658	保	HO / **preserve**	亻 (person)[K16] + 口 (mouth)[106] + 木 (tree)[43]	保
0659	査	SA / **investigate**	木 (tree)[43] + 且 (moreover)[331]	査
0660	柱	CHUU / **pillar**	木 (tree)[43] + 主 (master)[642]	柱
0661	丙	HEI / **third**	一 (one)[01] + 内 (inside)[225]	丙
0662	柄	HEI / **pattern; handle**	木 (tree)[43] + 丙 (third)[661]	柄
0663	甘	KAN / **sweet**	Something on tongue in mouth	甘
0664	某	BOO / **a certain**	甘 (sweet)[663] + 木 (tree)[43]	某
0665	桜	OO / **cherry**	木 (tree)[43] + *falling* + 女 (woman)[337]	桜
0666	校	KOO / **school**	木 (tree)[43] + 交 (exchange)[596]	校
0667	案	AN / **plan, proposal**	安 (peaceful)[340] + 木 (tree)[43]	案
0668	桃	TOO / **peach**	木 (tree)[43] + 兆 (sign)[21]	桃
0669	根	KON / **root, base**	木 (tree)[43] + 良 (*good*)[398]	根
0670	朱	SHU / **vermilion**	未 (not yet)[44] + ノ (accent)[K2]	朱
0671	株	KABU / **stock**	木 (tree)[43] + 朱 (vermilion)[670]	株
0672	森	SHIN / **woods**	木 (three trees)[43]	森

Day four: writing practice

困	松	枝	采	柳	枯	保
困	松	枝	采	柳	枯	保

査	柱	丙	柄	甘	某	桜
査	柱	丙	柄	甘	某	桜

校	案	桃	根	朱	株	森
校	案	桃	根	朱	株	森

Day five: story sketch

困	difficulty: 囗 (enclosure) + 木 (tree) + KONfusing
松	pine: 木 (tree) + 公 (public) + Source HOusehold Oils
枝	branch: 木 (tree) + 支 (branch) + Stem Has Increment
采	gather: 爫 (claw) + 木 (tree) + Slowly Accumulate Items
柳	willow: 木 (tree) + *supple branches* + Readily Yield Until Undulating
枯	wither: 木 (tree) + 古 (old) + Kontract Organically
保	preserve: 亻 (person) + 口 (mouth) + 木 (tree) + HOld
查	investigate: 木 (tree) + 且 (moreover) + Study Assiduously
柱	pillar: 木 (tree) + 主 (master) + Column HUge Upright
丙	third: 一 (one) + 内 (inside) + Hierarchy Enumerates Inferior
柄	pattern: 木 (tree) + 丙 (third) + Has Exemplary Impression
甘	sweet: (something on tongue in mouth) + KANdy
某	a certain: 甘 (sweet) + 木 (tree) + Believe One Observable
桜	cherry: 木 (tree) + *falling* + 女 (woman) + Off-white Offspring
校	school: 木 (tree) + 交 (exchange) + Kourses On Offer
案	plan: 安 (peaceful) + 木 (tree) + Aim Necessitates
桃	peach: 木 (tree) + 兆 (sign) + Tender Oriental Orb
根	root: 木 (tree) + 良 (*good*) + Kause ONe
朱	vermilion: 未 (not yet) + 丿 (accent) + Scarlet HUe
株	stock: 木 (tree) + 朱 (vermilion) + KApital Buyer Unit
森	woods: 木 (three trees) + SHaded INterior

Day six: character clusters

I   Complete the characters using the clues.

1	一	Hierarchy Enumerates Inferior (HEI)
2	木	Stem Has Increment (SHI)
3	ノ	Scarlet HUe (SHU)
4	木	Kontract Organically (KO)
5	甘	Believe One Observable (BOO)

II   Compose the compounds using the clues.

1	(OO) 横 side	+	(HEI) ____	=	_____ (arrogance)
2	(KON) ____	+	(KYO) 拠 basis	=	_____ (grounds)
3	(EN) 円 round	+	(CHUU) ____	=	_____ (column)
4	(SHIN) ____	+	(RIN) 林 forest	=	_____ (forest)
5	(KAS) 喝 shout	+	(SAI) ____	=	_____ (cheers)

III   Complete the sentences using the clues.

1   空港で手荷物を検＿＿ました。
Kuukoo de tenimotsu o kenSA shimashita.
The baggage was inspected at the airport.

2   この古い本は安全な所に＿＿存しなさい。
Kono furui hon wa anzen-na tokoro ni HOzon shinasai.
Store this old book in a safe place.

3   娘は自転車で学＿＿に通っている。
Musume wa jitensha de gakKOO ni kayotte iru.
My daughter goes to school by bicycle.

4   外国語を習得するのは＿＿難です。
Gaikokugo o shuutoku suru no wa KONnan desu.
It is very difficult to master a foreign language.

5   友人は町を＿＿内してくれました。
Yuujin wa machi o ANnai shite kuremashita.
My friend guided me around the town.

33

PERSONAL IDENTITY

Day one: crossword puzzle

Across
2. Serve His Interest
4. Stated HItherto
12. Support Associate
13. Kin Entangled In
15. Handsome Amusing Individual
17. However Inverse
18. Issue
19. Shape And KUt
20. Kost Attribute
21. Southpaw Aspect

Down
1. Normally INcumbent (D)
3. Konvey YOur Overture
5. Dispense ENergy
6. Joint Urban Use (R)
7. Join In (A)
8. Klarifies Ambiguity (W)
9. Joyful INclination (B)
10. Help ANother (A)
11. Joint Image
14. Kurtailed Activity (T)
16. Ruling Individual

Day two: acrostics

1   Duty: N _ _ _ _ _ _ _   I N _ _ _ _ _ _ _

2   Use: S _ _ _ _   H _ _   I _ _ _ _ _ _ _

3   Offer: K _ _ _ _ _   Y O _ _   O _ _ _ _ _ _ _

4   History: S _ _ _ _ _ _   H I _ _ _ _ _ _

5   Transmit: D _ _ _ _ _ _ _   E N _ _ _ _

6   Reside: J _ _ _ _   U _ _ _ _   U _ _

7   Attend: J _ _ _   I _

8   What: K _ _ _ _ _ _ _ _   A _ _ _ _ _ _ _

9   Benevolence: J _ _ _ _ _   I N _ _ _ _ _ _ _ _ _

10   Accompany: H _ _ _   A N _ _ _ _ _

11   Resemble: J _ _ _ _   I _ _ _ _

12   Assist: S _ _ _ _ _ _   A _ _ _ _ _ _ _ _

13   Connection: K _ _   E _ _ _ _ _ _ _ _   I _

14   Temporary: K _ _ _ _ _ _ _ _   A _ _ _ _ _ _ _

15   Actor: H _ _ _ _ _ _ _   A _ _ _ _ _ _   I _ _ _ _ _ _ _ _ _

16   Official: R _ _ _ _ _   I _ _ _ _ _ _ _ _ _

17   Not: H _ _ _ _ _ _   I _ _ _ _ _ _

18   From: I _ _ _ _

19   Make: S _ _ _ _   A _ _   K U _

20   Price: K _ _ _   A _ _ _ _ _ _ _ _

21   Left: S _ _ _ _ _ _ _   A _ _ _ _ _

Day three: componential analysis

Course Number	Kanji	ON Reading(s) / Core Concept(s)	Primary Components	Kanji Canvas
0673	仁	JIN / benevolence	イ (person)[K16] + 二 (two)[02]	仁
0674	任	NIN / duty; entrust	イ (person)[K16] + ノ (accent)[K2] + 士 (samurai)[67]	任
0675	仮	KA / temporary; false	イ (person)[K16] + 反 (oppose)[58]	仮
0676	伝	DEN / transmit	イ (person)[K16] + 二 (two)[02] + ム (self)[K18]	伝
0677	伴	HAN, BAN / accompany	イ (person)[K16] + 半 (half)[493]	伴
0678	作	SAKU, SA / make	イ (person)[K16] + 乍 (hacksaw)[K76]	作
0679	住	JUU / reside	イ (person)[K16] + 主 (master)[642]	住
0680	何	KA / what; how many	イ (person)[K16] + 可 (possible)[109]	何
0681	以	I / from	ム (*self*)[K18] + 人 (*person*)[64]	以
0682	似	JI / resemble	イ (person)[K16] + 以 (from)[681]	似
0683	左	SA / left	手 (*hand*)[85] + 工 (work)[26]	左
0684	佐	SA / assist	イ (person)[K16] + 左 (left)[683]	佐
0685	供	KYOO, KU / offer	イ (person)[K16] + 共 (together)[499]	供
0686	価	KA / price, value	イ (person)[K16] + 西 (*west*)[354]	価
0687	侍	JI / attend	イ (person)[K16] + 寺 (temple)[171]	侍
0688	史	SHI / history	口 (mouth)[106] + 人 (*person*)[64]	史
0689	吏	RI / official	一 (one)[01] + 史 (history)[688]	吏
0690	使	SHI / use	イ (person)[K16] + 吏 (official)[689]	使
0691	係	KEI / connection	イ (person)[K16] + 系 (lineage)[212]	係
0692	非	HI / not; wrong	Wings of bird from above	非
0693	俳	HAI / actor	イ (person)[K16] + 非 (not)[692]	俳

Day four: writing practice

仁	任	仮	伝	伴	作	住
仁	任	仮	伝	伴	作	住
何	以	似	左	佐	供	価
何	以	似	左	佐	供	価
侍	史	吏	使	係	非	俳
侍	史	吏	使	係	非	俳

Day five: story sketch

仁	benevolence: 亻 (person) + 二 (two) + Joyful INclination
任	duty: 亻 (person) + ノ (accent) + 士 (samurai) + Normally INcumbent
仮	temporary: 亻 (person) + 反 (oppose) + Kurtailed Activity
伝	transmit: 亻 (person) + 二 (two) + ム (self) + Dispense ENergy
伴	accompany: 亻 (person) + 半 (half) + Help ANother
作	make: 亻 (person) + 乍 (hacksaw) + Shape And KUt
住	reside: 亻 (person) + 主 (master) + Joint Urban Use
何	what: 亻 (person) + 可 (possible) + Klarifies Ambiguity
以	from: ム (*self*) + 人 (*person*) + Issue
似	resemble: 亻 (person) + 以 (from) + Joint Image
左	left: 手 (*hand*) + 工 (work) + Southpaw Aspect
佐	assist: 亻 (person) + 左 (left) + Support Associate
供	offer: 亻 (person) + 共 (together) + Konvey YOur Overture
価	price: 亻 (person) + 西 (*west*) + Kost Attribute
侍	attend: 亻 (person) + 寺 (temple) + Join In
史	history: 口 (mouth) + 人 (*person*) + Stated HItherto
吏	official: 一 (one) + 史 (history) + Ruling Individual
使	use: 亻 (person) + 吏 (official) + Serve His Interest
係	connection: 亻 (person) + 系 (lineage) + Kin Entangled In
非	not: (wings of bird from above) + However Inverse
俳	actor: 亻 (person) + 非 (not) + Handsome Amusing Individual

Day six: character clusters

I   Complete the characters using the clues.

1	亻	Join In (JI)
2	一	Ruling Individual (RI)
3	亻	Normally INcumbent (NIN)
4	工	Southpaw Aspect (SA)
5	亻	Klarifies Ambiguity (KA)

II   Compose the compounds using the clues.

1   (TEI) 提   +   (KYOO) ____   =   _____ (offer)
       present

2   (JUU) ____   +   (SHO) 所   =   _____ (address)
                                  place

3   (DEN) ____   +   (TOO) 統   =   _____ (tradition)
                                  lineage

4   (KAN) 関   +   (KEI) ____   =   _____ (relationship)
       concerning

5   (KA) ____   +   (MEN) 面   =   _____ (mask)
                                  face

III   Complete the sentences using the clues.

1   その建物は百万ドルと評＿＿されました。
    Sono tatemono wa hyaku man doru to hyooKA saremashita.
    That building was valued at one million dollars.

2   日本語で家族について＿＿文を書いた。
    Nihongo de kazoku ni tsuite SAKUbun o kaita.
    I wrote a composition about my family in Japanese.

3   エジプトの歴＿＿はとても長いです。
    Ejiputo no rekiSHI wa totemo nagai desu.
    Egyptian history is very long.

4   この廊下の突き当たりには＿＿常口があります。
    Kono rooka no tsukiatari ni wa HIjooguchi ga arimasu.
    At the end of this hall is an emergency exit.

5   子供の時＿＿来ドイツに住んでいる。
    Kodomo no toki Irai doitsu ni sunde iru.
    I have lived in Germany since I was a child.

34

HAND OUT

Day one: crossword puzzle

Across

3. Honor An Idol
6. Troubles Assume Now
8. BAldly Take SUbstance (E)
10. Open Openhandedly
12. YOu Kontrol Urge
13. Brighten YOur Outline (D)
14. Attend To SUbject KArefully
16. Konvey Your Offer (R)
17. Surrender Holdings Absolutely
20. Klosely ATtach SUndries (B)
21. HOld Onto

Down

1. Hold Overtly Over (W)
2. Success Opposite Now
4. Summon HOme Officially
5. Keep Attentive Now
7. Select Hand Indicator (F)
9. Harshly Interpret
11. KOnfiscate Object
15. Set Hand Upon Ultimately (two words: P/U)
18. Set Out
19. Join Intimately

Day two: acrostics

1 Wrap: H _ _ _   O _ _ _ _ _ _   O _ _ _

2 Loss: S _ _ _ _ _ _   O _ _ _ _ _ _   N _ _

3 Worship: H _ _ _ _   A _   I _ _ _

4 Invite: S _ _ _ _ _   H O _ _   O _ _ _ _ _ _ _ _

5 Watch: K _ _ _   A _ _ _ _ _ _ _ _   N _ _

6 Bear: T _ _ _ _ _ _ _   A _ _ _ _ _   N _ _

7 Finger: S _ _ _ _ _   H _ _ _   I _ _ _ _ _ _ _ _

8 Extract: B A _ _ _ _   T _ _ _   S U _ _ _ _ _ _

9 Criticize: H _ _ _ _ _ _   I _ _ _ _ _ _ _ _

10 Push: O _ _ _   O _ _ _ _ _ _ _ _ _ _

11 Seize: K O _ _ _ _ _ _ _ _   O _ _ _ _ _

12 Restrain: Y O _   K _ _ _ _ _ _   U _ _ _

13 Depict: B _ _ _ _ _ _ _   Y O _ _   O _ _ _ _ _

14 Handle: A _ _ _ _ _   T _   S U _ _ _ _ _   K A _ _ _ _ _ _ _ (U)

15 Pick Up: S _ _   H _ _ _   U _ _ _   U _ _ _ _ _ _ _ _

16 Raise: K _ _ _ _ _   Y _ _ _   O _ _ _ _

17 Discard: S _ _ _ _ _ _ _ _   H _ _ _ _ _ _ _   A _ _ _ _ _ _ _ _ _

18 Place: S _ _   O _ _

19 Hold: J _ _ _   I _ _ _ _ _ _ _ _ _

20 Bundle: K _ _ _ _ _ _   A T _ _ _ _   S U _ _ _ _ _ _

21 Embrace: H O _ _   O _ _ _

Day three: componential analysis

Course Number	Kanji	ON Reading(s) / Core Concept(s)	Primary Components	Kanji Canvas
0694	扱	atsuka(u) / handle	扌 (hand)[K21] + 及 (reach)[463]	扱
0695	抑	YOKU / restrain	扌 (hand)[K21] + 卬 (measured bow)[K42]	抑
0696	抜	BATSU / extract	扌 (hand)[K21] + 友 (friend)[465]	抜
0697	拝	HAI / worship	扌 (hand)[K21] + *spray*	拝
0698	担	TAN / bear, shoulder	扌 (hand)[K21] + 旦 (dawn)[148]	担
0699	押	OO / push	扌 (hand)[K21] + 甲 (first)[618]	押
0700	招	SHOO / invite	扌 (hand)[K21] + 召 (summon)[116]	招
0701	拘	KOO / seize	扌 (hand)[K21] + 句 (phrase)[110]	拘
0702	批	HI / criticize	扌 (hand)[K21] + 比 (compare)[532]	批
0703	包	HOO / wrap	勹 (wrap)[K25] + 己 (self)[132]	包
0704	抱	HOO / embrace	扌 (hand)[K21] + 包 (wrap)[703]	抱
0705	持	JI / hold	扌 (hand)[K21] + 寺 (temple)[171]	持
0706	拾	SHUU / pick up	扌 (hand)[K21] + 合 (fit)[118]	拾
0707	指	SHI / finger; point	扌 (hand)[K21] + 旨 (purport)[150]	指
0708	看	KAN / watch	手 (hand)[85] + 目 (eye)[62]	看
0709	括	KATSU / bundle	扌 (hand)[K21] + 舌 (tongue)[209]	括
0710	挙	KYO / raise; perform	⅍ (ornate)[K63] + 丆 (platform)[K65] + 手 (hand)[85]	挙
0711	捨	SHA / discard	扌 (hand)[K21] + 舎 (house)[389]	捨
0712	描	BYOO / depict	扌 (hand)[K21] + 苗 (seedling)[246]	描
0713	措	SO / place	扌 (hand)[K21] + 昔 (past)[245]	措
0714	損	SON / loss	扌 (hand)[K21] + 員 (member)[363]	損

Day four: writing practice

扱	抑	拔	拜	担	押	招
扱	抑	拔	拜	担	押	招
拘	批	包	抱	持	拾	指
拘	批	包	抱	持	拾	指
看	括	举	捨	描	措	損
看	括	举	捨	描	措	損

Day five: story sketch

扱	handle: 扌 (hand) + 及 (reach) + Attend To SUbject KArefully
抑	restrain: 扌 (hand) + 卬 (measured bow) + YOu Kontrol Urge
抜	extract: 扌 (hand) + 友 (friend) + BAldly Take SUbstance
拝	worship: 扌 (hand) + *spray* + Honor An Idol
担	bear: 扌 (hand) + 旦 (dawn) + Troubles Assume Now
押	push: 扌 (hand) + 甲 (first) + Open Openhandedly
招	invite: 扌 (hand) + 召 (summon) + Summon HOme Officially
拘	seize: 扌 (hand) + 句 (phrase) + KOnfiscate Object
批	criticize: 扌 (hand) + 比 (compare) + Harshly Interpret
包	wrap: 勹 (wrap) + 己 (self) + Hold Overtly Over
抱	embrace: 扌 (hand) + 包 (wrap) + HOld Onto
持	hold: 扌 (hand) + 寺 (temple) + Join Intimately
拾	pick up: 扌 (hand) + 合 (fit) + Set Hand Upon Ultimately
指	finger: 扌 (hand) + 旨 (purport) + Select Hand Indicator
看	watch: 手 (hand) + 目 (eye) + Keep Attentive Now
括	bundle: 扌 (hand) + 舌 (tongue) + Klosely ATtach SUndries
挙	raise: ⋎ (ornate) + 丆 (platform) + 手 (hand) + Konvey Your Offer
捨	discard: 扌 (hand) + 舎 (house) + Surrender Holdings Absolutely
描	depict: 扌 (hand) + 苗 (seedling) + Brighten YOur Outline
措	place: 扌 (hand) + 昔 (past) + Set Out
損	loss: 扌 (hand) + 員 (member) + Success Opposite Now

Day six: character clusters

I   Complete the characters using the clues.

1	扌	Set Out (SO)
2	勹	Hold Overtly Over (HOO)
3	合	Set Hand Upon Ultimately (SHUU)
4	目	Keep Attentive Now (KAN)
5	扌	Surrender Holdings Absolutely (SHA)

II   Compose the compounds using the clues.

1   (SHI) ____   +   (MON) 紋   =   _____ (fingerprint)
                            pattern

2   (BATSU) ____   +   (GUN) 群   =   _____ (outstanding)
                            group

3   (SUU) 崇   +   (HAI) ____   =   _____ (worship)
      revere

4   (BYOO) ____   +   (SHA) 写   =   _____ (description)
                            copy

5   (SON) ____   +   (GAI) 害   =   _____ (damage)
                            harm

III   Complete the sentences using the clues.

1   映画は新聞で___評された。
     Eiga wa shinbun de HIhyoo sareta.
     The movie was criticized in the newspaper.

2   四年ごとに選___が行われる。
     Yo nen goto ni senKYO ga okonawareru.
     An election is held every four years.

3   費用を二人で分___しよう。
     Hiyoo o futari de bunTAN shiyoo.
     Let's share the expenses between the two of us.

4   だれも計画を支___しませんでした。
     Dare mo keikaku o shiJI shimasen deshita.
     No one supported the plan.

5   彼女は私を昼食に___待した。
     Kanojo wa watashi o chuushoku ni SHOOtai shita.
     She invited me to lunch.

35

MOUTHFUL

Day one: crossword puzzle

Across

1. Digestion Aid
4. Initiates Neck
5. KYOto Once
7. KOurt Overlord
9. SUspend Indefinitely (H)
10. Kry Out
12. TEstament To Sound Understanding
17. Still HOnor One (F)
18. Turbulent Outflow (V)
19. Greatly INtone
20. Koincidental Is CHance Incident
21. SHOut Often (C)

Down

2. Keeps Yogi's Underbelly Upright (I)
3. Fully Unable
6. KOmmunicate Klear Understanding
8. Keen YOur Outcry
11. Mere Existence Is
13. SUck Inverse
14. Jinx Unpleasant (C)
15. Have Invalidated (D)
16. KApture Illegally

Day two: acrostics

1 Saliva: D _ _ _ _ _ _ _ _   A _ _

2 Inhale: K _ _ _ _   Y _ _ _ _   U _ _ _ _ _ _ _ _ _   U _ _ _ _ _ _

3 Not: F _ _ _ _   U _ _ _ _ _

4 Throat: I _ _ _ _ _ _ _ _   N _ _ _

5 Capital: K Y O _ _   O _ _ _

6 Inform: K O _ _ _ _ _ _ _ _   K _ _ _ _   U _ _ _ _ _ _ _ _ _ _ _

7 Empress: K O _ _ _   O _ _ _ _ _ _ _

8 Shout: K _ _ _   Y O _ _   O _ _ _ _ _

9 Hang: S U _ _ _ _ _   I _ _ _ _ _ _ _ _ _ _

10 Call: K _ _   O _ _

11 Life: M _ _ _   E _ _ _ _ _ _ _ _   I _

12 Wisdom: T E _ _ _ _ _ _ _   T _   S _ _ _ _   U _ _ _ _ _ _ _ _ _ _ _

13 Blow: S U _ _   I _ _ _ _ _ _

14 Curse: J _ _ _   U _ _ _ _ _ _ _ _ _

15 Deny: H _ _ _   I _ _ _ _ _ _ _ _ _ _

16 Kidnap: K A _ _ _ _ _ _   I _ _ _ _ _ _ _ _

17 Furthermore: S _ _ _ _   H O _ _ _   O _ _

18 Vomit: T _ _ _ _ _ _ _ _   O _ _ _ _ _ _

19 Recite: G _ _ _ _ _ _   I N _ _ _ _

20 Lucky: K _ _ _ _ _ _ _ _ _ _ _   I _   C H _ _ _ _   I _ _ _ _ _ _ _

21 Chant: S H O _ _   O _ _ _ _

Day three: componential analysis

Course Number	Kanji	ON Reading(s) / Core Concept(s)	Primary Components	Kanji Canvas
0715	后	KOO / empress	*tribute* + 口 (mouth)[106]	后
0716	吉	KICHI / lucky	士 (samurai)[67] + 口 (mouth)[106]	吉
0717	吸	KYUU / inhale, suck	口 (mouth)[106] + 及 (reach)[463]	吸
0718	吹	SUI / blow	口 (mouth)[106] + 欠 (lack)[427]	吹
0719	叫	KYOO / shout	口 (mouth)[106] + 丩 (fork)[K38]	叫
0720	吐	TO / vomit	口 (mouth)[106] + 土 (ground)[169]	吐
0721	告	KOKU / inform	止 (*stop*)[165] + 口 (mouth)[106]	告
0722	吟	GIN / recite	口 (mouth)[106] + 今 (now)[139]	吟
0723	不	FU / not	Surface and roots	不
0724	否	HI / deny	不 (not)[723] + 口 (mouth)[106]	否
0725	京	KYOO / capital	亠 (top)[K1] + 口 (mouth)[106] + 小 (small)[31]	京
0726	命	MEI / life	口 (mouth)[106] + 令 (order)[380]	命
0727	呼	KO / call	口 (mouth)[106] + 乎 (level)[207]	呼
0728	尚	SHOO / furthermore	⺌ (small)[K44] + 冂 (border)[K27] + 口 (mouth)[106]	尚
0729	拐	KAI / kidnap	扌 (hand)[K21] + 口 (mouth)[106] + 刀 (sword)[115]	拐
0730	呪	JU / curse	口 (mouth)[106] + 兄 (older brother)[117]	呪
0731	咽	IN / throat	口 (mouth)[106] + 因 (cause)[356]	咽
0732	哲	TETSU / wisdom	折 (break)[90] + 口 (mouth)[106]	哲
0733	唱	SHOO / chant; recite	口 (mouth)[106] + 日 (two days)[17]	唱
0734	垂	SUI / hang	千 (thousand)[10] + ⺗ (plants)[K29] + 土 (ground)[169]	垂
0735	唾	DA / saliva	口 (mouth)[106] + 垂 (hang)[734]	唾

Day four: writing practice

后	吉	吸	吹	叫	吐	告
后	吉	吸	吹	叫	吐	告

吟	不	否	京	命	呼	尚
吟	不	否	京	命	呼	尚

拐	呪	咽	哲	唱	垂	唾
拐	呪	咽	哲	唱	垂	唾

Day five: story sketch

后	empress: *tribute* + 口 (mouth) + KOurt Overlord
吉	lucky: 士 (samurai) + 口 (mouth) + Koincidental Is CHance Incident
吸	inhale: 口 (mouth) + 及 (reach) + Keeps Yogi's Underbelly Upright
吹	blow: 口 (mouth) + 欠 (lack) + SUck Inverse
叫	shout: 口 (mouth) + 丩 (fork) + Keen YOur Outcry
吐	vomit: 口 (mouth) + 土 (ground) + Turbulent Outflow
告	inform: 止 (*stop*) + 口 (mouth) + KOmmunicate Klear Understanding
吟	recite: 口 (mouth) + 今 (now) + Greatly INtone
不	not: (surface and roots) + Fully Unable
否	deny: 不 (not) + 口 (mouth) + Have Invalidated
京	capital: 亠 (top) + 口 (mouth) + 小 (small) + KYOto Once
命	life: 口 (mouth) + 令 (order) + Mere Existence Is
呼	call: 口 (mouth) + 乎 (level) + Kry Out
尚	furthermore: ⺍ (small) + 冂 (border) + 口 (mouth) + Still HOnor One
拐	kidnap: 扌 (hand) + 口 (mouth) + 刀 (sword) + KApture Illegally
呪	curse: 口 (mouth) + 兄 (older brother) + Jinx Unpleasant
咽	throat: 口 (mouth) + 因 (cause) + Initiates Neck
哲	wisdom: 折 (break) + 口 (mouth) + TEstament To Sound Understanding
唱	chant: 口 (mouth) + 日 (two days) + SHOut Often
垂	hang: 千 (thousand) + 艹 (plants) + 土 (ground) + SUspend Indefinitely
唾	saliva: 口 (mouth) + 垂 (hang) + Digestion Aid

Day six: character clusters

I   Complete the characters using the clues.

1	口	Koincidental Is CHance Incident (KICHI)
2	扌	KApture Illegally (KAI)
3	冂	Still HOnor One (SHOO)
4	丩	Keen YOur Outcry (KYOO)
5	口	KOurt Overlord (KOO)

II   Compose the compounds using the clues.

1   (GAS) 合   +   (SHOO) ____   =   _____ (chorus)
       combine

2   (TETSU) ____   +   (GAKU) 学   =   _____ (philosophy)
                             learning

3   (SUI) ____   +   (CHOKU) 直   =   _____ (vertical)
                             straight

4   (TOO) 東   +   (KYOO) ____   =   _____ (Tokyo)
       east

5   (JU) ____   +   (MON) 文   =   _____ (spell)
                             writing

III   Complete the sentences using the clues.

1   上司に報___を提出した。
    Jooshi ni hooKOKU o teishutsu shita.
    I submitted the report to my boss.

2   彼らは同じ運___にあった。
    Karera wa onaji unMEI ni atta.
    They suffered the same fate.

3   このスポンジは水をよく___収する。
    Kono suponji wa mizu o yoku KYUUshuu suru.
    This sponge absorbs water well.

4   彼女は私の言うことを___定した。
    Kanojo wa watashi no iu koto o HItei shita.
    She denied what I said.

5   将来に少し___安を感じている。
    Shoorai ni sukoshi FUan o kanjite iru.
    I am feeling a little uneasy about the future.

REVIEW: LESSONS 31–35

I   Given the character and meaning, write the pronunciation.

1 治 govern_____   2 松 pine _____   3 住 reside_____

4 担 bear _____   5 吉 lucky _____   6 洗 wash _____

7 株 stock _____   8 非 not _____   9 描 depict_____

10 垂 hang _____   11 波 wave _____   12 柳 willow_____

13 何 what _____   14 抜 handle_____   15 叫 shout _____

16 洪 flood _____   17 桃 peach_____   18 俳 actor_____

19 措 place _____   20 咽 throat_____   21 沼 swamp_____

22 采 gather_____   23 佐 assist _____   24 拘 seize_____

25 吐 vomit _____   26 洞 cave_____   27 根 root _____

28 侍 attend_____   29 損 loss _____   30 呪 curse _____

II   Given the character and pronunciation, write the meaning.

1 沖 CHUU_____   2 困 KON _____   3 抜 BATSU_____

4 抑 YOKU_____   5 尚 SHOO _____   6 泥 DEI _____

7 丙 HEI _____   8 伴 HAN _____   9 拝 HAI _____

10 唾 DA _____   11 泌 HITSU_____   12 某 BOO _____

13 係 KIN_____   14 抱 HOO _____   15 后 KOO _____

16 注 CHUU_____   17 桜 OO _____   18 吏 RI _____

19 看 KAN _____   20 哲 TETSU_____   21 尼 NI _____

22 査 SA _____ 23 史 SHI _____ 24 挙 KYO _____

25 拐 KAI _____ 26 柄 HEI _____ 27 供 KYOO _____

28 捨 SHA _____ 29 批 HI _____ 30 仮 KA _____

III Given the meaning and pronunciation, write the character.

1 along	EN	_____	2 branch	SHI	_____
3 benevolence	JIN	_____	4 push	OO	_____
5 blow	SUI	_____	6 precede	SEN	_____
7 woods	SHIN	_____	8 price	KA	_____
9 pick up	SHUU	_____	10 capital	KYOO	_____
11 sweet	KAN	_____	12 from	I	_____
13 invite	SHOO	_____	14 vermilion	SHU	_____
15 transmit	DEN	_____	16 use	SHI	_____
17 left	SA	_____	18 school	KOO	_____
19 leave	KYO	_____	20 pillar	CHUU	_____
21 resemble	JI	_____	22 finger	SHI	_____
23 wither	KO	_____	24 inform	KOKU	_____
25 master	SHU	_____			

IV Compose compounds using the following characters.

包 命 況 決 汚 括 任 作 持 案 法 不 染 活 吟 保 吸 唱 否 呼

1 (KO) ____	+	(KYUU) ____	=	_____ (breathing)
2 (GIN) ____	+	(SHOO) ____	=	_____ (intonation)
3 (HO) ____	+	(JI) ____	=	_____ (hold, retain)
4 (HI) ____	+	(KETSU) ____	=	_____ (rejection)
5 (O) ____	+	(SEN) ____	=	_____ (pollution)
6 (HOO) ____	+	(KATSU) ____	=	_____ (comprehend)
7 (FU) ____	+	(SAKU) ____	=	_____ (bad harvest)
8 (HOO) ____	+	(AN) ____	=	_____ (bill)
9 (KAK) ____	+	(KYOO) ____	=	_____ (rally)
10 (NIN) ____	+	(MEI) ____	=	_____ (appointment)

36

FROM THE BOTTOM OF ONE'S HEART

Day one: crossword puzzle

Across

3. Kondition Acute Now (S)
5. Romance ENtrance
7. Koncerns Your Ominous Ordeal (F)
8. Kind Agreeable Individual
9. Konveys Your Undue Urgency
10. Assistant (S)
14. Great Unease
16. AKt Unacceptable (B)
17. Obliging Nature
18. Type Always Inactive
20. Sad Experience KIndles
21. Banal ONe (C)

Down

1. Kooks Use SHarp Impaler (S)
2. Grasp Outright (C)
4. Fabric Unfurled
6. Formidable Unease
11. Heartbroken Indication
12. Intellect
13. Display Outrage
15. Kontains Offended Nature
19. Elation That's SUperior

Day two: acrostics

1 Skewer: K _ _ _ _   U _ _   S H _ _ _   I _ _ _ _ _ _

2 Comprehend: G _ _ _ _   O _ _ _ _ _ _ _

3 Sick: K _ _ _ _ _ _ _ _   A _ _ _ _   N _ _

4 Cloth: F _ _ _ _ _   U _ _ _ _ _ _ _

5 Love: R _ _ _ _ _ _   E N _ _ _ _ _ _

6 Fear: F _ _ _ _ _ _ _ _   U _ _ _ _ _

7 Fear: K _ _ _ _ _ _ _   Y _ _ _   O _ _ _ _ _ _   O _ _ _ _ _

8 Pleasant: K _ _ _   A _ _ _ _ _ _ _ _   I _ _ _ _ _ _ _ _

9 Hurry: K _ _ _ _ _ _   Y _ _ _   U _ _ _ _   U _ _ _ _ _ _

10 Subordinate: A _ _ _ _ _ _ _ _

11 Sad: H _ _ _ _ _ _ _ _ _ _   I _ _ _ _ _ _ _ _ _

12 Mind: I _ _ _ _ _ _ _ _

13 Anger: D _ _ _ _ _ _   O _ _ _ _ _ _

14 Apprehension: G _ _ _ _   U _ _ _ _ _

15 Resent: K _ _ _ _ _ _ _   O _ _ _ _ _ _ _   N _ _ _ _ _

16 Bad: A K _   U _ _ _ _ _ _ _ _ _ _

17 Gratitude: O _ _ _ _ _ _ _   N _ _ _ _ _

18 Idle: T _ _ _   A _ _ _ _ _   I _ _ _ _ _ _ _

19 Joy: E _ _ _ _ _ _   T _ _ _ _   S U _ _ _ _ _ _

20 Regret: S _ _   E _ _ _ _ _ _ _ _ _   K I _ _ _ _ _

21 Common: B _ _ _ _   O N _

Day three: componential analysis

Course Number	Kanji	ON Reading(s) / Core Concept(s)	Primary Components	Kanji Canvas
0736	快	KAI **pleasant**	忄 (heart)[K31] + 央 (center)[234]	快
0737	布	FU **cloth; spread**	手 (*hand*)[85] + 巾 (cloth)[395]	布
0738	怖	FU **fear**	忄 (heart)[K31] + 布 (spread)[737]	怖
0739	急	KYUU **hurry; sudden**	⺈ (bending)[K55] + ⺕ (open hand)[K54] + 心 (heart)[127]	急
0740	怒	DO **anger**	奴 (slave)[338] + 心 (heart)[127]	怒
0741	怠	TAI **idle; neglect**	台 (stand)[114] + 心 (heart)[127]	怠
0742	悦	ETSU **joy**	忄 (heart)[K31] + ⸜ (out)[K35] + 兄 (older brother)[117]	悦
0743	恨	KON **resent**	忄 (heart)[K31] + 艮 (*good*)[398]	恨
0744	恩	ON **gratitude**	因 (cause)[356] + 心 (heart)[127]	恩
0745	恋	REN **love**	亦 (again)[K77] + 心 (heart)[127]	恋
0746	悟	GO **comprehend**	忄 (heart)[K31] + 五 (five)[13] + 口 (mouth)[106]	悟
0747	凡	BON **common**	几 (table)[K11] + 丶 (accent)[K2]	凡
0748	恐	KYOO **fear**	工 (work)[26] + 凡 (common)[747] + 心 (heart)[127]	恐
0749	惜	SEKI **regret**	忄 (heart)[K31] + 昔 (past)[245]	惜
0750	串	kushi **skewer**	Two items pierced	串
0751	患	KAN **sick**	串 (skewer)[750] + 心 (heart)[127]	患
0752	惧	GU **apprehension**	忄 (heart)[K31] + 具 (*equipment*)[515]	惧
0753	亜	A **subordinate**	工 (work)[26] + 中 (middle)[77]	亜
0754	悪	AKU **bad; evil**	亜 (subordinate)[753] + 心 (heart)[127]	悪
0755	悲	HI **sad**	非 (wrong)[692] + 心 (heart)[127]	悲
0756	意	I **mind; thought**	音 (sound)[159] + 心 (heart)[127]	意

Day four: writing practice

快	布	怖	急	怒	怠	悦
快	布	怖	急	怒	怠	悦

恨	恩	恋	悟	凡	恐	惜
恨	恩	恋	悟	凡	恐	惜

串	患	惧	亜	悪	悲	意
串	患	惧	亜	悪	悲	意

Day five: story sketch

快	pleasant: 忄 (heart) + 央 (center) + Kind Agreeable Individual
布	cloth: 手 (*hand*) + 巾 (cloth) + Fabric Unfurled
怖	fear: 忄 (heart) + 布 (spread) + Formidable Unease
急	hurry: ⺈ (bending) + ヨ (open hand) + 心 (heart) + Konveys Your Undue Urgency
怒	anger: 奴 (slave) + 心 (heart) + Display Outrage
怠	idle: 台 (stand) + 心 (heart) + Type Always Inactive
悦	joy: 忄 (heart) + ﹅ (out) + 兄 (older brother) + Elation That's SUperior
恨	resent: 忄 (heart) + 艮 (*good*) + Kontains Offended Nature
恩	gratitude: 因 (cause) + 心 (heart) + Obliging Nature
恋	love: 亦 (again) + 心 (heart) + Romance ENtrance
悟	comprehend: 忄 (heart) + 五 (five) + 口 (mouth) + Grasp Outright
凡	common: 几 (table) + 丶 (accent) + Banal ONe
恐	fear: 工 (work) + 凡 (common) + 心 (heart) + Koncerns Your Ominous Ordeal
惜	regret: 忄 (heart) + 昔 (past) + Sad Experience KIndles
串	skewer: (two items pierced) + Kooks Use SHarp Impaler
患	sick: 串 (skewer) + 心 (heart) + Kondition Acute Now
惧	apprehension: 忄 (heart) + 具 (*equipment*) + Great Unease
亜	subordinate: 工 (work) + 中 (middle) + Assistant
悪	bad: 亜 (subordinate) + 心 (heart) + AKt Unacceptable
悲	sad: 非 (wrong) + 心 (heart) + Heartbroken Indication
意	mind: 音 (sound) + 心 (heart) + Intellect

Day six: character clusters

I   Complete the characters using the clues.

1	忄	Kontains Offended Nature (KON)
2	台	Type Always Inactive (TAI)
3	忄	Sad Experience KIndles (SEKI)
4	凡	Koncerns Your Ominous Ordeal (KYOO)
5	忄	Elation That's SUperior (ETSU)

II   Compose the compounds using the clues.

1   (MOO) 毛   +   (FU) ____   =   _____ (blanket)
        hair

2   (ON) ____   +   (JIN) 人   =   _____ (benefactor)
                               person

3   (SAI) 最   +   (AKU) ____   =   _____ (worst)
        most

4   (KAN) ____   +   (JA) 者   =   _____ (patient)
                               person

5   (KAKU) 覚   +   (GO) ____   =   _____ (prepared)
        remember

III   Complete the sentences using the clues.

1   大阪への＿＿行は15分ごとにあります。
    Oosaka e no KYUUkoo wa juugo-fun goto ni arimasu.
    The express (train) to Osaka runs every fifteen minutes.

2   二人は＿＿愛中のようです。
    Futari wa RENai-chuu no yoo desu.
    It looks like those two are in love.

3   平＿＿な作家にはなりたくない。
    HeiBONna sakka ni wa naritakunai.
    I don't want to become an ordinary writer.

4   小さくてもこの椅子は＿＿適だ。
    Chiisakutemo kono isu wa KAIteki da.
    Even though it is small, this chair is comfortable.

5   この企画について＿＿見はどうですか。
    Kono kikaku ni tsuite Iken wa doo desu ka.
    What is your opinion about this plan?

37

DAY AFTER DAY

Day one: crossword puzzle

Across

1. Sum AKtions Until (P)
4. KONjugality (M)
7. Elaborate Nosh (B)
8. Superior Organization Officer
14. June Unit Number (two words: T/P)
17. Oven Nearby
18. SAndwich Rests Atop
21. Reckoning Yields Only One

Down

2. Journey Interval
3. KOckroach Namely
5. FUrther KUstom
6. Find Usually (G)
9. Komes Around Konfines Inside
10. Stuff Oblong Object
11. Karefree Activity (L)
12. Horizontal Every Individual
13. Surname Honors Individual
15. Trade Alternate Items
16. At Night
19. KOunt Over
20. Blackened Outcome (D)

Day two: acrostics

1 Past: S _ _ A K _ _ _ _ _ U _ _ _ _

2 Time: J _ _ _ _ _ _ I _ _ _ _ _ _

3 Insect: K O _ _ _ _ _ _ _ N _ _ _ _ _

4 Marriage: K O N _ _ _ _ _ _ _

5 Repeat: F U _ _ _ _ _ K U _ _ _ _

6 Generally: F _ _ _ U _ _ _ _ _ _

7 Banquet: E _ _ _ _ _ _ _ _ N _ _ _

8 Official: S _ _ _ _ _ _ _ O _ _ _ _ _ _ _ _ _ _ O _ _ _ _ _ _

9 Fence: K _ _ _ _ A _ _ _ _ _ K _ _ _ _ _ _ _ I _ _ _ _ _

10 Insert: S _ _ _ _ O _ _ _ _ _ O _ _ _ _ _

11 Leisure: K _ _ _ _ _ _ _ A _ _ _ _ _ _ _

12 Row: H _ _ _ _ _ _ _ _ _ E _ _ _ _ I _ _ _ _ _ _ _ _ _

13 Family: S _ _ _ _ _ _ _ H _ _ _ _ _ I _ _ _ _ _ _ _ _ _

14 Ten-day Period: J _ _ _ U _ _ _ N _ _ _ _ _

15 Exchange: T _ _ _ _ A _ _ _ _ _ _ _ _ I _ _ _ _

16 Dark: A _ N _ _ _ _

17 Warm: O _ _ _ N _ _ _ _ _

18 Dish: S A _ _ _ _ _ _ R _ _ _ _ A _ _ _

19 Again: K O _ _ _ O _ _ _

20 Dusk: B _ _ _ _ _ _ _ _ O _ _ _ _ _ _

21 Quantity: R _ _ _ _ _ _ _ _ Y _ _ _ _ _ O _ _ _ O _ _

Day three: componential analysis

Course Number	Kanji	ON Reading(s) / Core Concept(s)	Primary Components	Kanji Canvas
0757	旬	JUN / **ten-day period**	勹 (wrap)^{K25} + 日 (day)^{17}	旬
0758	更	KOO / **again**	一 (one)^{01} + 日 (day)^{17} + 人 (*person*)^{64}	更
0759	昨	SAKU / **past**	日 (day)^{17} + 乍 (hacksaw)^{K76}	昨
0760	垣	kaki / **fence**	土 (ground)^{169} + 二 (two)^{02} + 日 (day)^{17}	垣
0761	昆	KON / **insect; descendants**	日 (day)^{17} + 比 (compare)^{532}	昆
0762	時	JI / **time**	日 (day)^{17} + 寺 (temple)^{171}	時
0763	宴	EN / **banquet**	宀 (roof)^{K51} + 日 (day)^{17} + 女 (woman)^{337}	宴
0764	挿	SOO / **insert**	扌 (hand)^{K21} + 千 (thousand)^{10} + 日 (day)^{17}	挿
0765	曹	SOO / **official**	艹 (*plants*)^{K29} + 日 (day)^{17} + 日 (day)^{17}	曹
0766	氏	SHI / **family**	Crest (depicts sword resting against base of cliff)	氏
0767	婚	KON / **marriage**	女 (woman)^{337} + 氏 (family)^{766} + 日 (day)^{17}	婚
0768	替	TAI / **exchange**	夫 (two men)^{94} + 日 (day)^{17}	替
0769	量	RYOO / **quantity**	日 (day)^{17} + 一 (one)^{01} + 里 (village)^{181}	量
0770	復	FUKU / **repeat**	彳 (go)^{K47} + 人 (*person*)^{64} + 日 (day)^{17} + 夂 (step)^{K13}	復
0771	皿	sara / **dish, plate**	Fancy plate	皿
0772	温	ON / **warm**	氵 (water)^{K6} + 日 (day)^{17} + 皿 (dish)^{771}	温
0773	並	HEI / **row**	立 (stand)^{37} + 立 (stand)^{37}	並
0774	普	FU / **generally**	並 (row)^{773} + 日 (day)^{17}	普
0775	暗	AN / **dark**	日 (day)^{17} + 音 (sound)^{159}	暗
0776	暇	KA / **leisure**	日 (day)^{17} + 戸 (*door*)^{306} + 又 (hand)^{K15}	暇
0777	暮	BO / **dusk; live**	莫 (gone)^{K78} + 日 (day)^{17}	暮

Day four: writing practice

旬	更	昨	垣	昆	時	宴
旬	更	昨	垣	昆	時	宴
挿	曹	氏	婚	替	量	復
挿	曹	氏	婚	替	量	復
皿	温	並	普	暗	暇	暮
皿	温	並	普	暗	暇	暮

Day five: story sketch

旬	ten-day period: 勹 (wrap) + 日 (day) + June Unit Number
更	again: 一 (one) + 日 (day) + 人 (*person*) + KOunt Over
昨	past: 日 (day) + 乍 (hacksaw) + Sum AKtions Until
垣	fence: 土 (ground) + 二 (two) + 日 (day) + Komes Around Konfines Inside
昆	insect: 日 (day) + 比 (compare) + KOckroach Namely
時	time: 日 (day) + 寺 (temple) + Journey Interval
宴	banquet: 宀 (roof) + 日 (day) + 女 (woman) + Elaborate Nosh
挿	insert: 扌 (hand) + 千 (thousand) + 日 (day) + Stuff Oblong Object
曹	official: 艹 (*plants*) + 日 (day) + 日 (day) + Superior Organization Officer
氏	family: (crest) + Surname Honors Individual
婚	marriage: 女 (woman) + 氏 (family) + 日 (day) + KONjugality
替	exchange: 夫 (two men) + 日 (day) + Trade Alternate Items
量	quantity: 日 (day) + 一 (one) + 里 (village) + Reckoning Yields Only One
復	repeat: 彳 (go) + 人 (*person*) + 日 (day) + 夊 (step) + FUrther KUstom
皿	dish: (fancy plate) + SAndwich Rests Atop
温	warm: 氵 (water) + 日 (day) + 皿 (dish) + Oven Nearby
並	row: 立 (stand) + 立 (stand) + Horizontal Every Individual
普	generally: 並 (row) + 日 (day) + Find Usually
暗	dark: 日 (day) + 音 (sound) + At Night
暇	leisure: 日 (day) + 戸 (*door*) + 又 (hand) + Karefree Activity
暮	dusk: 莫 (gone) + 日 (day) + Blackened Outcome

Day six: character clusters

I   Complete the characters using the clues.

1	扌	Stuff Oblong Object (SOO)
2	日	Reckoning Yields Only One (RYOO)
3	ケ丁	June Unit Number (JUN)
4	口	Trade Alternate Items (TAI)
5	日	Sum AKtions Until (SAKU)

II   Compose the compounds using the clues.

1   (AN) ____   +   (GOO) 号   =   _____ (code)
                        sign

2   (ON) ____   +   (DO) 度   =   _____ (temperature)
                        degree

3   (KYUU) 休   +   (KA) ____   =   _____ (vacation)
      rest

4   (SHI) ____   +   (MEI) 名   =   _____ (full name)
                        name

5   (EN) ____   +   (KAI) 会   =   _____ (banquet)
                        meet

III   Complete the sentences using the clues.

1   ここから名古屋まで二___間かかる。
    Koko kara nagoya made ni-JIkan kakaru.
    It is two hours to Nagoya from here.

2   ___通はずいぶん早く起きる。
    FUtsuu wa zuibun hayaku okiru.
    I usually get up very early.

3   妹はアメリカ人と結___した。
    Imooto wa amerika-jin to kekKON shita.
    My younger sister got married to an American.

4   来月免許を___新しなければならない。
    Raigetsu menkyo o KOOshin shinakereba naranai.
    I have to renew my license next month.

5   チャーリーは回___が遅い。
    Chaarii wa kaiFUKU ga osoi.
    Charlie is making a slow recovery.

38

GROUND LEVEL

Day one: crossword puzzle

Across

2. Stretches Across Inlet
4. Totally ENclose
6. The Square Unit Between Openings (M)
10. Take Action To SUcceed
14. Reinforcement Upholding Infantry
15. Burial Opening
16. Tall Observable Object
19. Ground Along Island
20. Your Ordinary Ovine
21. Koordinates INdicate

Down

1. DOrmitory Ordinarily (H)
3. Kondition Attractive (F)
5. Cobra's Habitat Is (G)
7. Zapped Ankle
8. Ground At Intersection (S)
9. Zebra Armchair
11. Thin Overlay (C)
12. Kornerstone Intent
13. Hinders Entry Into (W)
17. SExy Kiss Imprint
18. Make An Interment

Day two: acrostics

1 Hall: D O _ _ _ _ _ _ _   O _ _ _ _ _ _ _ _

2 Cape: S _ _ _ _ _ _ _ _   A _ _ _ _ _   I _ _ _ _

3 Fine: K _ _ _ _ _ _ _ _   A _ _ _ _ _ _ _ _

4 Fill: T _ _ _ _ _ _   E N _ _ _ _ _

5 Ground: C _ _ _ _ _ _   H _ _ _ _ _ _   I _

6 Measure: T _ _   S _ _ _ _ _   U _ _ _   B _ _ _ _ _ _   O _ _ _ _ _ _ _

7 Sprain: Z _ _ _ _ _ _   A _ _ _ _

8 Street: G _ _ _ _ _   A _   I _ _ _ _ _ _ _ _ _ _

9 Seat: Z _ _ _ _   A _ _ _ _ _ _ _

10 Attain: T _ _ _   A _ _ _ _ _   T _   S U _ _ _ _ _

11 Coat: T _ _ _   O _ _ _ _ _ _

12 Base: K _ _ _ _ _ _ _ _ _ _   I _ _ _ _ _

13 Wall: H _ _ _ _ _ _   E _ _ _ _   I _ _ _

14 Fort: R _ _ _ _ _ _ _ _ _ _ _   U _ _ _ _ _ _ _ _   I _ _ _ _ _ _ _

15 Grave: B _ _ _ _ _   O _ _ _ _ _ _

16 Tower: T _ _ _   O _ _ _ _ _ _ _ _ _   O _ _ _ _ _

17 Red: S E _ _   K _ _ _   I _ _ _ _ _ _

18 Bury: M _ _ _   A _   I _ _ _ _ _ _ _ _

19 Limit: G _ _ _ _ _   A _ _ _ _   I _ _ _ _ _

20 Sheep: Y _ _ _   O _ _ _ _ _ _ _   O _ _ _ _

21 Equal: K _ _ _ _ _ _ _ _ _ _   I N _ _ _ _ _ _

Day three: componential analysis

Course Number	Kanji	ON Reading(s) / Core Concept(s)	Primary Components	Kanji Canvas
0778	地	CHI / ground	土 (ground)[169] + 也 (serpent)[K7]	地
0779	赤	SEKI / red	土 (ground)[169] + 亦 (*again*)[K77]	赤
0780	均	KIN / equal	土 (ground)[169] + 勹 (cover)[K25] + 二 (*two*)[02]	均
0781	佳	KA / fine	亻 (person)[K16] + 圭 (raised)[K37]	佳
0782	坪	tsubo / measure	土 (ground)[169] + 平 (level)[207]	坪
0783	座	ZA / seat, sit	广 (building)[K24] + 人 (two persons)[64] + 土 (ground)[169]	座
0784	埋	MAI / bury	土 (ground)[169] + 里 (village)[181]	埋
0785	挫	ZA / sprain	扌 (hand)[K21] + 人 (two persons)[64] + 土 (ground)[169]	挫
0786	堂	DOO / hall	尚 (esteem)[728] + 土 (ground)[169]	堂
0787	基	KI / base	其 (ladder)[K79] + 土 (ground)[169]	基
0788	涯	GAI / limit; shore	氵 (water)[K6] + 厂 (cliff)[K14] + 圭 (raised)[K37]	涯
0789	埼	sai / cape	土 (ground)[169] + 奇 (strange)[627]	埼
0790	街	GAI / street; town	行 (go)[297] + 圭 (raised)[K37]	街
0791	塔	TOO / tower	土 (ground)[169] + 艹 (plants)[K29] + 合 (join)[118]	塔
0792	塁	RUI / fort; base	田 (field)[60] + ⋊⋉ (marks)[K66] + 土 (ground)[169]	塁
0793	塀	HEI / wall, fence	土 (ground)[169] + 尸 (bent body)[K59] + 丶 (away)[K35] + 井 (*well*)[184]	塀
0794	羊	YOO / sheep	Sheep's head and horns	羊
0795	達	TATSU / attain	辶 (move)[K41] + 土 (ground)[169] + 羊 (sheep)[794]	達
0796	墓	BO / grave	莫 (gone)[K78] + 土 (ground)[169]	墓
0797	塗	TO / coat, paint	氵 (water)[K6] + 余 (excess)[386] + 土 (ground)[169]	塗
0798	填	TEN / fill	土 (ground)[169] + 真 (true)[516]	填

Day four: writing practice

地	赤	均	佳	坪	座	埋
地	赤	均	佳	坪	座	埋

挫	堂	基	涯	埼	街	塔
挫	堂	基	涯	埼	街	塔

塁	塀	羊	達	墓	塗	填
塁	塀	羊	達	墓	塗	填

Day five: story sketch

地	ground: 土 (ground) + 也 (serpent) + Cobra's Habitat Is
赤	red: 土 (ground) + 亦 (*again*) + SExy Kiss Imprint
均	equal: 土 (ground) + 勹 (cover) + 二 (*two*) + Koordinates INdicate
佳	fine: 亻 (person) + 圭 (raised) + Kondition Attractive
坪	measure: 土 (ground) + 平 (level) + The Square Unit Between Openings
座	seat: 广 (building) + 人 (two persons) + 土 (ground) + Zebra Armchair
埋	bury: 土 (ground) + 里 (village) + Make An Interment
挫	sprain: 扌 (hand) + 人 (two persons) + 土 (ground) + Zapped Ankle
堂	hall: 尚 (esteem) + 土 (ground) + DOrmitory Ordinarily
基	base: 其 (ladder) + 土 (ground) + Kornerstone Intent
涯	limit: 氵 (water) + 厂 (cliff) + 圭 (raised) + Ground Along Island
埼	cape: 土 (ground) + 奇 (strange) + Stretches Across Inlet
街	street: 行 (go) + 圭 (raised) + Ground At Intersection
塔	tower: 土 (ground) + 艹 (plants) + 合 (join) + Tall Observable Object
塁	fort: 田 (field) + ⽶ (marks) + 土 (ground) + Reinforcement Upholding Infantry
塀	wall: 土 (ground) + 尸 (bent body) + 丶 (away) + 井 (*well*) + Hinders Entry Into
羊	sheep: (sheep's head and horns) + Your Ordinary Ovine
達	attain: 辶 (move) + 土 (ground) + 羊 (sheep) + Take Action To SUcceed
墓	grave: 莫 (gone) + 土 (ground) + Burial Opening
塗	coat: 氵 (water) + 余 (excess) + 土 (ground) + Thin Overlay
填	fill: 土 (ground) + 真 (true) + Totally ENclose

Day six: character clusters

I   Complete the characters using the clues.

1	土	Thin Overlay (TO)
2	里	Make An Interment (MAI)
3	合	Tall Observable Object (TOO)
4	亻	Kondition Attractive (KA)
5	土	Burial Opening (BO)

II   Compose the compounds using the clues.

1   (HEI) 平   +   (KIN) ____   =   _____ (average)
     level

2   (YOO) ____   +   (MOO) 毛   =   _____ (wool)
                              hair

3   (KI) ____   +   (KIN) 金   =   _____ (fund)
                              money

4   (NEN) 捻   +   (ZA) ____   =   _____ (sprain)
     twist

5   (SEKI) ____   +   (DOO) 道   =   _____ (equator)
                              way

III   Complete the sentences using the clues.

1   電車の___席を予約した。
    Densha no ZAseki o yoyaku shita.
    I reserved a seat on the train.

2   ソファーは無料で配___してもらう。
    Sofaa wa muryoo de haiTATSU shite morau.
    The sofa will be delivered free of charge.

3   サンフランシスコでは土___が高すぎる。
    Sanfuranshisuko de wa toCHI ga taka-sugiru.
    Land in San Francisco is very expensive.

4   山本さんは生___に六冊の本を書きました。
    Yamamoto-san wa shooGAI ni roku-satsu no hon o kakimashita.
    Mr. Yamamoto wrote six books in his lifetime.

5   食___の食べ物はあまりおいしくない。
    ShokuDOO no tabemono wa amari oishikunai.
    The food in the cafeteria is not very good.

39

SPEAR CARRIER

Day one: crossword puzzle

Across

2. WAnder Kourse Unclear (C)
7. Belligerent Union
9. Kount Indefinite (two words: H/M)
10. Gradually Erode Number
13. Gains Assurance
15. Influence
16. Simply ENact (I)
17. Superficial ENtity
20. JUst Unsturdy
21. Military Utensil

Down

1. Keenly Aware Now (F)
3. Skeletal ANatomy
4. SOck Kovers Up
5. Settle An Issue (J)
6. Kongress Inhabits (C)
8. SElect KIn
11. Must Undertake
12. Intentional Kountry Isolate (A)
14. Sow Area Intently
18. KAution Individual
19. Shape Entirely Into

Day two: acrostics

1   Feeling: K _ _ _ _ _   A _ _ _ _   N _ _

2   Confused: W A _ _ _ _   K _ _ _ _ _   U _ _ _ _ _

3   Frame: S _ _ _ _ _ _ _   A N _ _ _ _ _

4   Foot: S O _ _   K _ _ _ _ _   U _

5   Judge: S _ _ _ _ _   A _   I _ _ _ _

6   Capital: K _ _ _ _ _ _   I _ _ _ _ _ _ _

7   Military: B _ _ _ _ _ _ _ _ _   U _ _ _ _

8   Relatives: S E _ _ _ _   K I _

9   How Many: K _ _ _ _   I _ _ _ _ _ _ _ _

10   Decrease: G _ _ _ _ _ _ _   E _ _ _ _   N _ _ _ _ _

11   Duty: M _ _ _   U _ _ _ _ _ _ _

12   Area: I _ _ _ _ _ _ _ _ _   K _ _ _ _ _ _   I _ _ _ _ _ _

13   Self: G _ _ _ _   A _ _ _ _ _ _ _

14   Plant: S _ _   A _ _ _   I _ _ _ _ _ _ _

15   Authority: I _ _ _ _ _ _ _ _

16   Implement: S _ _ _ _ _   E N _ _ _

17   Shallow: S _ _ _ _ _ _ _ _ _   E N _ _ _ _

18   Warn: K A _ _ _ _ _   I _ _ _ _ _ _ _ _

19   Form: S _ _ _ _   E _ _ _ _ _ _ _   I _ _ _

20   Soft: J U _ _   U _ _ _ _ _ _

21   Spear: M _ _ _ _ _ _ _   U _ _ _ _ _ _

Day three: componential analysis

Course Number	Kanji	ON Reading(s) / Core Concept(s)	Primary Components	Kanji Canvas
0799	矛	MU / spear	Barbed halberd	矛
0800	成	SEI / form, become	刀 (sword)[115] + 戈 (spear)[K20]	成
0801	我	GA / self	手 (*hand*)[85] + 戈 (spear)[K20]	我
0802	戒	KAI / warn	廾 (two hands)[K3] + 戈 (spear)[K20]	戒
0803	武	BU / military	止 (stop)[165] + 戈 (*spear*)[K20]	武
0804	浅	SEN / shallow	氵 (water)[K6] + 二 (two)[02] + 戈 (spear)[K20]	浅
0805	威	I / authority; threaten	一 (one)[01] + 女 (woman)[337] + 戈 (spear)[K20]	威
0806	柔	JUU / soft, weak	矛 (spear)[799] + 木 (tree)[43]	柔
0807	栽	SAI / plant	十 (ten)[06] + 木 (tree)[43] + 戈 (spear)[K20]	栽
0808	桟	SAN / frame	木 (wood)[43] + 二 (two)[02] + 戈 (spear)[K20]	桟
0809	務	MU / duty	矛 (spear)[799] + 攵 (strike)[K46] + 力 (strength)[07]	務
0810	域	IKI / area, region	土 (ground)[169] + 口 (mouth)[106] + 一 (one)[01] + 戈 (spear)[K20]	域
0811	戚	SEKI / relatives	上 (up)[474] + 小 (small)[31] + 戈 (spear)[K20]	戚
0812	惑	WAKU / confused	口 (mouth)[106] + 一 (one)[01] + 戈 (spear)[K20] + 心 (heart)[127]	惑
0813	幾	KI / how many	幺 (two short threads)[K64] + 人 (person)[64] + 戈 (spear)[K20]	幾
0814	裁	SAI / judge; cut	十 (ten)[06] + 衣 (clothes)[397] + 戈 (spear)[K20]	裁
0815	減	GEN / decrease	氵 (water)[K6] + 一 (one)[01] + 口 (open)[106] + 戈 (spear)[K20]	減
0816	感	KAN / feeling	一 (one)[01] + 口 (mouth)[106] + 戈 (spear)[K20] + 心 (heart)[127]	感
0817	足	SOKU / foot, leg; suffice	Ankle, heel and toes	足
0818	践	SEN / implement	足 (foot)[817] + 二 (two)[02] + 戈 (spear)[K20]	践
0819	畿	KI / capital	幺 (two short threads)[K64] + 田 (field)[60] + 戈 (spear)[K20]	畿

Day four: writing practice

矛	成	我	戒	武	浅	威
矛	成	我	戒	武	浅	威
柔	栽	栈	務	域	戚	惑
柔	栽	栈	務	域	戚	惑
幾	裁	減	感	足	踐	畿
幾	裁	減	感	足	踐	畿

Day five: story sketch

矛	spear: (barbed halberd) + Military Utensil
成	form: 刀 (sword) + 戈 (spear) + Shape Entirely Into
我	self: 手 (*hand*) + 戈 (spear) + Gains Assurance
戒	warn: 廾 (two hands) + 戈 (spear) + KAution Individual
武	military: 止 (stop) + 戈 (*spear*) + Belligerent Union
浅	shallow: 氵 (water) + 二 (two) + 戈 (spear) + Superficial ENtity
威	authority: 一 (one) + 女 (woman) + 戈 (spear) + Influence
柔	soft: 矛 (spear) + 木 (tree) + JUst Unsturdy
栽	plant: 十 (ten) + 木 (tree) + 戈 (spear) + Sow Area Intently
栈	frame: 木 (wood) + 二 (two) + 戈 (spear) + Skeletal ANatomy
務	duty: 矛 (spear) + 攵 (strike) + 力 (strength) + Must Undertake
域	area: 土 (ground) + 口 (mouth) + 一 (one) + 戈 (spear) + Intentional Kountry Isolate
戚	relatives: 上 (up) + 小 (small) + 戈 (spear) + SElect KIn
惑	confused: 口 (mouth) + 一 (one) + 戈 (spear) + 心 (heart) + WAnder Kourse Unclear
幾	how many: 幺 (two short threads) + 人 (person) + 戈 (spear) + Kount Indefinite
裁	judge: 十 (ten) + 衣 (clothes) + 戈 (spear) + Settle An Issue
减	decrease: 氵 (water) + 一 (one) + 口 (open) + 戈 (spear) + Gradually Erode Number
感	feeling: 一 (one) + 口 (mouth) + 戈 (spear) + 心 (heart) + Keenly Aware Now
足	foot: (ankle, heel and toes) + SOck Kovers Up
践	implement: 足 (foot) + 二 (two) + 戈 (spear) + Simply ENact
畿	capital: 幺 (two short threads) + 田 (field) + 戈 (spear) + Kongress Inhabits

Day six: character clusters

I Complete the characters using the clues.

1	氵	Gradually Erode Number (GEN)
2	戈	KAution Individual (KAI)
3	木	JUst Unsturdy (JUU)
4	氵	Superficial ENtity (SEN)
5	戈	Sow Area Intently (SAI)

II Compose the compounds using the clues.

1 (KYOO) 脅   +   (I) _____   =   _____ (threat)
   threaten

2 (MU) _____   +   (JUN) 盾   =   _____ (contradiction)
                       shield

3 (SEI) _____   +   (BUN) 分   =   _____ (ingredient)
                       divide

4 (CHUU) 仲   +   (SAI) _____   =   _____ (arbitration)
   relationship

5 (BU) _____   +   (KI) 器   =   _____ (weapon)
                       implement

III Complete the sentences using the clues.

1 デイビッドの勇気に＿＿心した。
   Deibiddo no yuuki ni KANshin shita.
   I was impressed by David's courage.

2 大変ご迷＿＿をかけてすみません。
   Taihen go-meiWAKU o kakete sumimasen.
   I'm sorry to have given you so much trouble.

3 あの先生には＿＿慢できない。
   Ano sensei ni wa GAman dekinai.
   I have no patience with that teacher.

4 子供たちは奈良へ遠＿＿に行きました。
   Kodomo-tachi wa nara e enSOKU ni ikimashita.
   The children went on an excursion to Nara.

5 すべての人は借金を払う義＿＿がある。
   Subete no hito wa shakkin o harau giMU ga aru.
   Everyone is obliged to pay their debts.

40

BUILDING BLOCKS

Day one: crossword puzzle

Across

2. Just Opening
8. Top End Inverted
9. YOre
10. KOntented Occurrence
12. Time Oriental Opulence
13. Konsolidate ENtirely
15. Select Hues Ornament Outline (M)
17. Trade Exhibit Need
19. Sleep HOrizontally On
20. Carefully Handles Official Orders
21. ROofed Opening

Down

1. MArijuana
3. Functions Urban (two words)
4. Tended Edible Island
5. Real ENtirely (H)
6. HAppen To Stand Up (S)
7. The Entourage Imperial (C)
11. Your One Occupation (U)
14. ROmantic Other (H)
16. YOu're Ordinary
18. HAve Isolated (A)

Day two: acrostics

1 Hemp: M A _ _ _ _ _ _ _

2 Beginning: J _ _ _   O _ _ _ _ _ _

3 Government Office: F _ _ _ _ _ _ _ _   U _ _ _ _

4 Garden: T _ _ _ _ _   E _ _ _ _ _   I _ _ _ _ _

5 Honest: R _ _ _   E N _ _ _ _ _ _

6 Start: H A _ _ _ _   T _   S _ _ _ _   U _

7 Court: T _ _   E _ _ _ _ _ _ _ _   I _ _ _ _ _ _ _

8 Bottom: T _ _   E _ _   I _ _ _ _ _ _ _

9 Prior: Y O _ _

10 Peaceful: K O _ _ _ _ _ _ _   O _ _ _ _ _ _ _ _

11 Use: Y _ _ _   O _ _   O _ _ _ _ _ _ _ _

12 Tang: T _ _ _   O _ _ _ _ _ _ _   O _ _ _ _ _ _ _

13 Combine: K _ _ _ _ _ _ _ _ _ _   E N _ _ _ _ _ _

14 Husband: R O _ _ _ _ _ _   O _ _ _ _

15 Makeup: S _ _ _ _ _ _   H _ _ _   O _ _ _ _ _ _ _   O _ _ _ _ _ _

16 Mediocre: Y O _ _ _   O _ _ _ _ _ _ _

17 Store: T _ _ _ _   E _ _ _ _ _ _   N _ _ _

18 Abandon: H A _ _   I _ _ _ _ _ _ _

19 Bed: S _ _ _ _   H O _ _ _ _ _ _ _ _ _ _   O _

20 Agency: C _ _ _ _ _ _ _ _   H _ _ _ _ _ _   O _ _ _ _ _ _ _   O _ _ _ _ _

21 Corridor: R O _ _ _ _   O _ _ _ _ _ _

Day three: componential analysis

Course Number	Kanji	ON Reading(s) / Core Concept(s)	Primary Components	Kanji Canvas
0820	庁	CHOO **agency**	广 (building)^{K24} + 丁 (exact)^{87}	庁
0821	床	SHOO **bed; floor**	广 (building)^{K24} + 木 (wood)^{43}	床
0822	予	YO **prior**	Spear without ax	予
0823	序	JO **beginning; order**	广 (building)^{K24} + 予 (prior)^{822}	序
0824	店	TEN **store, shop**	广 (building)^{K24} + 占 (occupy)^{112}	店
0825	府	FU **government office**	广 (building)^{K24} + 付 (attach)^{69}	府
0826	底	TEI **bottom**	广 (building)^{K24} + 氏 (family)^{766} + 一 (one)^{01}	底
0827	廷	TEI **court**	廴 (move)^{K41} + ノ (accent)^{K2} + 士 (samurai)^{67}	廷
0828	庭	TEI **garden**	广 (building)^{K24} + 廷 (court)^{827}	庭
0829	唐	TOO **Tang**	广 (building)^{K24} + ヨ (open hand)^{K54} + ｜ (tool)^{K80} + 口 (open)^{106}	唐
0830	康	KOO **peaceful**	广 (building)^{K24} + ヨ (open hand)^{K54} + ｜ (tool)^{K80} + 水 (water)^{22}	康
0831	用	YOO **use**	Fencing	用
0832	庸	YOO **mediocre**	广 (building)^{K24} + ヨ (open hand)^{K54} + ｜ (tool)^{K80} + 用 (use)^{831}	庸
0833	麻	MA **hemp**	广 (building)^{K24} + 林 (forest)^{54}	麻
0834	粧	SHOO **makeup**	米 (rice)^{269} + 广 (building)^{K24} + 土 (ground)^{169}	粧
0835	発	HATSU **start, leave**	*upturned feet* (cf. 1759) + 二 (two)^{02} + 儿 (boy)^{K5}	発
0836	廃	HAI **abandon; abolish**	广 (building)^{K24} + 発 (start)^{835}	廃
0837	郎	ROO **husband**	良 (*good*)^{398} + 阝 (village)^{K81}	郎
0838	廊	ROO **corridor**	广 (building)^{K24} + 郎 (husband)^{837}	廊
0839	兼	KEN **combine**	ヨ (open hand)^{K54} + 米 (*two rice plants*)^{269}	兼
0840	廉	REN **honest; cheap**	广 (building)^{K24} + 兼 (combine)^{839}	廉

Day four: writing practice

庁	床	予	序	店	府	底
庁	床	予	序	店	府	底
廷	庭	唐	康	用	庸	麻
廷	庭	唐	康	用	庸	麻
粧	発	廃	郎	廊	兼	廉
粧	発	廃	郎	廊	兼	廉

Day five: story sketch

庁	agency: 广 (building) + 丁 (exact) + Carefully Handles Official Orders
床	bed: 广 (building) + 木 (wood) + Sleep HOrizontally On
予	prior: (spear without ax) + YOre
序	beginning: 广 (building) + 予 (prior) + Just Opening
店	store: 广 (building) + 占 (occupy) + Trade Exhibit Need
府	government office: 广 (building) + 付 (attach) + Functions Urban
底	bottom: 广 (building) + 氏 (family) + 一 (one) + Top End Inverted
廷	court: 廴 (move) + ノ (accent) + 士 (samurai) + The Entourage Imperial
庭	garden: 广 (building) + 廷 (court) + Tended Edible Island
唐	Tang: 广 (building) + ヨ (open hand) + ｜ (tool) + 口 (open) + Time Oriental Opulence
康	peaceful: 广 (building) + ヨ (open hand) + ｜ (tool) + 水 (water) + KOntented Occurrence
用	use: (fencing) + Your One Occupation
庸	mediocre: 广 (building) + ヨ (open hand) + ｜ (tool) + 用 (use) + YOu're Ordinary
麻	hemp: 广 (building) + 林 (forest) + MArijuana
粧	makeup: 米 (rice) + 广 (building) + 土 (ground) + Select Hues Ornament Outline
発	start: *upturned feet* + 二 (two) + 儿 (boy) + HAppen To Stand Up
廃	abandon: 广 (building) + 発 (start) + HAve Isolated
郎	husband: 良 (*good*) + 阝 (village) + ROmantic Other
廊	corridor: 广 (building) + 郎 (husband) + ROofed Opening
兼	combine: ヨ (open hand) + 米 (*two rice plants*) + Konsolidate ENtirely
廉	honest: 广 (building) + 兼 (combine) + Real ENtirely

Day six: character clusters

I   Complete the characters using the clues.

1	广	Carefully Handles Official Orders (CHOO)
2	夂	The Entourage Imperial (TEI)
3	广	Sleep HOrizontally On (SHOO)
4	用	YOu're Ordinary (YOO)
5	广	Time Oriental Opulence (TOO)

II   Compose the compounds using the clues.

1   (KA) 家   +   (TEI) ____   =   _____ (home, family)
    house

2   (JO) ____   +   (BUN) 文   =   _____ (preface)
                               writing

3   (HAI) ____   +   (SHI) 止   =   _____ (abolition)
                               stop

4   (SEI) 政   +   (FU) ____   =   _____ (government)
    government

5   (ROO) ____   +   (KA) 下   =   _____ (corridor)
                               down

III   Complete the sentences using the clues.

1   適度な運動は健___にいいです。
    Tekidona undoo wa kenKOO ni ii desu.
    Moderate exercise is good for your health.

2   誰が電球を___明しましたか。
    Dare ga denkyuu o HATSUmei shimashita ka.
    Who invented the light bulb?

3   公立の図書館をよく利___します。
    Kooritsu no toshokan o yoku riYOO shimasu.
    I often use the public library.

4   虫歯の___防に歯を磨きなさい。
    Mushiba no YOboo ni ha o migakinasai.
    Brush your teeth to prevent tooth decay.

5   弟は___員のアルバイトをしている。
    Otooto wa TENin no arubaito o shite iru.
    My younger brother works part-time as a salesclerk.

REVIEW: LESSONS 36–40

I   Given the character and meaning, write the pronunciation.

1 怒 anger _____   2 更 again _____   3 佳 fine _____

4 戒 warn _____   5 廷 court _____   6 悪 bad _____

7 並 row _____   8 塁 fort _____   9 畿 capital _____

10 廉 honest _____   11 悦 joy _____   12 挿 insert _____

13 挫 sprain _____   14 栽 plant _____   15 発 start _____

16 恨 resent _____   17 垣 fence _____   18 座 seat _____

19 我 self _____   20 予 prior _____   21 怠 idle _____

22 復 repeat _____   23 街 street _____   24 域 area _____

25 店 store _____   26 暮 dusk _____   27 桟 frame _____

28 均 equal _____   29 暗 dark _____   30 柔 soft _____

II   Given the character and pronunciation, write the meaning.

1 恩 ON _____   2 旬 JUN _____   3 坪 tsubo _____

4 威 I _____   5 廃 HAI _____   6 悟 GO _____

7 婚 KON _____   8 埼 sai _____   9 戚 SEKI _____

10 兼 KEN _____   11 惧 GU _____   12 暇 KA _____

13 塀 HEI _____   14 減 GEN _____   15 庸 YOO _____

16 患 KAN _____   17 府 FU _____   18 堂 DOO _____

19 践 SEN _____   20 康 KOO _____   21 恋 REN _____

22 宴 EN _____   23 塔 TOO _____   24 幾 KI _____

25 廊 ROO _____   26 曹 SOO _____   27 填 TEN _____

28 粧 SHOO_____   29 惑 WAKU _____   30 務 MU _____

III Given the meaning and pronunciation, write the character.

1 hurry	KYUU	_____	2 generally	FU	_____
3 beginning	JO	_____	4 spear	MU	_____
5 agency	CHOO	_____	6 exchange	TAI	_____
7 dish	sara	_____	8 limit	GAI	_____
9 shallow	SEN	_____	10 Tang	TOO	_____
11 skewer	kushi	_____	12 family	SHI	_____
13 bury	MAI	_____	14 military	BU	_____
15 garden	TEI	_____	16 common	BON	_____
17 time	JI	_____	18 husband	ROO	_____
19 sad	HI	_____	20 red	SEKI	_____
21 regret	SEKI	_____	22 insect	KON	_____
23 sheep	YOO	_____	24 foot	SOKU	_____
25 past	SAKU	_____			

IV Compose compounds using the following characters.

恐 量 温 亜 地 成 墓 用 怖 底 床 感 意 麻 塗 快 裁 達 布 基

1 (ON) _____ + (SHOO) _____ = _____ (hotbed)

2 (SAI) _____ + (RYOO) _____ = _____ (discretion)

3 (KYOO) _____ + (FU) _____ = _____ (fear)

4 (KI) _____ + (TEI) _____ = _____ (base)

5 (YOO) _____ + (I) _____ = _____ (preparation)

6 (TO) _____ + (FU) _____ = _____ (application)

7 (KAI) _____ + (KAN) _____ = _____ (pleasure)

8 (BO) _____ + (CHI) _____ = _____ (graveyard)

9 (TAS) _____ + (SEI) _____ = _____ (achievement)

10 (A) _____ + (MA) _____ = _____ (flax)

41

BIG AND SMALL

Day one: crossword puzzle

Across

3. Thump On Object
6. Kontrived Item
8. Konsistently Overstate
10. Support HOpeful Outlook
13. This Ample Increase
14. Kommit Earnest Intent (P)
15. Scent HUnt Unpleasant
17. REverts Itself
18. Naturally Act
20. TO Thrust SUddenly (L)

Down

1. Shrine Attend Now (V)
2. Tranquil AIr
4. Outermost Opposite
5. SOng Offering (P)
7. Kountry ENtity (P)
9. Stimulate Once Over (R)
11. SHOuts Orders
12. Oneself REfer
16. Gap Extensive Kuts Inward
19. HOld Out (O)
21. Shelter Osprey Occupy

Day two: acrostics

1 Visit: S _ _ _ _ _   A _ _ _ _ _   N _ _

2 Calm: T _ _ _ _ _ _ _   A I _

3 Hit: T _ _ _ _   O _   O _ _ _ _ _

4 Innermost: O _ _ _ _ _ _ _ _   O _ _ _ _ _ _

5 Play: S O _ _   O _ _ _ _ _ _

6 Implement: K _ _ _ _ _ _ _ _   I _ _ _

7 Prefecture: K _ _ _ _ _ _   E N _ _ _ _

8 Boast: K _ _ _ _ _ _ _ _ _ _   O _ _ _ _ _ _ _

9 Refresh: S _ _ _ _ _ _ _ _   O _ _ _   O _ _ _

10 Encourage: S _ _ _ _ _ _   H O _ _ _ _ _   O _ _ _ _ _ _

11 Commander: S H O _ _ _   O _ _ _ _ _

12 Me: O _ _ _ _ _ _   R E _ _ _

13 Fat: T _ _ _   A _ _ _ _   I _ _ _ _ _ _ _

14 Pledge: K _ _ _ _ _   E _ _ _ _ _ _   I _ _ _ _ _

15 Odor: S _ _ _ _   H U _   U _ _ _ _ _ _ _ _

16 Crevice: G _ _   E _ _ _ _ _ _ _ _   K _ _ _   I _ _ _ _ _

17 Return: R E _ _ _ _ _   I _ _ _ _ _

18 How: N _ _ _ _ _ _ _ _   A _ _

19 Offer: H O _ _   O _ _

20 Lunge: T O   T _ _ _ _ _   S U _ _ _ _ _ _

21 Nest: S _ _ _ _ _ _   O _ _ _ _ _   O _ _ _ _ _

Day three: componential analysis

Course Number	**Kanji**	ON Reading(s) / Core Concept(s)	Primary Components	Kanji Canvas
0841	太	TAI **fat, big, thick**	大 (big)[233] + 丶 (accent)[K2]	太
0842	当	TOO **hit; this**	⺌ (small)[K44] + ヨ (open hand)[K54]	当
0843	戻	REI **return**	戸 (door)[284] + 大 (big)[233]	戻
0844	参	SAN **visit; participate**	ム (self)[K18] + 大 (big)[233] + 彡 (delicate)[K12]	参
0845	突	TOTSU **lunge**	穴 (hole)[316] + 大 (big)[233]	突
0846	奉	HOO **offer**	二 (two)[02] + 大 (big)[233] + 手 (*hand*)[85]	奉
0847	奈	NA **how**	大 (big)[233] + 示 (altar)[176]	奈
0848	県	KEN **prefecture**	目 (eye)[62] + 乚 (corner)[K30] + 小 (small)[31]	県
0849	契	KEI **pledge**	生 (*life*)[142] + 刀 (knife)[115] + 大 (big)[233]	契
0850	臭	SHUU **odor**	自 (self)[146] + 大 (big)[233]	臭
0851	奏	SOO **play**	二 (two)[02] + 大 (big)[233] + 天 (heaven)[261]	奏
0852	泰	TAI **calm**	二 (two)[02] + 大 (big)[233] + 水 (water)[22]	泰
0853	俺	ore **me, I**	亻 (person)[K16] + 大 (big)[233] + 申 (*state*)[230]	俺
0854	爽	SOO **refresh**	大 (big)[233] + 㐅 (four marks)[K49]	爽
0855	巣	SOO **nest**	⺍ (ornate)[K63] + 果 (fruit)[61]	巣
0856	隙	GEKI **crevice**	阝 (hill)[K68] + 小 (small)[31] + 日 (sun)[17] + 小 (small)[31]	隙
0857	奥	OO **innermost**	ノ (accent)[K2] + 凵 (*container*)[K48] + 米 (rice)[269] + 大 (big)[233]	奥
0858	将	SHOO **commander**	丬 (side)[K40] + ⺤ (claw)[K53] + 寸 (measure)[11]	将
0859	奨	SHOO **encourage**	将 (commander)[858] + 大 (big)[233]	奨
0860	誇	KO **boast**	言 (words)[190] + 大 (big)[233] + 亏 (emerge)[K28]	誇
0861	器	KI **implement; container**	口 (four mouths)[106] + 大 (big)[233]	器

Day four: writing practice

太	当	戻	参	突	奉	奈
太	当	戻	参	突	奉	奈
県	契	臭	奏	泰	俺	爽
県	契	臭	奏	泰	俺	爽
巣	隙	奥	将	奨	誇	器
巣	隙	奥	将	奨	誇	器

Day five: story sketch

太	fat: 大 (big) + 丶 (accent) + This Ample Increase
当	hit: 丷 (small) + ヨ (open hand) + Thump On Object
戻	return: 戸 (door) + 大 (big) + REverts Itself
参	visit: 厶 (self) + 大 (big) + 彡 (delicate) + Shrine Attend Now
突	lunge: 穴 (hole) + 大 (big) + TO Thrust SUddenly
奉	offer: 二 (two) + 大 (big) + 手 (*hand*) + HOld Out
奈	how: 大 (big) + 示 (altar) + Naturally Act
県	prefecture: 目 (eye) + ﹂ (corner) + 小 (small) + Kountry ENtity
契	pledge: 生 (*life*) + 刀 (knife) + 大 (big) + Kommit Earnest Intent
臭	odor: 自 (self) + 大 (big) + Scent HUnt Unpleasant
奏	play: 二 (two) + 大 (big) + 天 (heaven) + SOng Offering
泰	calm: 二 (two) + 大 (big) + 水 (water) + Tranquil AIr
俺	me: 亻 (person) + 大 (big) + 申 (*state*) + Oneself REfer
爽	refresh: 大 (big) + ✕ (four marks) + Stimulate Once Over
巣	nest: 丷 (ornate) + 果 (fruit) + Shelter Osprey Occupy
隙	crevice: 阝 (hill) + 小 (small) + 日 (sun) + 小 (small) + Gap Extensive Kuts Inward
奥	innermost: 丿 (accent) + 凵 (*container*) + 米 (rice) + 大 (big) + Outermost Opposite
将	commander: 丬 (side) + 爫 (claw) + 寸 (measure) + SHOuts Orders
奨	encourage: 将 (commander) + 大 (big) + Support HOpeful Outlook
誇	boast: 言 (words) + 大 (big) + 丂 (emerge) + Konsistently Overstate
器	implement: 口 (four mouths) + 大 (big) + Kontrived Item

Day six: character clusters

I   Complete the characters using the clues.

1	阝	Gap Extensive Kuts Inward (GEKI)
2	大	Scent HUnt Unpleasant (SHUU)
3	戸	REverts Itself (REI)
4	目	Kountry ENtity (KEN)
5	亻	Oneself REfer (ORE)

II   Compose the compounds using the clues.

1   (EN) 演   +   (SOO) _____   =   _____ (performance)
        perform

2   (SHOO) _____   +   (RAI) 来   =   _____ (future)
                               come

3   (KO) _____   +   (CHOO) 張   =   _____ (exaggeration)
                                stretch

4   (BU) 武   +   (KI) _____   =   _____ (weapon)
        military

5   (HOO) _____   +   (SHI) 仕   =   _____ (service)
                               serve

III   Complete the sentences using the clues.

1   たくさんの選手がオリンピックに___加する。
      Takusan no senshu ga orinpikku ni SANka suru.
      Many athletes participate in the Olympics.

2   ___陽は照っていたけど雨が降り出した。
      TAIyoo wa tette ita kedo ame ga furidashita.
      Even though the sun was shining, it began to rain.

3   友達と釣りをして本___に楽しかった。
      Tomodachi to tsuri o shite honTOO ni tanoshikatta.
      I really enjoyed fishing with my friends.

4   この___約は延長できません。
      Kono KEIyaku wa enchoo dekimasen.
      This contract cannot be extended.

5   ヘンリーの辞職は___然のことだった。
      Henrii no jishoku wa TOTSUzen no koto datta.
      Henry's resignation was sudden.

42

DOG TAGS

Day one: crossword puzzle

Across
2. JUngle Ungulate (B)
5. Kontinue Exercise Intently
8. Rabidly YOu Outfox (H)
9. Guards Oversee KUlprits
10. Face Unseen Keep Uniform
11. Beast YOu Own
14. Creature HUndreds Unlike
16. Set Objective
17. Konstricted YOur Opening
19. Emulator Nimble (M)
20. Harmed ANother
21. Yet Utterly Undecided

Down
1. Set Hounds Upon
3. MOuth Kept Unopened
4. Krazy YOur Obsession (M)
6. JOint Outlook (C)
7. MOngrel Onslaught (F)
12. DO Kome Unaccompanied
13. Konfer ENtity (O)
15. Start HUman Undertaking
    (two words)
18. Kologne You Uncover
    Unpleasant

Day two: acrostics

1 Hunt: S _ _   H _ _ _ _ _   U _ _ _

2 Beast: J U _ _ _ _   U _ _ _ _ _ _ _

3 Silent: M O _ _ _   K _ _ _   U _ _ _ _ _ _ _

4 Mad: K _ _ _ _   Y O _ _   O _ _ _ _ _ _ _

5 Practice: K _ _ _ _ _ _ _   E _ _ _ _ _ _ _   I _ _ _ _ _ _ _

6 Condition: J O _ _ _   O _ _ _ _ _ _

7 Fierce: M O _ _ _ _ _   O _ _ _ _ _ _ _ _

8 Hunting: R _ _ _ _ _ _ _   Y O _   O _ _ _ _ _

9 Prison: G _ _ _ _ _   O _ _ _ _ _ _   K U _ _ _ _ _ _

10 Prostrate: F _ _ _   U _ _ _ _ _   K _ _ _   U _ _ _ _ _ _

11 Cat: B _ _ _ _   Y O _   O _ _

12 Alone: D O   K _ _ _   U _ _ _ _ _ _ _ _ _ _ _

13 Offer: K _ _ _ _ _   E N _ _ _ _

14 Insect: C _ _ _ _ _ _ _   H U _ _ _ _ _ _   U _ _ _ _ _

15 Take Up: S _ _ _ _   H U _ _ _   U _ _ _ _ _ _ _ _ _

16 Aim: S _ _   O _ _ _ _ _ _ _ _

17 Narrow: K _ _ _ _ _ _ _ _ _ _   Y O _ _   O _ _ _ _ _

18 Smell: K _ _ _ _ _ _   Y _ _   U _ _ _ _ _ _   U _ _ _ _ _ _ _ _

19 Monkey: E _ _ _ _ _ _ _   N _ _ _ _ _

20 Crime: H _ _ _ _ _   A N _ _ _ _ _

21 Delay: Y _ _   U _ _ _ _ _ _   U _ _ _ _ _ _ _ _

Day three: componential analysis

Course Number	Kanji	ON Reading(s) / Core Concept(s)	Primary Components	Kanji Canvas
0862	犯	HAN **crime**	犭 (dog)[K82] + 㔾 (slumped)[K8]	犯
0863	伏	FUKU **prostrate**	亻 (person)[K16] + 犬 (dog)[438]	伏
0864	状	JOO **condition; form; letter**	丬 (side)[K40] + 犬 (dog)[438]	状
0865	狂	KYOO **mad**	犭 (dog)[K82] + 王 (king)[155]	狂
0866	狙	SO **aim**	犭 (dog)[K82] + 且 (moreover)[331]	狙
0867	狩	SHU **hunt**	犭 (dog)[K82] + 守 (protect)[317]	狩
0868	狭	KYOO **narrow**	犭 (dog)[K82] + 来 (between)[K75]	狭
0869	虫	CHUU **insect**	Antenna, head and tail	虫
0870	独	DOKU **alone**	犭 (dog)[K82] + 虫 (insect)[869]	独
0871	猛	MOO **fierce**	犭 (dog)[K82] + 子 (child)[320] + 皿 (dish)[771]	猛
0872	猟	RYOO **hunting**	犭 (dog)[K82] + ⺌ (ornate)[K63] + 用 (*use*)[831]	猟
0873	猫	BYOO **cat**	犭 (dog)[K82] + 苗 (seedling)[246]	猫
0874	就	SHUU **take up**	京 (capital)[725] + 犬 (*dog*)[438]	就
0875	献	KEN **offer, dedicate**	南 (south)[513] + 犬 (dog)[438]	献
0876	猶	YUU **delay**	犭 (dog)[K82] + ⺍ (out)[K35] + 酉 (alcohol)[K83]	猶
0877	嗅	KYUU **smell**	口 (mouth)[106] + 自 (self)[146] + 犬 (dog)[438]	嗅
0878	猿	EN **monkey**	犭 (dog)[K82] + 哀 (*pity*)[407]	猿
0879	獄	GOKU **prison**	犭 (dog)[K82] + 言 (words)[190] + 犬 (dog)[438]	獄
0880	黙	MOKU **silent**	里 (village)[181] + 犬 (dog)[438] + 灬 (fire)[K61]	黙
0881	稽	KEI **practice**	禾 (grain)[K33] + 犬 (dog)[438] + 匕 (sitting)[K17] + 日 (day)[17]	稽
0882	獣	JUU **beast**	⺍ (ornate)[K63] + 田 (field)[60] + 一 (one)[01] + 口 (open)[106] + 犬 (dog)[438]	獣

Day four: writing practice

犯	伏	状	狂	狙	狩	狭
犯	伏	状	狂	狙	狩	狭
虫	独	猛	猟	猫	就	献
虫	独	猛	猟	猫	就	献
猶	嗅	猿	獄	黙	稽	獣
猶	嗅	猿	獄	黙	稽	獣

Day five: story sketch

犯	crime: 犭 (dog) + 㔾 (slumped) + Harmed ANother
伏	prostrate: 亻 (person) + 犬 (dog) + Face Unseen Keep Uniform
状	condition: 丬 (side) + 犬 (dog) + JOint Outlook
狂	mad: 犭 (dog) + 王 (king) + Krazy YOur Obsession
狙	aim: 犭 (dog) + 且 (moreover) + Set Objective
狩	hunt: 犭 (dog) + 守 (protect) + Set Hounds Upon
狭	narrow: 犭 (dog) + 来 (between) + Konstricted YOur Opening
虫	insect: (antenna, head and tail) + Creature HUndreds Unlike
独	alone: 犭 (dog) + 虫 (insect) + DO Kome Unaccompanied
猛	fierce: 犭 (dog) + 子 (child) + 皿 (dish) + MOngrel Onslaught
猟	hunting: 犭 (dog) + 丷 (ornate) + 用 (*use*) + Rabidly YOu Outfox
猫	cat: 犭 (dog) + 苗 (seedling) + Beast YOu Own
就	take up: 京 (capital) + 犬 (*dog*) + Start HUman Undertaking
献	offer: 南 (south) + 犬 (dog) + Konfer ENtity
猶	delay: 犭 (dog) + 丷 (out) + 酉 (alcohol) + Yet Utterly Undecided
嗅	smell: 口 (mouth) + 自 (self) + 犬 (dog) + Kologne You Uncover Unpleasant
猿	monkey: 犭 (dog) + 哀 (*pity*) + Emulator Nimble
獄	prison: 犭 (dog) + 言 (words) + 犬 (dog) + Guards Oversee KUlprits
黙	silent: 里 (village) + 犬 (dog) + 灬 (fire) + MOuth Kept Unopened
稽	practice: 禾 (grain) + 犬 (dog) + 匕 (sitting) + 日 (day) + Kontinue Exercise Intently
獣	beast: 丷 (ornate) + 田 (field) + 一 (one) + 口 (open) + 犬 (dog) + JUngle Ungulate

Day six: character clusters

I Complete the characters using the clues.

1	犭	Beast YOu Own (BYOO)
2	犬	Kologne You Uncover Unpleasant (KYUU)
3	京	Start HUman Undertaking (SHUU)
4	子	MOngrel Onslaught (MOO)
5	犭	Konstricted YOur Opening (KYOO)

II Compose the compounds using the clues.

1 (KOO) 降   +   (FUKU) ____   =   _____ (surrender)
    descend

2 (JUU) ____   +   (I) 医   =   _____ (veterinarian)
                medicine

3 (KYOO) ____   +   (KI) 気   =   _____ (madness)
                spirit

4 (JI) 地   +   (GOKU) ____   =   _____ (hell)
    ground

5 (KEN) ____   +   (SHIN) 身   =   _____ (devotion)
                body

III Complete the sentences using the clues.

1 インターネット＿＿罪は増加している。
    Intaanetto HANzai wa zooka shite iru.
    Crime on the Internet is increasing.

2 政治家はその事件について沈＿＿を守った。
    Seijika wa sono jiken ni tsuite chinMOKU o mamotta.
    The politician kept silent about the incident.

3 そんな＿＿態では車の運転できない。
    Sonna JOOtai de wa kuruma no unten dekinai.
    You cannot drive a car in that condition.

4 毎日ギターの＿＿古をします。
    Mainichi gitaa no KEIko o shimasu.
    I practice playing the guitar every day.

5 由美ちゃんはプールを＿＿占していた。
    Yumi-chan wa puuru o DOKUsen shite ita.
    Yumi had the swimming pool all to herself.

43

STEPPINGSTONES

Day one: crossword puzzle

Across

1. Movement Amends (P)
5. Triumph Offends (J)
7. Keep ENhancing (S)
9. HOwitzer Outright
10. Surely Handle Obstacle (two words)
11. Hit Apart
12. Supports Object (F)
16. Bread's Ample Komponent Ultimately
17. Honors Immortal
19. SHOal Obscurity
20. Take Acre KUltivate
21. Smash Asymmetric Items

Down

2. Shore Accumulation
3. Konfirmed AKcurate Understanding (C)
4. Time Of Overcoats
6. Sear HOt Object
8. Just Irresistible (M)
13. Salt Hard On Outside
14. Game Oriental
15. Rock Yellowish Used Unpleasantly (S)
18. KOncrete Object

Day two: acrostics

1 Polish: M _ _ _ _ _ _ _ _   A _ _ _ _ _

2 Sand: S _ _ _ _   A _ _ _ _ _ _ _ _ _ _

3 Certain: K _ _ _ _ _ _ _ _   A K _ _ _ _ _ _   U _ _ _ _ _ _ _ _ _ _ _

4 Winter: T _ _ _   O _   O _ _ _ _ _ _ _

5 Jealous: T _ _ _ _ _ _   O _ _ _ _ _ _

6 Scorch: S _ _ _   H O _   O _ _ _ _ _

7 Sharpen: K _ _ _   E N _ _ _ _ _ _ _

8 Magnetic: J _ _ _   I _ _ _ _ _ _ _ _ _ _

9 Cannon: H O _ _ _ _ _ _   O _ _ _ _ _ _ _

10 Deal With: S _ _ _ _ _ _   H _ _ _ _ _   O _ _ _ _ _ _ _

11 Break: H _ _   A _ _ _ _

12 Foundation: S _ _ _ _ _ _ _   O _ _ _ _ _

13 Niter: S _ _ _   H _ _ _   O _   O _ _ _ _ _

14 Go: G _ _ _   O _ _ _ _ _ _ _

15 Sulfur: R _ _ _   Y _ _ _ _ _ _ _ _   U _ _ _   U _ _ _ _ _ _ _ _ _ _

16 Wheat: B _ _ _ _ _ _   A _ _ _ _   K _ _ _ _ _ _ _ _   U _ _ _ _ _ _ _ _ _

17 Monument: H _ _ _ _ _   I _ _ _ _ _ _ _

18 Hard: K O _ _ _ _ _ _   O _ _ _ _ _

19 Reef: S H O _ _   O _ _ _ _ _ _ _

20 Reclaim: T _ _ _   A _ _ _   K U _ _ _ _ _ _ _

21 Crush: S _ _ _ _   A _ _ _ _ _ _ _ _ _   I _ _ _ _

Day three: componential analysis

Course Number	Kanji	ON Reading(s) / Core Concept(s)	Primary Components	Kanji Canvas
0883	処	SHO / **deal with**	夂 (step)[K13] + 几 (table)[K11]	処
0884	冬	TOO / **winter**	夂 (step)[K13] + 冫 (ice)[K84]	冬
0885	麦	BAKU / **wheat**	生 (life)[142] + 夂 (step)[K13]	麦
0886	拓	TAKU / **reclaim**	扌 (hand)[K21] + 石 (stone)[614]	拓
0887	妬	TO / **jealous**	女 (woman)[337] + 石 (stone)[614]	妬
0888	研	KEN / **sharpen**	石 (stone)[614] + 井 (well)[184]	研
0889	砂	SA / **sand**	石 (stone)[614] + 少 (little)[32]	砂
0890	砕	SAI / **crush**	石 (stone)[614] + 九 (nine)[05] + 十 (ten)[06]	砕
0891	破	HA / **break; tear**	石 (stone)[614] + 皮 (skin)[409]	破
0892	砲	HOO / **cannon; gun**	石 (stone)[614] + 包 (wrap)[703]	砲
0893	硫	RYUU / **sulfur**	石 (stone)[614] + 亠 (top)[K1] + ㄙ (self)[K18] + 川 (river)[198]	硫
0894	硬	KOO / **hard**	石 (stone)[614] + 更 (again)[758]	硬
0895	硝	SHOO / **niter**	石 (stone)[614] + 肖 (resemble)[277]	硝
0896	碁	GO / **go**	其 (ladder)[K79] + 石 (stone)[614]	碁
0897	磁	JI / **magnetic**	石 (stone)[614] + 玄 (obscure + dark = *mysterious*)[495] (cf. 1117)	磁
0898	碑	HI / **monument**	石 (stone)[614] + 卑 (humble)[514]	碑
0899	確	KAKU / **certain**	石 (stone)[614] + *crane* (crested bird with outstretched neck)	確
0900	磨	MA / **polish**	麻 (hemp)[833] + 石 (stone)[614]	磨
0901	焦	SHOO / **scorch**	隹 (bird)[K67] + 灬 (fire)[K61]	焦
0902	礁	SHOO / **reef**	石 (stone)[614] + 焦 (scorch)[901]	礁
0903	礎	SO / **foundation**	石 (stone)[614] + 林 (forest)[54] + 正 (correct)[166]	礎

Day four: writing practice

処	冬	麦	拓	姤	研	砂
処	冬	麦	拓	姤	研	砂
砕	破	砲	硫	硬	硝	碁
砕	破	砲	硫	硬	硝	碁
磁	碑	確	磨	焦	礁	礎
磁	碑	確	磨	焦	礁	礎

Day five: story sketch

处	deal with: 夂 (step) + 几 (table) + Surely Handle Obstacle
冬	winter: 夂 (step) + 冫 (*ice*) + Time Of Overcoats
麦	wheat: 生 (*life*) + 夂 (step) + Bread's Ample Komponent Ultimately
拓	reclaim: 扌 (hand) + 石 (stone) + Take Acre KUltivate
妬	jealous: 女 (woman) + 石 (stone) + Triumph Offends
研	sharpen: 石 (stone) + 井 (*well*) + Keep ENhancing
砂	sand: 石 (stone) + 少 (little) + Shore Accumulation
砕	crush: 石 (stone) + 九 (nine) + 十 (ten) + Smash Asymmetric Items
破	break: 石 (stone) + 皮 (skin) + Hit Apart
砲	cannon: 石 (stone) + 包 (wrap) + HOwitzer Outright
硫	sulfur: 石 (stone) + 亠 (top) + 厶 (self) + 川 (river) + Rock Yellowish Used Unpleasantly
硬	hard: 石 (stone) + 更 (again) + KOncrete Object
硝	niter: 石 (stone) + 肖 (resemble) + Salt Hard On Outside
碁	go: 其 (ladder) + 石 (stone) + Game Oriental
磁	magnetic: 石 (stone) + 玄 (obscure) + 玄 (dark) + Just Irresistible
碑	monument: 石 (stone) + 卑 (humble) + Honors Immortal
確	certain: 石 (stone) + *crane* + Konfirmed AKcurate Understanding
磨	polish: 麻 (hemp) + 石 (stone) + Movement Amends
焦	scorch: 隹 (bird) + 灬 (fire) + Sear HOt Object
礁	reef: 石 (stone) + 焦 (scorch) + SHOal Obscurity
礎	foundation: 石 (stone) + 林 (forest) + 正 (correct) + Supports Object

Day six: character clusters

I Complete the characters using the clues.

<table>
<tr><td>1</td><td>石</td><td>KOncrete Object (KOO)</td></tr>
<tr><td>2</td><td>石</td><td>Movement Amends (MA)</td></tr>
<tr><td>3</td><td>女</td><td>Triumph Offends (TO)</td></tr>
<tr><td>4</td><td>夂</td><td>Bread's Ample Komponent Ultimately (BAKU)</td></tr>
<tr><td>5</td><td>九</td><td>Smash Asymmetric Items (SAI)</td></tr>
</table>

II Compose the compounds using the clues.

1 (KAI) 開 + (TAKU) ____ = _____ (reclamation)
   open

2 (SA) ____ + (TOO) 糖 = _____ (sugar)
                      sugar

3 (HA) ____ + (HEN) 片 = _____ (fragment)
                     piece

4 (TAI) 大 + (HOO) ____ = _____ (cannon)
   big

5 (TOO) ____ + (MIN) 眠 = _____ (hibernation)
                     sleep

III Complete the sentences using the clues.

1 電話でレンタカーの予約を＿認した。
  Denwa de rentakaa no yoyaku o KAKUnin shita.
  I confirmed the rent-a-car reservation by telephone.

2 このごみをどう＿分しましょうか。
  Kono gomi o doo SHObun shimashoo ka.
  How shall we dispose of this garbage?

3 西田先生はがんを＿究している。
  Nishida-sensei wa gan o KENkyuu shite iru.
  Professor Nishida is doing research on cancer.

4 花にカメラの＿点を合わせた。
  Hana ni kamera no SHOOten o awaseta.
  I focused my camera on the flower.

5 マイケルはまだ数学の基＿を覚えてない。
  Maikeru wa mada suugaku no kiSO o oboetenai.
  Michael has not yet learned the basics of mathematics.

44

CUT FROM THE SAME CLOTH

Day one: crossword puzzle

Across

- 3. Tight Around Individual
- 7. Space Houses Industry
- 9. Kraving Intense
- 11. Just Ordinary One
- 12. Brought ATtendant Sanctions Upon (P)
- 18. Material Enhances Napkins
- 19. MAterial Konceals Utterly
- 20. BOnnet Originally
- 21. Catalogue HOnored Officially

Down

- 1. Transmit Each Item (R)
- 2. SUperior Individual (C)
- 4. SHOw Kolors Uncommon (D)
- 5. Yum Ultimately (P)
- 6. FUll Kapacity Unfolded (W)
- 8. Students Head Influence
- 10. Harness Air Navigator
- 13. BETter Split Up
- 14. Kolorfully INterwoven (B)
- 15. Kalcium Ossified Tissue SUbstance
- 16. SEt Keister Into
- 17. Honored Exchange Instrument

Day two: acrostics

1 Relay: T _ _ _ _ _ _ _   E _ _ _   I _ _ _

2 Commander: S U _ _ _ _ _ _   I _ _ _ _ _ _ _ _ _

3 Belt: T _ _ _ _   A _ _ _ _ _   I _ _ _ _ _ _ _ _

4 Decorate: S H O _   K _ _ _ _ _   U _ _ _ _ _ _ _

5 Pleasure: Y _ _   U _ _ _ _ _ _ _ _

6 Width: F U _ _   K _ _ _ _ _ _ _   U _ _ _ _ _ _

7 City: S _ _ _ _   H _ _ _ _ _   I _ _ _ _ _ _

8 Teacher: S _ _ _ _ _ _ _   H _ _ _   I _ _ _ _ _ _ _

9 Desire: K _ _ _ _ _ _   I _ _ _ _ _ _

10 Sail: H _ _ _ _ _ _   A _ _   N _ _ _ _ _ _ _ _

11 Normal: J _ _ _   O _ _ _ _ _ _ _   O _ _

12 Punishment: B _ _ _ _ _ _   A T _ _ _ _ _ _ _   S _ _ _ _ _ _ _ _   U _ _ _

13 Separate: B E T _ _ _   S _ _ _ _   U _

14 Brocade: K _ _ _ _ _ _ _ _ _   I N _ _ _ _ _ _ _

15 Bone: K _ _ _ _ _ _   O _ _ _ _ _ _ _   T _ _ _ _ _   S U _ _ _ _ _ _ _

16 Seat: S E _   K _ _ _ _ _ _   I _ _ _

17 Money: H _ _ _ _ _ _   E _ _ _ _ _ _ _   I _ _ _ _ _ _ _ _ _

18 Cotton: M _ _ _ _ _ _ _   E _ _ _ _ _ _ _   N _ _ _ _ _ _

19 Curtain: M A _ _ _ _ _ _   K _ _ _ _ _ _ _   U _ _ _ _ _ _

20 Hat: B O _ _ _ _   O _ _ _ _ _ _ _ _

21 Register: C _ _ _ _ _ _ _ _   H O _ _ _ _ _   O _ _ _ _ _ _ _ _

Day three: componential analysis

Course Number	Kanji	ON Reading(s) / Core Concept(s)	Primary Components	Kanji Canvas
0904	市	SHI / city; market	亠 (top)[K1] + 巾 (cloth)[395]	市
0905	帆	HAN / sail	巾 (cloth)[395] + 凡 (common)[747]	帆
0906	希	KI / desire; rare	メ (mark)[K49] + 手 (*hand*)[85] + 巾 (cloth)[395]	希
0907	骨	KOTSU / bone	Spinal column	骨
0908	別	BETSU / separate	骨 (*bone*)[907] + 刂 (cut)[K36]	別
0909	席	SEKI / seat	广 (building)[K24] + 廿 (twenty)[K62] + 巾 (cloth)[395]	席
0910	帯	TAI / belt	*buckle* + 冖 (cover)[K26] + 巾 (cloth)[395]	帯
0911	帥	SUI / commander	𠂤 (buttocks)[K52] + 巾 (cloth)[395]	帥
0912	師	SHI / teacher	𠂤 (buttocks)[K52] + 一 (one)[01] + 巾 (cloth)[395]	師
0913	逓	TEI / relay; successive	辶 (move)[K41] + 厂 (cliff)[K14] + 二 (two)[02] + 巾 (cloth)[395]	逓
0914	常	JOO / normal, usual	尚 (esteem)[728] + 巾 (cloth)[395]	常
0915	帳	CHOO / register	巾 (cloth)[395] + 長 (long)[402]	帳
0916	帽	BOO / hat, cap	巾 (cloth)[395] + 冒 (risk)[161]	帽
0917	幅	FUKU / width	巾 (cloth)[395] + 畐 (full)[K72]	幅
0918	愉	YU / pleasure	忄 (heart)[K31] + 人 (*cover*)[K26] + 月 (meat)[274] + 刂 (cut)[K36]	愉
0919	幕	MAKU / curtain	莫 (gone)[K78] + 巾 (cloth)[395]	幕
0920	綿	MEN / cotton	糸 (thread)[211] + 白 (white)[18] + 巾 (cloth)[395]	綿
0921	飾	SHOKU / decorate	食 (food)[399] + 人 (*person*)[64] + 巾 (cloth)[395]	飾
0922	罰	BATSU / punishment	罒 (net)[K56] + 言 (words)[190] + 刂 (cut)[K36]	罰
0923	幣	HEI / money	巾 (cloth)[395] + ソ (pieces)[K66] + 攵 (strike)[K46] + 巾 (cloth)[395]	幣
0924	錦	KIN / brocade	金 (gold)[388] + 白 (white)[18] + 巾 (cloth)[395]	錦

Day four: writing practice

市	帆	希	骨	別	席	帯
市	帆	希	骨	別	席	帯

帥	師	逓	常	帳	帽	幅
帥	師	逓	常	帳	帽	幅

愉	幕	綿	飾	罰	幣	錦
愉	幕	綿	飾	罰	幣	錦

Day five: story sketch

市	city: 亠 (top) + 巾 (cloth) + Space Houses Industry
帆	sail: 巾 (cloth) + 凡 (common) + Harness Air Navigator
希	desire: ㄨ (mark) + 手 (*hand*) + 巾 (cloth) + Kraving Intense
骨	bone: (spinal column) + Kalcium Ossified Tissue SUbstance
別	separate: 骨 (*bone*) + 刂 (cut) + BETter Split Up
席	seat: 广 (building) + 廿 (twenty) + 巾 (cloth) + SEt Keister Into
帯	belt: *buckle* + 冖 (cover) + 巾 (cloth) + Tight Around Individual
帥	commander: 𠂤 (buttocks) + 巾 (cloth) + SUperior Individual
師	teacher: 𠂤 (buttocks) + 一 (one) + 巾 (cloth) + Students Head Influence
逓	relay: 辶 (move) + 厂 (cliff) + 二 (two) + 巾 (cloth) + Transmit Each Item
常	normal: 尚 (esteem) + 巾 (cloth) + Just Ordinary One
帳	register: 巾 (cloth) + 長 (long) + Catalogue HOnored Officially
帽	hat: 巾 (cloth) + 冒 (risk) + BOnnet Originally
幅	width: 巾 (cloth) + 畐 (full) + FUll Kapacity Unfolded
愉	pleasure: 忄 (heart) + 亼 (*cover*) + 月 (meat) + 刂 (cut) + Yum Ultimately
幕	curtain: 莫 (gone) + 巾 (cloth) + MAterial Konceals Utterly
綿	cotton: 糸 (thread) + 白 (white) + 巾 (cloth) + Material Enhances Napkins
飾	decorate: 食 (food) + 人 (*person*) + 巾 (cloth) + SHOw Kolors Uncommon
罰	punishment: 罒 (net) + 言 (words) + 刂 (cut) + Brought ATtendant Sanctions Upon
幣	money: 巾 (cloth) + ㇒< (pieces) + 攵 (strike) + 巾 (cloth) + Honored Exchange Instrument
錦	brocade: 金 (gold) + 白 (white) + 巾 (cloth) + Kolorfully INterwoven

Day six: character clusters

I Complete the characters using the clues.

1	自	Students Head Influence (SHI)
2	巾	Just Ordinary One (JOO)
3	長	Catalogue HOnored Officially (CHOO)
4	白	Material Enhances Napkins (MEN)
5	辶	Transmit Each Item (TEI)

II Compose the compounds using the clues.

1 (SA) 差   +   (BETSU) _____   =   _____ (discrimination)
    difference

2 (HOO) 包   +   (TAI) _____   =   _____ (bandage)
    wrap

3 (KOS) _____   +   (SETSU) 折   =   _____ (fracture)
                   break

4 (JI) 字   +   (MAKU) _____   =   _____ (captions)
    character

5 (YU) _____   +   (KAI) 快   =   _____ (pleasure)
                   pleasant

III Complete the sentences using the clues.

1 みんなすべての___望を失ったらしい。
Minna subete no KIboo o ushinatta rashii.
It seems that everyone has lost all hope.

2 エミリーは素敵な___子をかぶっている。
Emirii wa suteki na BOOshi o kabutte iru.
Emily is wearing a nice hat.

3 なぜ先週学校を欠___しましたか。
Naze senshuu gakkoo o kesSEKI shimashita ka.
Why were you absent from school last week?

4 スピード違反の___金は一万円です。
Supiido ihan no BAKkin wa ichiman-en desu.
The fine for speeding is ten thousand yen.

5 トロントはカナダで一番大きな都___だ。
Toronto wa kanada de ichiban ookina toSHI da.
Toronto is the largest city in Canada.

45

BOWS AND ARROWS

Day one: crossword puzzle

Across

4. Great Incredulity
5. Kurved Yielding Upraised Unloader
7. Kurve Open
9. Making Immense (I)
12. Directly Attacks Nemesis (P)
15. Invigorates (M)
16. Uplifters
18. WAtery Nook
20. TAll Not
21. Just AKt Unstable

Down

1. Induce Near
2. Korrect YOur Order (S)
3. Condolences HOnor One (M)
6. Cord HOld Outwards (S)
8. Guitar ENtanglement (S)
10. Zone Of Kin Union
11. Comprehension Hits Instantly
13. King's Official Overseer
14. TOfu Origin
17. Kan YOke Oxen
19. SHoot It

Day two: acrostics

1   Pull: I _ _ _ _ _   N _ _ _

2   Straighten: K _ _ _ _ _ _   Y O _ _   O _ _ _ _

3   Mourn: C _ _ _ _ _ _ _ _ _   H O _ _ _   O _ _

4   Doubt: G _ _ _ _   I _ _ _ _ _ _ _ _ _

5   Bow: K _ _ _ _ _   Y _ _ _ _ _ _ _   U _ _ _ _ _ _ _   U _ _ _ _ _ _ _

6   Stretch: C _ _ _   H O _ _   O _ _ _ _ _ _ _

7   Arc: K _ _ _ _   O _ _ _

8   String: G _ _ _ _ _   E N _ _ _ _ _ _ _ _ _ _

9   Increasingly: M _ _ _ _ _   I _ _ _ _ _ _

10   Family: Z _ _ _   O _   K _ _   U _ _ _ _

11   Know: C _ _ _ _ _ _ _ _ _ _ _   H _ _ _   I _ _ _ _ _ _ _ _

12   Projectile: D _ _ _ _ _ _ _   A _ _ _ _ _ _   N _ _ _ _ _ _

13   Lord: K _ _ _ _   O _ _ _ _ _ _ _   O _ _ _ _ _ _

14   Bean: T O _ _   O _ _ _ _ _

15   Medicine: I _ _ _ _ _ _ _ _ _

16   Wings: U _ _ _ _ _ _ _ _

17   Strong: K _ _   Y O _ _   O _ _ _

18   Bay: W A _ _ _ _   N _ _ _

19   Arrow: S H _ _ _   I _

20   Short: T A _ _   N _ _

21   Weak: J _ _ _   A K _   U _ _ _ _ _ _ _

Day three: componential analysis

Course Number	Kanji	ON Reading(s) / Core Concept(s)	Primary Components	Kanji Canvas
0925	弓	KYUU / **bow**	Bow without string	弓
0926	引	IN / **pull**	弓 (bow)^{925} + | (string)^{K69}	引
0927	弔	CHOO / **mourn**	弓 (bow)^{925} + | (string)^{K69}	弔
0928	矢	SHI / **arrow**	ノ (accent)^{K2} + 天 (heaven)^{261}	矢
0929	医	I / **medicine**	匚 (container)^{K48} + 矢 (arrow)^{928}	医
0930	弦	GEN / **string**	弓 (bow)^{925} + 玄 (obscure)^{495}	弦
0931	弧	KO / **arc**	弓 (bow)^{925} + *melon* (cf. 1789)	弧
0932	弥	MI / **increasingly**	弓 (bow)^{925} + ノ (accent)^{K2} + 丁 (exact)^{87} + 八 (*eight*)^{04}	弥
0933	知	CHI / **know**	矢 (arrow)^{928} + 口 (mouth)^{106}	知
0934	侯	KOO / **lord; marquis**	亻 (person)^{K16} + *target* + 矢 (arrow)^{928}	侯
0935	羽	U / **wings, feathers**	Pair of flapping wings	羽
0936	弱	JAKU / **weak**	弓 (two bows)^{925} + 羽 (two wings)^{935}	弱
0937	強	KYOO, GOO / **strong**	弓 (bow)^{925} + 厶 (self)^{K18} + 虫 (insect)^{869}	強
0938	張	CHOO / **stretch**	弓 (bow)^{925} + 長 (long)^{402}	張
0939	族	ZOKU / **family, clan**	方 (direction)^{174} + 人 (*person*)^{64} + 矢 (arrow)^{928}	族
0940	弾	DAN / **projectile; spring**	弓 (bow)^{925} + 単 (single)^{486}	弾
0941	湾	WAN / **bay**	氵 (water)^{K6} + 亦 (again)^{K77} + 弓 (bow)^{925}	湾
0942	豆	TOO / **bean; miniature**	Food container on stand	豆
0943	短	TAN / **short**	矢 (arrow)^{928} + 豆 (bean)^{942}	短
0944	疑	GI / **doubt**	匕 (sitting)^{K17} + 矢 (arrow)^{928} + マ (bent arm)^{K85} + 疋 (correct)^{166}	疑
0945	矯	KYOO / **straighten**	矢 (arrow)^{928} + 天 (heaven)^{261} + 高 (*high*)^{586}	矯

Day four: writing practice

弓	引	弔	矢	医	弦	弧
弓	引	弔	矢	医	弦	弧

弥	知	侯	羽	弱	強	張
弥	知	侯	羽	弱	強	張

族	弾	湾	豆	短	疑	矯
族	弾	湾	豆	短	疑	矯

Day five: story sketch

弓	bow: (bow without string) + Kurved Yielding Upraised Unloader
引	pull: 弓 (bow) + | (string) + Induce Near
弔	mourn: 弓 (bow) + | (string) + Condolences HOnor One
矢	arrow: ⼃ (accent) + 天 (heaven) + SHoot It
医	medicine: 匚 (container) + 矢 (arrow) + Invigorates
弦	string: 弓 (bow) + 玄 (obscure) + Guitar ENtanglement
弧	arc: 弓 (bow) + *melon* + Kurve Open
弥	increasingly: 弓 (bow) + ⼃ (accent) + 丁 (exact) + 八 (*eight*) + Making Immense
知	know: 矢 (arrow) + 口 (mouth) + Comprehension Hits Instantly
侯	lord: 亻 (person) + *target* + 矢 (arrow) + King's Official Overseer
羽	wings: (pair of flapping wings) + Uplifters
弱	weak: 弓 (two bows) + 羽 (two wings) + Just AKt Unstable
強	strong: 弓 (bow) + 厶 (self) + 虫 (insect) + Kan YOke Oxen
張	stretch: 弓 (bow) + 長 (long) + Cord HOld Outwards
族	family: 方 (direction) + 人 (*person*) + 矢 (arrow) + Zone Of Kin Union
弾	projectile: 弓 (bow) + 単 (single) + Directly Attacks Nemesis
湾	bay: 氵 (water) + 亦 (again) + 弓 (bow) + WAtery Nook
豆	bean: (food container on stand) + TOfu Origin
短	short: 矢 (arrow) + 豆 (bean) + TAll Not
疑	doubt: 匕 (sitting) + 矢 (arrow) + ⼇ (bent arm) + 疋 (correct) + Great Incredulity
矯	straighten: 矢 (arrow) + 天 (heaven) + 高 (*high*) + Korrect YOur Order

Day six: character clusters

I Complete the characters using the clues.

1	氵	WAtery Nook (WAN)
2	亻	King's Official Overseer (KOO)
3	弓	Condolences HOnor One (CHOO)
4	天	Korrect YOur Order (KYOO)
5	匚	Invigorating (I)

II Compose the compounds using the clues.

1 (SHU) 主　　　　　+　　　(CHOO) ____　　　=　　　_____ (insistence)
　　　master

2 (KYUU) ____　　　+　　　(JUTSU) 術　　　=　　　_____ (archery)
　　　　　　　　　　　　　　　　technique

3 (TAN) ____　　　　+　　　(KI) 期　　　　=　　　_____ (short term)
　　　　　　　　　　　　　　　period

4 (BAKU) 爆　　　　+　　　(DAN) ____　　　=　　　_____ (bomb)
　　　explode

5 (JAKU) ____　　　+　　　(TEN) 点　　　=　　　_____ (shortcoming)
　　　　　　　　　　　　　　　point

III Complete the sentences using the clues.

1 国を出るように＿＿制されました。
   Kuni o deru yoo ni KYOOsei saremashita.
   I was forced to leave the country.

2 ご家＿＿はどこに住んでいますか。
   Go-kaZOKU wa doko ni sunde imasu ka.
   Where does your family live?

3 この言葉はシェークスピアからの＿＿用です。
   Kono kotoba wa sheekusupia kara no INyoo desu.
   These words are a quotation from Shakespeare.

4 リンダが成功するかどうか＿＿問に思う。
   Rinda ga seikoo suru ka doo ka GImon ni omou.
   I doubt whether Linda will succeed.

5 教授はアフリカについて広い＿＿識がある。
   Kyooju wa afurika ni tsuite hiroi CHIshiki ga aru.
   The professor has extensive knowledge of Africa.

REVIEW: LESSONS 41–45

I   Given the character and meaning, write the pronunciation.

1 戻 return_____   2 狂 mad _____   3 麦 wheat_____

4 骨 bone _____   5 弔 mourn _____   6 誇 boast _____

7 嗅 smell _____   8 礁 reef _____   9 幣 money _____

10 疑 doubt _____   11 泰 calm _____   12 献 offer_____

13 碁 go _____   14 幅 width _____   15 湾 bay _____

16 奈 how _____   17 猶 delay _____   18 硝 niter_____

19 帯 belt _____   20 弧 arc _____   21 俺 me _____

22 黙 silent _____   23 焦 scorch _____   24 帆 sail _____

25 弦 string _____   26 参 visit_____   27 狙 aim _____

28 砂 sand_____   29 逓 relay_____   30 侯 lord _____

II   Given the character and pronunciation, write the meaning.

1 県 KEN _____   2 伏 FUKU _____   3 硫 RYUU _____

4 帥 SUI _____   5 張 CHOO _____   6 奨 SHOO _____

7 稽 KEI _____   8 礎 SO _____   9 愉 YU _____

10 豆 TOO _____   11 爽 SOO_____   12 狭 KYOO_____

13 碑 HI _____   14 幕 MAKU _____   15 羽 U _____

16 契 KEI _____   17 就 SHUU _____   18 希 KI _____

19 綿 MEN _____   20 弥 MI _____   21 短 TAN_____

22 奉 HOO _____   23 隙 GEKI _____   24 猿 EN _____

25 錦 KIN_____   26 弓 KYUU _____   27 奥 OO _____

28 帳 CHOO _____   29 席 SEKI _____   30 矯 KYOO_____

III   Given the meaning and pronunciation, write the character.

1	odor	SHUU	_____	2	condition	JOO	_____
3	crush	SAI	_____	4	nest	SOO	_____
5	commander	SHOO	_____	6	hit	TOO	_____
7	insect	CHUU	_____	8	reclaim	TAKU	_____
9	separate	BETSU	_____	10	pull	IN	_____
11	weak	JAKU	_____	12	prison	GOKU	_____
13	city	SHI	_____	14	know	CHI	_____
15	fat	TAI	_____	16	crime	HAN	_____
17	jealous	TO	_____	18	hat	BOO	_____
19	certain	KAKU	_____	20	family	ZOKU	_____
21	cat	BYOO	_____	22	arrow	SHI	_____
23	winter	TOO	_____	24	normal	JOO	_____
25	decorate	SHOKU	_____				

IV   Compose compounds using the following characters.

狩 砲 奏 医 猟 強 罰 磁 独 硬 突 師 猛 器 破 磨 獣 研 処 弾

1 (I) _____   +   (SHI) _____   =   _____ (doctor)

2 (MOO) _____   +   (JUU) _____   =   _____ (wild animal)

3 (JI) _____   +   (KI) _____   =   _____ (porcelain)

4 (KYOO) _____   +   (KOO) _____   =   _____ (strong, firm)

5 (SHU) _____   +   (RYOO) _____   =   _____ (hunting)

6 (TOP) _____   +   (PA) _____   =   _____ (breakthrough)

7 (DOKU) _____   +   (SOO) _____   =   _____ (solo)

8 (SHO) _____   +   (BATSU) _____   =   _____ (punishment)

9 (HOO) _____   +   (DAN) _____   =   _____ (shell)

10 (KEN) _____   +   (MA) _____   =   _____ (grind)

46

BAMBOO SHOOTS

Day one: crossword puzzle

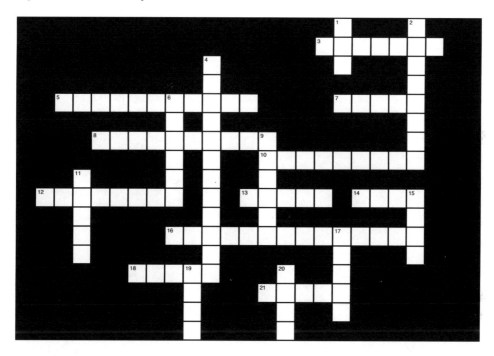

Across

3. Kontain ANother
5. Sum Amount Numerated (C)
7. Stationery ENtity
8. HAndy Sticks Help Ingestion
10. SOmething KUrrent
12. Tubular Object Ordinarily
13. Kontact Area Nowhere
14. Komponent Alone (I)
16. The Eldest's Inferior (two words: Y/B)
18. SHOw Overjoy
21. Tubular Euphonic Key Instrument

Down

1. HAuling KOntainer (B)
2. Some Extreme Temperament SUppressed (M)
4. HIstorically The Scribe's Utensil (two words: W/B)
6. Talk Opposite Other
9. Koncise ANswer
11. Types Often Organized (C)
15. Figure Usually
17. Degrees Arranged In
19. Main Opening North
20. Strategic Aim Karefully Undertaken

Day two: acrostics

1   Box: H A _ _ _ _ _ _   K O _ _ _ _ _ _ _ _

2   Moderate: S _ _ _   E _ _ _ _ _ _ _   T _ _ _ _ _ _ _ _ _ _ _   S U _ _ _ _ _ _ _ _

3   Control: K _ _ _ _ _ _ _   A N _ _ _ _ _ _

4   Writing Brush: H I _ _ _ _ _ _ _ _ _ _   T _ _   S _ _ _ _ _ _   U _ _ _ _ _ _

5   Calculation: S _ _   A _ _ _ _ _ _   N _ _ _ _ _ _ _ _

6   Answer: T _ _ _ _   O _ _ _ _ _ _ _   O _ _ _ _

7   Paper: S _ _ _ _ _ _ _ _ _   E N _ _ _ _

8   Chopsticks: H A _ _ _   S _ _ _ _ _ _   H _ _ _   I _ _ _ _ _ _ _ _

9   Simple: K _ _ _ _ _ _ _   A N _ _ _ _

10   Immediate: S O _ _ _ _ _ _ _   K U _ _ _ _ _

11   Class: T _ _ _ _   O _ _ _ _   O _ _ _ _ _ _ _ _

12   Cylinder: T _ _ _ _ _ _   O _ _ _ _ _   O _ _ _ _ _ _ _ _ _

13   Space: K _ _ _ _ _ _ _   A _ _ _   N _ _ _ _ _ _

14   Item: K _ _ _ _ _ _ _ _   A _ _ _ _

15   Mark: F _ _ _ _ _ _   U _ _ _ _ _ _

16   Younger Brother: T _ _   E _ _ _ _ _ _ _   I _ _ _ _ _ _ _

17   Order: D _ _ _ _ _ _   A _ _ _ _ _ _ _ _   I _

18   Laugh: S H O _   O _ _ _ _ _ _

19   Gate: M _ _ _   O _ _ _ _ _ _   N _ _ _ _

20   Plan: S _ _ _ _ _ _ _ _   A _ _   K _ _ _ _ _ _ _ _   U _ _ _ _ _ _ _ _ _

21   Flute: T _ _ _ _ _ _   E _ _ _ _ _ _ _   K _ _   I _ _ _ _ _ _ _ _ _

Day three: componential analysis

Course Number	Kanji	ON Reading(s) / Core Concept(s)	Primary Components	Kanji Canvas
0946	笑	SHOO **laugh, smile**	⺮ (bamboo)[K74] + 天 (heaven)[261]	笑
0947	符	FU **mark; tally**	⺮ (bamboo)[K74] + 付 (attach)[69]	符
0948	笛	TEKI **flute**	⺮ (bamboo)[K74] + 由 (reason)[39]	笛
0949	筆	HITSU **writing brush**	⺮ (bamboo)[K74] + ヨ (open hand)[K54] + 聿 (brush)[K86]	筆
0950	等	TOO **class; equal**	⺮ (bamboo)[K74] + 寺 (temple)[171]	等
0951	答	TOO **answer**	⺮ (bamboo)[K74] + 合 (fit)[118]	答
0952	策	SAKU **plan, policy**	⺮ (bamboo)[K74] + *tree with broken branches* (cf. 555)	策
0953	筒	TOO **cylinder**	⺮ (bamboo)[K74] + 同 (same)[119]	筒
0954	弟	TEI, DAI **younger brother**	弓 (bow)[925] + *broken arrow*	弟
0955	第	DAI **order; ordinal prefix**	⺮ (bamboo)[K74] + 弟 (younger brother)[954]	第
0956	即	SOKU **immediate**	良 (*good*)[398] + 卩 (bowing)[K57]	即
0957	節	SETSU **moderate; season**	⺮ (bamboo)[K74] + 即 (immediate)[956]	節
0958	管	KAN **control; pipe**	⺮ (bamboo)[K74] + 官 (government)[327]	管
0959	算	SAN **calculation**	⺮ (bamboo)[K74] + 目 (eye)[62] + 廾 (two hands)[K3]	算
0960	箇	KA **item; item counter**	⺮ (bamboo)[K74] + 固 (hard)[461]	箇
0961	箋	SEN **paper**	⺮ (bamboo)[K74] + 戈 (two spears)[K20]	箋
0962	箸	hashi **chopsticks**	⺮ (bamboo)[K74] + 者 (person)[152]	箸
0963	箱	hako **box**	⺮ (bamboo)[K74] + 相 (mutual)[63]	箱
0964	門	MON **gate**	Two doors	門
0965	間	KAN **space, interval**	門 (gate)[964] + 日 (sun)[17]	間
0966	簡	KAN **simple, brief**	⺮ (bamboo)[K74] + 間 (space)[965]	簡

Day four: writing practice

笑	符	笛	筆	等	答	策
笑	符	笛	筆	等	答	策
筒	弟	第	即	節	管	算
筒	弟	第	即	節	管	算
箇	箋	箸	箱	門	間	簡
箇	箋	箸	箱	門	間	簡

Day five: story sketch

笑	laugh: ⺮ (bamboo) + 天 (heaven) + SHOw Overjoy
符	mark: ⺮ (bamboo) + 付 (attach) + Figure Usually
笛	flute: ⺮ (bamboo) + 由 (reason) + Tubular Euphonic Key Instrument
筆	writing brush: ⺮ (bamboo) + 彐 (open hand) + 丰 (brush) + HIstorically The Scribe's Utensil
等	class: ⺮ (bamboo) + 寺 (temple) + Types Often Organized
答	answer: ⺮ (bamboo) + 合 (fit) + Talk Opposite Other
策	plan: ⺮ (bamboo) + *tree with broken branches* + Strategic Aim Karefully Undertaken
筒	cylinder: ⺮ (bamboo) + 同 (same) + Tubular Object Ordinarily
弟	younger brother: 弓 (bow) + *broken arrow* + The Eldest's Inferior
第	order: ⺮ (bamboo) + 弟 (younger brother) + Degrees Arranged In
即	immediate: 良 (*good*) + 卩 (bowing) + SOmething KUrrent
節	moderate: ⺮ (bamboo) + 即 (immediate) + Some Extreme Temperament SUppressed
管	control: ⺮ (bamboo) + 官 (government) + Kontain ANother
算	calculation: ⺮ (bamboo) + 目 (eye) + 廾 (two hands) + Sum Amount Numerated
箇	item: ⺮ (bamboo) + 固 (hard) + Komponent Alone
箋	paper: ⺮ (bamboo) + 戈 (two spears) + Stationery ENtity
箸	chopsticks: ⺮ (bamboo) + 者 (person) + HAndy Sticks Help Ingestion
箱	box: ⺮ (bamboo) + 相 (mutual) + HAuling KOntainer
門	gate: (two doors) + Main Opening North
間	space: 門 (gate) + 日 (sun) + Kontact Area Nowhere
簡	simple: ⺮ (bamboo) + 間 (space) + Koncise ANswer

Day six: character clusters

I Complete the characters using the clues.

1	⺮	Figure Usually (FU)
2	阝	SOmething KUrrent (SOKU)
3	⺮	Types Often Organized (TOO)
4	弓	The Eldest's Inferior (TEI)
5	⺮	HAuling KOntainer (HAKO)

II Compose the compounds using the clues.

1 (REI) 冷   +   (SHOO) ____   =   _____ (sneer)
    cold

2 (KA) ____   +   (SHO) 所   =   _____ (place)
                      place

3 (EN) 鉛   +   (PITSU) ____   =   _____ (pencil)
    lead

4 (KI) 期   +   (KAN) ____   =   _____ (period, term)
    period

5 (DAI) ____   +   (ICHI) 一   =   _____ (first)
                        one

III Complete the sentences using the clues.

1 政府はインフレ対___をとるべきだ。
Seifu wa infure taiSAKU o toru beki da.
The government should take measures against inflation.

2 ロバートは電気工学を専___にしている。
Robaato wa denki-koogaku o senMON ni shite iru.
Robert specializes in electrical engineering.

3 旅行の予___が足りないと思う。
Ryokoo no yoSAN ga tarinai to omou.
I think that the budget for the trip is not enough.

4 誰がその工場を___理していますか。
Dare ga sono koojoo o KANri shite imasu ka.
Who manages that factory?

5 封___に切手を貼らなければならない。
FuuTOO ni kitte o haranakereba naranai.
You must put a stamp on the envelope.

47

HEAD START

Day one: crossword puzzle

Across

1. Koncise Amount (F)
4. Gained Earliest Name (O)
8. Kant Evidently Indicates
9. Habitual INterval (F)
13. Designates Area Interest
15. Rules You Order Others
16. Yen Order
18. TOp Of
20. Should Use
21. Just UNinterrupted (O)

Down

2. Hike Onward
3. Hand Apportions Number
5. Great Aspiration Now (W)
6. Respectfully Attempt Inquiry
7. Great Adamant Nature (S)
10. KOncerning Recent Occasion
11. Terrible Outburst Now
12. Have ANxiety
14. HOllow Oval (C)
17. KOmponent One
19. Crest High Over One

Day two: acrostics

1 Few: K _ _ _ _ _ _   A _ _ _ _ _

2 Walk: H _ _ _   O _ _ _ _ _

3 Distribute: H _ _ _   A _ _ _ _ _ _ _ _ _   N _ _ _ _ _

4 Original: G _ _ _ _ _   E _ _ _ _ _ _ _   N _ _ _

5 Wish: G _ _ _ _   A _ _ _ _ _ _ _ _   N _ _

6 Request: R _ _ _ _ _ _ _ _ _   A _ _ _ _ _ _   I _ _ _ _ _ _

7 Stubborn: G _ _ _ _   A _ _ _ _ _ _   N _ _ _ _ _

8 Incline: K _ _ _   E _ _ _ _ _ _ _ _   I _ _ _ _ _ _ _ _

9 Frequently: H _ _ _ _ _ _ _   I N _ _ _ _ _ _

10 Time: K O _ _ _ _ _ _ _   R _ _ _ _ _   O _ _ _ _ _ _ _

11 Sudden: T _ _ _ _ _ _ _   O _ _ _ _ _ _ _   N _ _

12 Worry: H _ _ _   A N _ _ _ _ _

13 Subject: D _ _ _ _ _ _ _ _ _   A _ _ _   I _ _ _ _ _ _ _

14 Cheek: H O _ _ _ _   O _ _ _

15 Govern: R _ _ _ _   Y _ _   O _ _ _ _   O _ _ _ _ _

16 Deposit: Y _ _   O _ _ _ _

17 Item: K O _ _ _ _ _ _ _   O _ _

18 Head: T O _   O _

19 Top: C _ _ _ _   H _ _ _   O _ _ _   O _ _

20 Essential: S _ _ _ _ _ _   U _ _

21 Order: J _ _ _   U N _ _ _ _ _ _ _ _ _ _ _

Day three: componential analysis

Course Number	Kanji	ON Reading(s) / Core Concept(s)	Primary Components	Kanji Canvas
0967	頂	CHOO **top; receive**	丁 (exact)[87] + 頁 (head)[K87]	頂
0968	頃	koro **time; about**	匕 (sitting)[K17] + 頁 (head)[K87]	頃
0969	順	JUN **order, sequence**	川 (river)[198] + 頁 (head)[K87]	順
0970	項	KOO **item, clause**	工 (work)[26] + 頁 (head)[K87]	項
0971	須	SU **essential**	彡 (pattern)[K12] + 頁 (head)[K87]	須
0972	預	YO **deposit**	予 (prior)[822] + 頁 (head)[K87]	預
0973	傾	KEI **incline**	亻 (person)[K16] + 匕 (sitting)[K17] + 頁 (head)[K87]	傾
0974	煩	HAN **worry, trouble**	火 (fire)[421] + 頁 (head)[K87]	煩
0975	頒	HAN **distribute**	分 (divide)[219] + 頁 (head)[K87]	頒
0976	頑	GAN **stubborn**	元 (origin)[322] + 頁 (head)[K87]	頑
0977	頓	TON **sudden**	屯 (encampment)[223] + 頁 (head)[K87]	頓
0978	領	RYOO **govern; territory**	令 (order)[380] + 頁 (head)[K87]	領
0979	寡	KA **few; widow**	宀 (roof)[K51] + 頁 (head)[K87] + 力 (power)[07]	寡
0980	頬	hoo **cheek**	来 (between)[K75] + 頁 (head)[K87]	頬
0981	頭	TOO, ZU **head**	豆 (bean)[942] + 頁 (head)[K87]	頭
0982	頼	RAI **request; rely**	束 (bundle)[271] + 頁 (head)[K87]	頼
0983	歩	HO **walk, step**	止 (stop)[165] + 少 (few)[32]	歩
0984	頻	HIN **frequently**	歩 (walk)[983] + 頁 (head)[K87]	頻
0985	題	DAI **subject, title**	是 (right)[167] + 頁 (head)[K87]	題
0986	原	GEN **original**	厂 (cliff)[K14] + 白 (white)[18] + 小 (small)[31]	原
0987	願	GAN **wish; request**	原 (original)[986] + 頁 (head)[K87]	願

Day four: writing practice

頂	頃	順	項	須	預	傾
頂	頃	順	項	須	預	傾
煩	頒	頑	頓	領	寡	頮
煩	頒	頑	頓	領	寡	頮
頭	賴	步	頻	題	原	願
頭	賴	步	頻	題	原	願

Day five: story sketch

頂	top: 丁 (exact) + 頁 (head) + Crest High Over One
頃	time: 匕 (sitting) + 頁 (head) + KOncerning Recent Occasion
順	order: 川 (river) + 頁 (head) + Just UNinterrupted
項	item: 工 (work) + 頁 (head) + KOmponent One
須	essential: 彡 (pattern) + 頁 (head) + Should Use
預	deposit: 予 (prior) + 頁 (head) + Yen Order
傾	incline: 亻 (person) + 匕 (sitting) + 頁 (head) + Kant Evidently Indicates
煩	worry: 火 (fire) + 頁 (head) + Have ANxiety
頒	distribute: 分 (divide) + 頁 (head) + Hand Apportions Number
頑	stubborn: 元 (origin) + 頁 (head) + Great Adamant Nature
頓	sudden: 屯 (encampment) + 頁 (head) + Terrible Outburst Now
領	govern: 令 (order) + 頁 (head) + Rules You Order Others
寡	few: 宀 (roof) + 頁 (head) + 力 (power) + Koncise Amount
頬	cheek: 来 (between) + 頁 (head) + HOllow Oval
頭	head: 豆 (bean) + 頁 (head) + TOp Of
頼	request: 束 (bundle) + 頁 (head) + Respectfully Attempt Inquiry
歩	walk: 止 (stop) + 少 (few) + Hike Onward
頻	frequently: 歩 (walk) + 頁 (head) + Habitual INterval
題	subject: 是 (right) + 頁 (head) + Designates Area Interest
原	original: 厂 (cliff) + 白 (white) + 小 (small) + Gained Earliest Name
願	wish: 原 (original) + 頁 (head) + Great Aspiration Now

Day six: character clusters

I Complete the characters using the clues.

1	頁	Great Adamant Nature (GAN)
2	彡	Should Use (SU)
3	宀	Koncise Amount (KA)
4	分	Hand Apportions Number (HAN)
5	頁	KOmponent One (KOO)

II Compose the compounds using the clues.

1 (SAN) 山   + (CHOO) ____   = _____ (summit)
    mountain

2 (ZU) ____   + (TSUU) 痛   = _____ (headache)
                pain

3 (GEN) ____   + (SOKU) 則   = _____ (principle)
                rule

4 (I) 依   + (RAI) ____   = _____ (request)
    depend

5 (YO) ____   + (KIN) 金   = _____ (deposit)
                money

III Complete the sentences using the clues.

1 この都市はロシア軍が占＿＿している。
Kono toshi wa roshia-gun ga senRYOO shite iru.
The Russian army is occupying this city.

2 朝食のあとで犬を散＿＿させる。
Chooshoku no ato de inu o sanPO saseru.
After breakfast I walk the dog.

3 医者はすべての患者を＿＿番に診察した。
Isha wa subete no kanja o JUNban ni shinsatsu shita.
The doctor examined all the patients in turn.

4 今日の宿＿＿を終えたところです。
Kyoo no shukuDAI o oeta tokoro desu.
I have just finished today's homework.

5 祖父は寝過ぎる＿＿向がある。
Sofu wa ne-sugiru KEIkoo ga aru.
My grandfather tends to sleep too much.

48

WOODWORK

Day one: crossword puzzle

Across

3. ENcircled
5. Shaft Undulates Upon
6. Just INquire
9. Below Optimal Output (I)
10. KOnstruct One
15. KArefree Notion (L)
16. Style Has Ideal KInd (C)
17. Second Additional Instance
18. Klouds Unwind Under
19. Konnects You Over Obstacles
20. SHadow INward (D)
21. SHines ITs SUrface (L)

Down

1. Korpse Abode Normally
2. Konstructed Across (S)
4. Kolor Orbit Observed
7. KOmpetent Operation
8. Separate Amount (D)
11. Key Assistance Instrument
12. Holds Alcohol Inside
13. Krumbling Yields Utter Uselessness
14. Skillfully Oversee Operation

Day two: acrostics

1 Coffin: K _ _ _ _ _ _   A _ _ _ _   N _ _ _ _ _ _ _

2 Span: K _ _ _ _ _ _ _ _ _   A _ _ _ _ _

3 Round: E N _ _ _ _ _ _ _

4 Rainbow: K _ _ _ _   O _ _ _ _   O _ _ _ _ _ _ _

5 Pivot: S _ _ _ _   U _ _ _ _ _ _ _ _   U _ _ _

6 Ask: J _ _ _   I N _ _ _ _ _ _

7 Skill: K O _ _ _ _ _ _ _   O _ _ _ _ _ _ _ _

8 Difference: S _ _ _ _ _ _ _   A _ _ _ _ _

9 Insufficient: B _ _ _ _   O _ _ _ _ _ _   O _ _ _ _ _

10 Build: K O _ _ _ _ _ _ _   O _ _

11 Device: K _ _   A _ _ _ _ _ _ _ _ _   I _ _ _ _ _ _ _ _

12 Cup: H _ _ _ _   A _ _ _ _ _ _   I _ _ _ _ _

13 Decay: K _ _ _ _ _ _ _ _   Y _ _ _ _ _   U _ _ _ _   U _ _ _ _ _ _ _ _ _

14 Handle: S _ _ _ _ _ _ _ _   O _ _ _ _ _ _   O _ _ _ _ _ _ _ _

15 Leisure: K A _ _ _ _ _ _   N _ _ _ _ _

16 Ceremony: S _ _ _ _   H _ _   I _ _ _ _   K I _ _

17 Again: S _ _ _ _ _ _   A _ _ _ _ _ _ _ _ _   I _ _ _ _ _ _ _

18 Sky: K _ _ _ _ _   U _ _ _ _ _   U _ _ _ _

19 Bridge: K _ _ _ _ _ _ _   Y _ _   O _ _ _   O _ _ _ _ _ _ _ _

20 Deep: S H _ _ _ _   I N _ _ _ _

21 Lacquer: S H _ _ _ _   I T _   S U _ _ _ _ _

Day three: componential analysis

Course Number	Kanji	ON Reading(s) / Core Concept(s)	Primary Components	Kanji Canvas
0988	乏	BOO / **insufficient**	工 (work)[26] + 人 (*person*)[64]	乏
0989	巧	KOO / **skill**	工 (work)[26] + 丂 (emerge)[K28]	巧
0990	式	SHIKI / **ceremony**	工 (work)[26] + 弋 (stake)[K19]	式
0991	朽	KYUU / **decay**	木 (wood)[43] + 丂 (emerge)[K28]	朽
0992	空	KUU / **sky**	穴 (hole)[316] + 工 (work)[26]	空
0993	杯	HAI / **cup**	木 (wood)[43] + 不 (not)[723]	杯
0994	枢	SUU / **pivot**	木 (wood)[43] + 区 (ward)[303]	枢
0995	虹	KOO / **rainbow**	虫 (insect)[869] + 工 (work)[26]	虹
0996	架	KA / **span**	加 (add)[111] + 木 (wood)[43]	架
0997	差	SA / **difference**	羊 (sheep)[794] + 工 (work)[26]	差
0998	械	KAI / **device**	木 (wood)[43] + 戒 (warn)[802]	械
0999	深	SHIN / **deep**	氵 (water)[K6] + 穴 (*hole*)[316] + 木 (wood)[43]	深
1000	尋	JIN / **ask, seek**	ヨ (open hand)[K54] + 工 (work)[26] + 口 (mouth)[106] + 寸 (measure)[11]	尋
1001	閑	KAN / **leisure; quiet**	門 (gate)[964] + 木 (wood)[43]	閑
1002	棺	KAN / **coffin**	木 (wood)[43] + 官 (government)[327]	棺
1003	円	EN / **round; yen**	冂 (border)[K27] + *seal*	円
1004	再	SAI / **again; twice**	工 (work)[26] + 円 (round)[1003]	再
1005	構	KOO / **build**	木 (wood)[43] + 冓 (accumulate)[K88]	構
1006	漆	SHITSU / **lacquer**	氵 (water)[K6] + 木 (wood)[43] + 𠆢 (cover)[K26] + 水 (water)[22]	漆
1007	橋	KYOO / **bridge**	木 (wood)[43] + 夭 (heaven)[261] + 高 (*tall*)[586]	橋
1008	操	SOO / **handle**	扌 (hand)[K21] + 品 (goods)[126] + 木 (wood)[43]	操

Day four: writing practice

乏	巧	式	朽	空	杯	枢
乏	巧	式	朽	空	杯	枢
虹	架	差	械	深	尋	閑
虹	架	差	械	深	尋	閑
棺	円	再	構	漆	橋	操
棺	円	再	構	漆	橋	操

Day five: story sketch

乏	insufficient: 工 (work) + 人 (*person*) + Below Optimal Output
巧	skill: 工 (work) + 丂 (emerge) + KOmpetent Operation
式	ceremony: 工 (work) + 弋 (stake) + Style Has Ideal KInd
朽	decay: 木 (wood) + 丂 (emerge) + Krumbling Yields Utter Uselessness
空	sky: 穴 (hole) + 工 (work) + Klouds Unwind Under
杯	cup: 木 (wood) + 不 (not) + Holds Alcohol Inside
枢	pivot: 木 (wood) + 区 (ward) + Shaft Undulates Upon
虹	rainbow: 虫 (insect) + 工 (work) + Kolor Orbit Observed
架	span: 加 (add) + 木 (wood) + Konstructed Across
差	difference: 羊 (sheep) + 工 (work) + Separate Amount
械	device: 木 (wood) + 戒 (warn) + Key Assistance Instrument
深	deep: 氵 (water) + 穴 (*hole*) + 木 (wood) + SHadow INward
尋	ask: ヨ (open hand) + 工 (work) + 口 (mouth) + 寸 (measure) + Just INquire
閑	leisure: 門 (gate) + 木 (wood) + KArefree Notion
棺	coffin: 木 (wood) + 官 (government) + Korpse Abode Normally
円	round: 冂 (border) + *seal* + ENcircled
再	again: 工 (work) + 円 (round) + Second Additional Instance
構	build: 木 (wood) + 冓 (accumulate) + KOnstruct One
漆	lacquer: 氵 (water) + 木 (wood) + 𠆢 (cover) + 水 (water) + SHines ITs SUrface
橋	bridge: 木 (wood) + 夭 (heaven) + 高 (*tall*) + Konnects You Over Obstacles
操	handle: 扌 (hand) + 品 (goods) + 木 (wood) + Skillfully Oversee Operation

Day six: character clusters

I   Complete the characters using the clues.

1	氵	SHines ITs SUrface (SHITSU)
2	木	Shaft Undulates Upon (SUU)
3	ヨ	Just INquire (JIN)
4	木	Holds Alcohol Inside (HAI)
5	虫	Kolor Orbit Observed (KOO)

II   Compose the compounds using the clues.

1   (KI) 機   +   (KAI) ____   =   _____ (machine)
      machine

2   (BIN) 貧   +   (BOO) ____   =   _____ (poverty)
      poor

3   (KOO) ____   +   (SEI) 成   =   _____ (composition)
                              form

4   (TAI) 体   +   (SOO) ____   =   _____ (gymnastics)
      body

5   (TAN) 担   +   (KA) ____   =   _____ (stretcher)
      bear

III   Complete the sentences using the clues.

1   その会社は何年も女性を___別した。
    Sono kaisha wa nannen mo josei o SAbetsu shita.
    That company discriminated against women for many years.

2   左のタイヤに___気を入れて下さい。
    Hidari no taiya ni KUUki o irete kudasai.
    Please put some air in the left tire.

3   娘にお箸の正___な使い方を教えた。
    Musume ni o-hashi no seiSHIKI na tsukaikata o oshieta.
    I taught my daughter the proper way to use chopsticks.

4   試合は雨がやんだ後に___開されます。
    Shiai wa ame ga yanda ato ni SAIkai saremasu.
    The game will resume after the rain stops.

5   イエメンの水不足がずいぶん___刻です。
    Iemen no mizu-busoku ga zuibun SHINkoku desu.
    Yemen's water shortage is very serious.

49

ALTAR BOYS

Day one: crossword puzzle

Across

5. Kreator Invoke
6. Kandle Offers One
7. Standard Age Interval
9. Handwritten YOur Option (V)
13. Sanctify Absolute Intent (P)
14. Juvenile Individual
16. BOdy Outline
17. FUnds Kome Upon
19. KAlamity
21. Zazen ENlightens

Down

1. Sell Happily Obtain Other (T)
2. Ranked Entirely Inferior (S)
3. Society Honors Unusual KUstom (C)
4. Sufficient Happiness Implies
8. Sign HOnors Opulence
10. REspect Indicator (G)
11. Sire Older (A)
12. Spirit Holy INcarnate
15. Stare Has Intent
18. BArgain Item
20. Keen Eyes Notify

Day two: acrostics

1 Trade: S _ _ _   H _ _ _ _ _ _   O _ _ _ _ _   O _ _ _ _

2 Subordinate: R _ _ _ _ _   E _ _ _ _ _ _ _   I _ _ _ _ _ _ _

3 Celebrate: S _ _ _ _ _ _   H _ _ _ _ _   U _ _ _ _ _ _   K U _ _ _ _

4 Wellbeing: S _ _ _ _ _ _ _ _   H _ _ _ _ _ _ _ _   I _ _ _ _ _ _

5 Pray: K _ _ _ _ _ _   I _ _ _ _ _

6 Light: K _ _ _ _ _   O _ _ _ _ _   O _ _

7 Year: S _ _ _ _ _ _ _   A _ _   I _ _ _ _ _ _ _

8 Auspicious: S _ _ _   H O _ _ _ _   O _ _ _ _ _ _ _

9 Vote: H _ _ _ _ _ _ _ _ _ _   Y O _ _   O _ _ _ _ _

10 Gratitude: R E _ _ _ _ _   I _ _ _ _ _ _ _ _

11 Ancestor: S _ _ _   O _ _ _ _

12 God: S _ _ _ _ _   H _ _ _   I N _ _ _ _ _ _ _

13 Purification: S _ _ _ _ _ _ _   A _ _ _ _ _ _ _   I _ _ _ _ _

14 Child: J _ _ _ _ _ _ _   I _ _ _ _ _ _ _ _ _

15 Look: S _ _ _ _   H _ _   I _ _ _ _ _

16 Form: B O _ _   O _ _ _ _ _ _

17 Fortune: F U _ _ _   K _ _ _   U _ _ _

18 Sell: B A _ _ _ _ _   I _ _ _

19 Disaster: K A _ _ _ _ _ _

20 See: K _ _ _   E _ _ _   N _ _ _ _ _

21 Zen: Z _ _ _ _   E N _ _ _ _ _ _ _ _

Day three: componential analysis

Course Number	Kanji	ON Reading(s) Core Concept(s)	Primary Components	Kanji Canvas
1009	礼	REI **gratitude; propriety**	礻 (altar)^{K34} + 乚 (kneeling)^{K9}	礼
1010	光	KOO **light**	⺌ (small)^{K44} + 一 (one)^{01} + 儿 (boy)^{K5}	光
1011	売	BAI **sell**	士 (samurai)^{67} + 冖 (cover)^{K26} + 儿 (boy)^{K5}	売
1012	児	JI **child**	旧 (old)^{536} + 儿 (boy)^{K5}	児
1013	祈	KI **pray**	礻 (altar)^{K34} + 斤 (ax)^{55}	祈
1014	祉	SHI **wellbeing**	礻 (altar)^{K34} + 止 (stop)^{165}	祉
1015	神	SHIN **god**	礻 (altar)^{K34} + 申 (state)^{230}	神
1016	祖	SO **ancestor**	礻 (altar)^{K34} + 且 (moreover)^{331}	祖
1017	祝	SHUKU **celebrate**	礻 (altar)^{K34} + 兄 (older brother)^{117}	祝
1018	商	SHOO **trade**	亠 (top)^{K1} + 儿 (boy)^{K5} + 冂 (border)^{K27} + 口 (mouth)^{106}	商
1019	祥	SHOO **auspicious**	礻 (altar)^{K34} + 羊 (sheep)^{794}	祥
1020	票	HYOO **vote**	西 (west)^{354} + 示 (altar)^{176}	票
1021	見	KEN **see, look**	目 (eye)^{62} + 儿 (boy)^{K5}	見
1022	視	SHI **look, regard**	礻 (altar)^{K34} + 見 (see)^{1021}	視
1023	斎	SAI **purification**	斉 (equal)^{561} + 示 (altar)^{176}	斎
1024	福	FUKU **fortune**	礻 (altar)^{K34} + 畐 (full)^{K72}	福
1025	禅	ZEN **Zen**	礻 (altar)^{K34} + 単 (single)^{486}	禅
1026	歳	SAI **year**	止 (stop)^{165} + 示 (altar)^{176} + 戈 (spear)^{K20}	歳
1027	禍	KA **disaster**	礻 (altar)^{K34} + 咼 (excessive)^{K89}	禍
1028	貌	BOO **form**	豸 (beast)^{K90} + 白 (white)^{18} + 儿 (boy)^{K5}	貌
1029	隷	REI **inferior**	士 (samurai)^{67} + 示 (altar)^{176} + ヨ (open hand)^{K54} + ⼁ (tool)^{K80} + 水 (water)^{22}	隷

Day four: writing practice

礼	光	売	児	祈	祉	神
礼	光	売	児	祈	祉	神
祖	祝	商	祥	票	見	視
祖	祝	商	祥	票	見	視
斎	福	禅	歳	禍	貌	隷
斎	福	禅	歳	禍	貌	隷

Day five: story sketch

礼	gratitude: ネ (altar) + 乚 (kneeling) + REspect Indicator
光	light: ⺌ (small) + 一 (one) + 儿 (boy) + Kandle Offers One
売	sell: 士 (samurai) + 冖 (cover) + 儿 (boy) + BArgain Item
児	child: 旧 (old) + 儿 (boy) + Juvenile Individual
祈	pray: ネ (altar) + 斤 (ax) + Kreator Invoke
祉	wellbeing: ネ (altar) + 止 (stop) + Sufficient Happiness Implies
神	god: ネ (altar) + 申 (state) + Spirit Holy INcarnate
祖	ancestor: ネ (altar) + 且 (moreover) + Sire Older
祝	celebrate: ネ (altar) + 兄 (older brother) + Society Honors Unusual KUstom
商	trade: 亠 (top) + 儿 (boy) + 冂 (border) + 口 (mouth) + Sell Happily Obtain Other
祥	auspicious: ネ (altar) + 羊 (sheep) + Sign HOnors Opulence
票	vote: 西 (west) + 示 (altar) + Handwritten YOur Option
見	see: 目 (eye) + 儿 (boy) + Keen Eyes Notify
視	look: ネ (altar) + 見 (see) + Stare Has Intent
斎	purification: 斉 (equal) + 示 (altar) + Sanctify Absolute Intent
福	fortune: ネ (altar) + 畐 (full) + FUnds Kome Upon
禅	Zen: ネ (altar) + 単 (single) + Zazen ENlightens
歳	year: 止 (stop) + 示 (altar) + 戈 (spear) + Standard Age Interval
禍	disaster: ネ (altar) + 咼 (excessive) + KAlamity
貌	form: 豸 (beast) + 白 (white) + 儿 (boy) + BOdy Outline
隷	subordinate: 士 (samurai) + 示 (altar) + ヨ (open hand) + 丨 (tool) + 水 (water) + Ranked Entirely Inferior

Day six: character clusters

I   Complete the characters using the clues.

1	儿	Keen Eyes Notify (KEN)
2	ネ	Sufficient Happiness Implies (SHI)
3	豸	BOdy Outline (BOO)
4	ネ	Society Honors Unusual KUstom (SHUKU)
5	止	Standard Age Interval (SAI)

II   Compose the compounds using the clues.

1   (KOO) 幸   +   (FUKU) ____   =   _____ (happiness)
        happiness

2   (SHIN) ____   +   (WA) 話   =   _____ (myth)
                               speech

3   (YOO) 幼   +   (JI) ____   =   _____ (infant)
       infant

4   (SO) ____   +   (FU) 父   =   _____ (grandfather)
                           father

5   (TOO) 投   +   (HYOO) ____   =   _____ (vote)
     throw

III   Complete the sentences using the clues.

1   叔父さんはダイヤモンド＿＿人だ。
     Oji-san wa daiyamondo SHOOnin da.
     My uncle is a diamond merchant.

2   ハワイへ観＿＿に出かける。
     Hawai e kanKOO ni dekakeru.
     I'm going to Hawaii for sightseeing.

3   新しいテレビゲームは明日発＿＿されます。
     Atarashii terebi-geemu wa ashita hatsuBAI saremasu.
     The new video game will go on sale tomorrow.

4   パイロットの＿＿力は良くなければいけない。
     Pairotto no SHIryoku wa yoku nakereba ikenai.
     Pilots must have good eyesight.

5   彼女は誰に対しても＿＿儀正しい。
     Kanojo wa dare ni tai shite mo REIgi tadashii.
     She is polite to everyone.

50

ANYTHING GOES

Day one: crossword puzzle

Across

- 2. Subdue Enemy Instantly (C)
- 6. Glorifies One
- 8. Connotes Hidden Obscure Order (S)
- 11. Build Indistinct
- 12. Initiate Kareful Upbringing
- 15. To Enter The SUrface
- 16. Jog Ongoing (S)
- 19. Overall Retail Order Sells Huge Inventory
- 21. JUst Next

Down

- 1. Strike Hard Oncoming Object
- 3. Onward Objective
- 4. Trails Others
- 5. TOward Konduct Upright (V)
- 7. Gaining On (A)
- 9. Take Ownership KUrrently
- 10. Kharacter Expresses TAlly (D)
- 13. Joust UNder
- 14. JUnior Urged (F)
- 17. Rule ITself SUpreme
- 18. To Anticipate Inactively
- 20. Him Identified

Day two: acrostics

1 Collide: S _ _ _ _ _   H _ _ _   O _ _ _ _ _ _ _   O _ _ _ _ _

2 Conquer: S _ _ _ _ _   E _ _ _ _   I _ _ _ _ _ _ _ _

3 Go: O _ _ _ _ _   O _ _ _ _ _ _ _ _

4 Follower: T _ _ _ _ _   O _ _ _ _ _

5 Virtue: T O _ _ _ _   K _ _ _ _ _ _   U _ _ _ _ _ _

6 Honorific: G _ _ _ _ _ _ _   O _ _

7 After: G _ _ _ _ _ _   O _

8 Sign: C _ _ _ _ _ _ _   H _ _ _ _ _   O _ _ _ _ _ _   O _ _ _ _

9 Gain: T _ _ _   O _ _ _ _ _ _ _ _   K U _ _ _ _ _ _ _

10 Digit: K _ _ _ _ _ _ _ _   E _ _ _ _ _ _ _ _   T A _ _ _

11 Minute: B _ _ _ _   I _ _ _ _ _ _ _ _ _

12 Raise: I _ _ _ _ _ _ _   K _ _ _ _ _ _   U _ _ _ _ _ _ _ _

13 Shield: J _ _ _ _   U N _ _ _

14 Follow: J U _ _ _ _   U _ _ _ _

15 Through: T _   E _ _ _ _   T _ _   S U _ _ _ _ _

16 Slowly: J _ _   O _ _ _ _ _ _

17 Law: R _ _ _   I T _ _ _ _   S U _ _ _ _ _

18 Wait: T _   A _ _ _ _ _ _ _ _ _   I _ _ _ _ _ _ _ _

19 Wholesale: O _ _ _ _ _ _   R _ _ _ _ _   O _ _ _ _   S _ _ _ _   H _ _ _   I _ _ _ _ _ _ _ _

20 He: H _ _   I _ _ _ _ _ _ _ _

21 Follow: J U _ _   N _ _ _

Day three: componential analysis

Course Number	**Kanji**	ON Reading(s) Core Concept(s)	Primary Components	Kanji Canvas
1030	往	OO **go**	彳 (go)[K47] + 主 (master)[642]	往
1031	征	SEI **conquer; subjugate**	彳 (go)[K47] + 正 (correct)[166]	征
1032	彼	HI **he**	彳 (go)[K47] + 皮 (skin)[409]	彼
1033	後	GO, KOO **after, behind**	彳 (go)[K47] + 幺 (short thread)[K64] + 夂 (step)[K13]	後
1034	律	RITSU **law**	彳 (go)[K47] + ヨ (open hand)[K54] + ⺺ (brush)[K86]	律
1035	待	TAI **wait**	彳 (go)[K47] + 寺 (temple)[171]	待
1036	従	JUU **follow**	彳 (go)[K47] + 丷 (away)[K35] + 正 (correct)[166]	従
1037	徒	TO **follower**	彳 (go)[K47] + 走 (run)[179]	徒
1038	徐	JO **slowly**	彳 (go)[K47] + 余 (excess)[386]	徐
1039	桁	keta **digit**	木 (tree)[43] + 行 (go)[297]	桁
1040	得	TOKU **gain**	彳 (go)[K47] + 日 (day)[17] + 一 (one)[01] + 寸 (measure)[11]	得
1041	卸	oroshi **wholesale**	牛 (*cow*)[75] + 止 (stop)[165] + 卩 (bowing)[K57]	卸
1042	御	GO, GYO **honorific; control**	彳 (go)[K47] + 卸 (wholesale)[1041]	御
1043	盾	JUN **shield**	厂 (cliff)[K14] + 十 (ten)[06] + 目 (eye)[62]	盾
1044	循	JUN **follow**	彳 (go)[K47] + 盾 (shield)[1043]	循
1045	微	BI **minute**	彳 (go)[K47] + 山 (mountain)[71] + 一 (one)[01] + 儿 (*boy*)[K5] + 攵 (strike)[K46]	微
1046	徳	TOKU **virtue**	彳 (go)[K47] + 罒 (view)[K91] + 心 (heart)[127]	徳
1047	徴	CHOO **sign; summon**	彳 (go)[K47] + 山 (mountain)[71] + 王 (king)[155] + 攵 (strike)[K46]	徴
1048	衝	SHOO **collide**	行 (go)[297] + 重 (heavy)[607]	衝
1049	育	IKU **raise**	亠 (top)[K1] + 厶 (self)[K18] + 月 (body)[K43]	育
1050	徹	TETSU **through**	彳 (go)[K47] + 育 (raise)[1049] + 攵 (strike)[K46]	徹

Day four: writing practice

往	征	彼	後	律	待	從
往	征	彼	後	律	待	從
徒	徐	桁	得	卸	御	盾
徒	徐	桁	得	卸	御	盾
循	微	德	徵	衝	育	徹
循	微	德	徵	衝	育	徹

Day five: story sketch

往	go: 彳 (go) + 主 (master) + Onward Objective
征	conquer: 彳 (go) + 正 (correct) + Subdue Enemy Instantly
彼	he: 彳 (go) + 皮 (skin) + Him Identified
後	after: 彳 (go) + 幺 (short thread) + 夂 (step) + Gaining On
律	law: 彳 (go) + ヨ (open hand) + ⺀ (brush) + Rule ITself SUpreme
待	wait: 彳 (go) + 寺 (temple) + To Anticipate Inactively
從	follow: 彳 (go) + ⺀ (away) + 正 (correct) + JUnior Urged
徒	follower: 彳 (go) + 走 (run) + Trails Others
徐	slowly: 彳 (go) + 余 (excess) + Jog Ongoing
桁	digit: 木 (tree) + 行 (go) + Kharacter Expresses TAlly
得	gain: 彳 (go) + 日 (day) + 一 (one) + 寸 (measure) + Take Ownership KUrrently
卸	wholesale: 牛 (*cow*) + 止 (stop) + 卩 (bowing) + Overall Retail Order Sells Huge Inventory
御	honorific: 彳 (go) + 卸 (wholesale) + Glorifies One
盾	shield: 厂 (cliff) + 十 (ten) + 目 (eye) + Joust UNder
循	follow: 彳 (go) + 盾 (shield) + JUst Next
微	minute: 彳 (go) + 山 (mountain) + 一 (one) + 几 (*boy*) + 夊 (strike) + Build Indistinct
德	virtue: 彳 (go) + 𠃌 (view) + 心 (heart) + TOward Konduct Upright
徴	sign: 彳 (go) + 山 (mountain) + 王 (king) + 夊 (strike) + Connotes Hidden Obscure Order
衝	collide: 行 (go) + 重 (heavy) + Strike Hard Oncoming Object
育	raise: ⼇ (top) + 厶 (self) + 月 (body) + Initiate Kareful Upbringing
徹	through: 彳 (go) + 育 (raise) + 夊 (strike) + To Enter The SUrface

Day six: character clusters

I   Complete the characters using the clues.

1	亻	Take Ownership KUrrently (TOKU)
2	山	Build Indistinct (BI)
3	育	To Enter The SUrface (TETSU)
4	山	Connotes Hidden Obscure Order (CHOO)
5	亻	Him Identified (HI)

II   Compose the compounds using the clues.

1   (SEI) 生   +   (TO) ＿＿＿   =   ＿＿＿＿＿＿ (student)
    life

2   (MU) 矛   +   (JUN) ＿＿＿   =   ＿＿＿＿＿＿ (contradiction)
    spear

3   (SEI) ＿＿＿   +   (FUKU) 服   =   ＿＿＿＿＿＿ (conquest)
                         obey

4   (DOO) 道   +   (TOKU) ＿＿＿   =   ＿＿＿＿＿＿ (morality)
    way

5   (SAI) 最   +   (GO) ＿＿＿   =   ＿＿＿＿＿＿ (last, end)
    most

III   Complete the sentences using the clues.

1   このホテルは期＿＿＿していたよりずっといい。
    Kono hoteru wa kiTAI shite ita yori zutto ii.
    This hotel is much better than I had expected.

2   バイクがトラックに＿＿＿突された。
    Baiku ga torakku ni SHOOtotsu sareta.
    The motorcycle was hit by a truck.

3   病院の中での喫煙を禁止する法＿＿＿がある。
    Byooin no naka de no kitsuen o kinshi suru hooRITSU ga aru.
    There is a law against smoking in hospitals.

4   公立学校で良い教＿＿＿を受けました。
    Kooritsu gakko de yoi kyooIKU o ukemashita.
    I received a good education in public school.

5   ナイロビまでの＿＿＿復切符はいくらですか。
    Nairobi made no OOfuku kippu wa ikura desu ka.
    How much is a round-trip ticket to Nairobi?

REVIEW: LESSONS 46–50

I   Given the character and meaning, write the pronunciation.

1 符 mark _____   2 寡 few _____   3 朽 decay_____

4 票 vote _____   5 後 after _____   6 箱 box _____

7 頃 time _____   8 構 build _____   9 貌 form _____

10 徴 sign _____   11 第 order _____   12 煩 worry _____

13 尋 ask _____   14 視 look_____   15 得 gain_____

16 策 plan _____   17 領 govern _____   18 枢 pivot _____

19 歳 year _____   20 徳 virtue _____   21 箇 item_____

22 願 wish _____   23 円 round _____   24 神 god _____

25 律 law _____   26 等 class_____   27 頬 cheek _____

28 深 deep_____   29 祈 pray_____   30 従 follow _____

II   Given the character and pronunciation, write the meaning.

1 算 SAN _____   2 須 SU _____   3 乏 BOO _____

4 祥 SHOO _____   5 征 SEI _____   6 簡 KAN _____

7 頻 HIN _____   8 械 KAI _____   9 斎 SAI _____

10 徐 JO _____   11 箋 SEN _____   12 傾 KEI _____

13 差 SA _____   14 禍 KA _____   15 御 GO _____

16 弟 TEI _____   17 頓 TON _____   18 項 KOO _____

19 隷 REI _____   20 循 JUN _____   21 筒 TOO _____

22 頑 GAN _____ 23 桁 keta _____ 24 頒 HAN _____

25 衝 SHOO _____ 26 待 TAI _____ 27 棺 KAN _____

28 題 DAI _____ 29 頼 RAI _____ 30 微 BI _____

III Given the meaning and pronunciation, write the character.

1 control	KAN	_____	2 head	TOO	_____
3 rainbow	KOO	_____	4 chopsticks	hashi	_____
5 wholesale	oroshi	_____	6 laugh	SHOO	_____
7 ceremony	SHIKI	_____	8 lacquer	SHITSU	_____
9 gratitude	REI	_____	10 shield	JUN	_____
11 see	KEN	_____	12 original	GEN	_____
13 again	SAI	_____	14 ancestor	SO	_____
15 he	HI	_____	16 gate	MON	_____
17 top	CHOO	_____	18 skill	KOO	_____
19 through	TETSU	_____	20 flute	TEKI	_____
21 deposit	YO	_____	22 Zen	ZEN	_____
23 go	OO	_____	24 leisure	KAN	_____
25 light	KOO	_____			

IV Compose compounds using the following characters.

節 歩 架 間 順 売 杯 筆 福 児 即 橋 答 祉 徒 祝 空 操 商 育

1 (KUU) _____ + (KAN) _____ = _____ (space)

2 (TO) _____ + (HO) _____ = _____ (on foot)

3 (FUKU) _____ + (SHI) _____ = _____ (welfare)

4 (IKU) _____ + (JI) _____ = _____ (child care)

5 (SOKU) _____ + (TOO) _____ = _____ (prompt reply)

6 (SHUKU) _____ + (HAI) _____ = _____ (toast)

7 (SES) _____ + (SOO) _____ = _____ (integrity)

8 (SHOO) _____ + (BAI) _____ = _____ (business)

9 (HITSU) _____ + (JUN) _____ = _____ (stroke order)

10 (KA) _____ + (KYOO) _____ = _____ (bridge-building)

51
VEHICLE INSPECTION

Day one: crossword puzzle

Across
2. Joins Into Kar Undercarriage
6. Gets Enemy KIlled
7. Zealot ANnihilates
11. Kollects Objects
13. Konveys Edifice Number (two words: B/C)
16. His Associate Is
17. Rotation INvention
18. Twist ENtirely

Down
1. Not Adamant Nature (S)
3. Relation ENhances (L)
4. Kourse Indication (T)
5. Joint INstallation (E)
8. Karries Easily Itself
9. Kontain ATtack SUccessfully
10. Yonder Unload (T)
12. GUards Nation
14. Konsider AKin Unit
15. Have As Norm (M)

Day two: acrostics

1 Soft: N _ _   A _ _ _ _ _ _   N _ _ _ _ _

2 Axle: J _ _ _ _   I _ _ _   K _ _   U _ _ _ _ _ _ _ _ _ _

3 Link: R _ _ _ _ _ _ _   E N _ _ _ _ _ _

4 Track: K _ _ _ _ _   I _ _ _ _ _ _ _ _

5 Encampment: J _ _ _ _   I N _ _ _ _ _ _ _ _ _

6 Attack: G _ _ _   E _ _ _ _   K I _ _ _ _

7 Kill: Z _ _ _ _ _   A N _ _ _ _ _ _ _ _

8 Light: K _ _ _ _ _ _   E _ _ _ _ _   I _ _ _ _ _

9 Control: K _ _ _ _ _ _   A T _ _ _ _   S U _ _ _ _ _ _ _ _ _

10 Transport: Y _ _ _ _ _   U _ _ _ _ _

11 Storehouse: K _ _ _ _ _ _ _   O _ _ _ _ _ _

12 Military: G U _ _ _ _   N _ _ _ _ _

13 Building Counter: K _ _ _ _ _ _   E _ _ _ _ _ _   N _ _ _ _ _

14 Compare: K _ _ _ _ _ _ _   A K _ _   U _ _ _

15 Model: H _ _ _   A _   N _ _ _

16 Fellow: H _ _   A _ _ _ _ _ _ _ _   I _

17 Wheel: R _ _ _ _ _ _ _   I N _ _ _ _ _ _

18 Turn: T _ _ _ _   E N _ _ _ _ _ _

Day three: componential analysis

Course Number	Kanji	ON Reading(s) / Core Concept(s)	Primary Components	Kanji Canvas
1051	軍	GUN / **military**	冖 (cover)[K26] + 車 (vehicle)[524]	軍
1052	軌	KI / **track**	車 (vehicle)[524] + 九 (nine)[05]	軌
1053	連	REN / **link; consecutive**	辶 (move)[K41] + 車 (vehicle)[524]	連
1054	庫	KO / **storehouse**	广 (building)[K24] + 車 (vehicle)[524]	庫
1055	軒	KEN / **building counter**	車 (vehicle)[524] + 干 (dry)[24]	軒
1056	陣	JIN / **encampment**	阝 (hill)[K68] + 車 (vehicle)[524]	陣
1057	転	TEN / **turn**	車 (vehicle)[524] + 二 (two)[02] + 厶 (self)[K18]	転
1058	軟	NAN / **soft**	車 (vehicle)[524] + 欠 (lack)[427]	軟
1059	斬	ZAN / **kill, cut down**	車 (vehicle)[524] + 斤 (ax)[55]	斬
1060	軽	KEI / **light**	車 (vehicle)[524] + 又 (again)[57] + 土 (ground)[169]	軽
1061	軸	JIKU / **axle; axis**	車 (vehicle)[524] + 由 (reason)[39]	軸
1062	較	KAKU / **compare**	車 (vehicle)[524] + 交 (exchange)[596]	較
1063	輪	RIN / **wheel**	車 (vehicle)[524] + 侖 (align)[K92]	輪
1064	範	HAN / **model; limit**	⺮ (bamboo)[K74] + 車 (vehicle)[524] + 㔾 (slumped)[K8]	範
1065	撃	GEKI / **attack**	車 (vehicle)[524] + 殳 (club)[K23] + 手 (hand)[85]	撃
1066	輩	HAI / **fellow**	非 (wrong)[692] + 車 (vehicle)[524]	輩
1067	輸	YU / **transport**	車 (vehicle)[524] + 亼 (*cover*)[K26] + 月 (meat)[K43] + 刂 (cut)[K36]	輸
1068	轄	KATSU / **control**	車 (vehicle)[524] + 害 (harm)[336]	轄

Day four: writing practice

軍	軌	連		庫	軒	陣
軍	軌	連		庫	軒	陣
転	軟	斬		軽	軸	較
転	軟	斬		軽	軸	較
輪	範	撃		輩	輸	轄
輪	範	撃		輩	輸	轄

Day five: story sketch

軍	military: 冖 (cover) + 車 (vehicle) + GUards Nation
軌	track: 車 (vehicle) + 九 (nine) + Kourse Indication
連	link: 辶 (move) + 車 (vehicle) + Relation ENhances
庫	storehouse: 广 (building) + 車 (vehicle) + Kollects Objects
軒	building counter: 車 (vehicle) + 干 (dry) + Konveys Edifice Number
陣	encampment: 阝 (hill) + 車 (vehicle) + Joint INstallation
転	turn: 車 (vehicle) + 二 (two) + ム (self) + Twist ENtirely
軟	soft: 車 (vehicle) + 欠 (lack) + Not Adamant Nature
斬	kill: 車 (vehicle) + 斤 (ax) + Zealot ANnihilates
軽	light: 車 (vehicle) + 又 (again) + 土 (ground) + Karries Easily Itself
軸	axle: 車 (vehicle) + 由 (reason) + Joins Into Kar Undercarriage
較	compare: 車 (vehicle) + 交 (exchange) + Konsider AKin Unit
輪	wheel: 車 (vehicle) + 侖 (align) + Rotation INvention
範	model: ⺮ (bamboo) + 車 (vehicle) + 巳 (slumped) + Have As Norm
撃	attack: 車 (vehicle) + 殳 (club) + 手 (hand) + Gets Enemy KIlled
輩	fellow: 非 (wrong) + 車 (vehicle) + His Associate Is
輸	transport: 車 (vehicle) + 𠆢 (*cover*) + 月 (meat) + 刂 (cut) + Yonder Unload
轄	control: 車 (vehicle) + 害 (harm) + Kontain ATtack SUccessfully

Day six: character clusters

I Complete the characters using the clues.

1	車	Rotation INvention (RIN)
2	阝	Joint INstallation (JIN)
3	車	Zealot ANnihilates (ZAN)
4	手	Gets Enemy KIlled (GEKI)
5	車	Not Adamant Nature (NAN)

II Compose the compounds using the clues.

1 (ZAI) 在   +   (KO) ____   =   _____ (stock)
      be, reside

2 (HAN) ____   +   (I) 囲   =   _____ (range, scope)
                       surround

3 (KI) ____   +   (DOO) 道   =   _____ (orbit)
                       way

4 (KAI) 海   +   (GUN) ____   =   _____ (navy)
    sea

5 (KEI) ____   +   (SOTSU) 率   =   _____ (imprudence)
                       command

III Complete the sentences using the clues.

1 父はエレベーターの運＿＿の仕方が分かります。
Chichi wa erebeetaa no unTEN no shikata ga wakarimasu.
My father knows how to operate an elevator.

2 原画と複製では比＿＿にならない。
Genga to fukusei de wa hiKAKU ni naranai.
The reproduction cannot be compared to the original picture.

3 家族とメールで＿＿絡を取れる。
Kazoku to meeru de RENraku o toreru.
I am able to contact my family by email.

4 中井さんは三年先＿＿です。
Nakai-san wa sannen senPAI desu.
Mr. Nakai is senior to me by three years.

5 グアテマラは多くの国にコーヒーを＿＿出している。
Guatemara wa ooku no kuni ni koohii o YUshutsu shite iru.
Guatemala exports coffee to many countries.

Appendixes

APPENDIX 1

Kanji components

Components are comprised mostly of elements that do not appear as stand-alone characters. These include conventional radicals or determinatives and graphemic constituents or composites that have been devised for this book. Also included in this list are several Japanese non-general use characters and some that occur exclusively in Chinese.

K1: Top/ Lid 亠 (*cover with handle*)

0014	0045	0134	0239	0314	0455	0492	0495	0509	0518	0596
0725	0893	0904	1018	1049						

K2: Accent/ Emphasis (Very) ✓ ＼ (*mark indicates prominence*)

0016	0018	0023	0052	0120	0197	0203	0264	0265	0314	0318
0344	0435	0438	0514	0575	0642	0670	0674	0747	0827	0841
0857	0928	0932								

K3: Two Hands 廾 (*joined together in prayer*)

0016	0510	0802	0959							

K4: Enclosure 囗 (*area sealed off with barrier*)

0020	0356	0461	0579	0652					

K5: Boy 儿 (*short legs of person*)

0020	0117	0322	0436	0455	0519	0538	0539	0650	0835	1010
1011	1012	1018	1021	1028	1045				

K6: Water 氵 (*three drops*)

0025	0027	0028	0029	0030	0033	0034	0035	0036	0038	0040
0042	0299	0522	0631	0632	0633	0634	0635	0636	0637	0638
0639	0641	0643	0645	0646	0647	0648	0649	0651	0772	0788
0797	0804	0815	0941	0999	1006				

K7: Serpent 也 (*twisted body and long tail*)

0029	0070	0778							

K8: Slumped 巳 (*seated with upper body bent forward*)

0030	0862	1064							

K9: Kneeling ∟ (*side view of person kneeling*)

0046	1009								

K10: Divination 卜 (*rod pointed toward ground*)

0047	0112	0194	0361							

K11: Table 几 (*side view of table*)

0048	0276	0379	0747	0883						

K12: Pattern/Delicate 彡 (*three strands of hair*)

0049	0844	0971								

K13: Step 夂 (*leg extended forward*)

0050	0122	0530	0539	0542	0625	0770	0883	0884	0885	1033

K14: Cliff 厂 (*side view of cliff*)

0058	0170	0423	0595	0611	0614	0788	0913	0986	1043	

K15: (Right) Hand 又 (*thumb touching four fingers*)

0058	0079	0338	0390	0409	0463	0464	0465	0466	0467	0468
0469	0470	0471	0473	0475	0476	0477	0478	0479	0480	0481
0483	0776									

K16: Person 亻 (*side view of person leaning forward*)

0065	0066	0068	0069	0070	0072	0073	0074	0076	0078	0080
0081	0082	0084	0191	0390	0403	0609	0658	0673	0674	0675

0676	0677	0678	0679	0680	0682	0684	0685	0686	0687	0690
0691	0693	0781	0853	0863	0934	0973				

K17: Sitting 匕 (*with arms and legs stretched out*)

0065	0113	0150	0387	0532	0644	0881	0944	0968	0973	

K18: Self 厶 (*forefinger pointed toward forehead*)

0066	0086	0101	0114	0173	0205	0237	0383	0455	0541	0568
0640	0676	0681	0844	0893	0937	1049	1057			

K19: Stake 弋 (*planted firmly in the ground*)

0073	0990									

K20: Spear 戈 (*sharp blade unsheathed*)

0081	0247	0523	0525	0800	0801	0802	0803	0804	0805	0807
0808	0810	0811	0812	0813	0814	0815	0816	0818	0819	0961
1026										

K21: (Left) Hand 扌 (*making peace sign*)

0086	0088	0089	0090	0091	0092	0093	0095	0096	0098	0100
0102	0103	0104	0105	0172	0478	0694	0695	0696	0697	0698
0699	0700	0701	0702	0704	0705	0706	0707	0709	0711	0712

0713	0714	0729	0764	0785	0886	1008				

K22: Flat/ Straight 兀 (*top of table*)

0092	0180									

K23: Club 殳 (*blunt object in right hand*)

0096	0202	0283	0298	0299	0304	0305	0306	0310	0312	1065

K24: Building 广 (*side view of roof and outer wall*)

0101	0129	0433	0476	0783	0820	0821	0823	0824	0825	0826
0828	0829	0830	0832	0833	0834	0836	0838	0840	0909	1054

K25: Wrap/ Cover 勹 (*strip of adhesive tape*)

0110	0703	0757	0780							

K26: Cover 宀 ᐱ (*hard and soft variants*)

0118	0139	0379	0380	0382	0383	0384	0385	0386	0387	0388
0389	0390	0391	0392	0393	0394	0396	0399	0413	0467	0502
0910	0918	1006	1011	1051	1067					

K27: Border 冂 (*lines demarcate territory*)

0119	0120	0182	0225	0513	0610	0613	0728	1003	1018	

K28: Emerge 丂 (*floating weed on water surface*)

0121	0381	0631	0860	0989	0991					

K29: Plants ⺿ (*two sprouts*)

0131	0232	0235	0236	0237	0238	0239	0241	0242	0243	0244
0245	0246	0247	0248	0250	0251	0252	0411	0436	0469	0499
0519	0579	0602	0734	0765	0791					

K30: Corner └ ┐ (*two sides meet*)

0134	0139	0512	0848							

K31: Heart 忄 (*lines on an electrocardiogram*)

0136	0143	0145	0468	0736	0738	0742	0743	0746	0749	0752
0918										

K32: Old Man 耂 (*bending toward ground*)

0152										

K33: Grain 禾 (*leafy stalk*)

0163	0429	0549	0563	0568	0569	0570	0571	0572	0573	0574
0575	0576	0577	0578	0579	0581	0582	0584	0585	0587	0588
0881										

K34: Altar 礻 (*elaborate table with offering on top*)

0177	1009	1013	1014	1015	1016	1017	1019	1022	1024	1025
1027										

K35: Split/ Away/ Out 丶丿 (*lines of separation or division*)

0183	0207	0262	0267	0289	0294	0457	0493	0498	0513	0582
0603	0613	0742	0793	0876	1036					

K36: Cut 刂 (*sharp edge of knife*)

0185	0289	0359	0415	0547	0548	0549	0550	0551	0552	0553
0554	0555	0556	0557	0558	0559	0560	0562	0564	0565	0566
0567	0908	0918	0922	1067						

K37: Raised 圭 (*ground placed upon ground*)

0187	0781	0788	0790							

K38: Fork 丩 (*two prongs*)

0214	0466	0719								

K39: Measure 勺 (*interval mark on tape measure*)

0216										

K40: Side 丬 (*object split in half*)

0249	0858	0864								

K41: Move 辶 辵 辶 (*zigzagging trail*)

0253	0255	0256	0257	0258	0259	0260	0262	0263	0264	0266
0267	0268	0270	0272	0273	0795	0827	0913	1053		

K42: Measured Bow 卩 (*forefinger and thumb indicate bow*)

0260	0695									

K43: Meat/ Flesh/ Body 月 (*cut of marbled beef*)

0275	0276	0277	0278	0279	0280	0281	0282	0283	0285	0286
0287	0288	0289	0291	0292	0293	0294	0439	0470	0481	0599
0603	0606	0626	1049	1067						

K44: Small ⺌ (*tips of three fingers*)

0277	0728	0842	1010							

K45: Spiral Pattern 巴 (*winds around a central point*)

0282										

K46: Strike 攵 (*with stick in right hand*)

0295	0296	0300	0301	0302	0307	0308	0309	0313	0315	0368
0809	0923	1045	1047	1050						

K47: Go 彳 (*one person after another*)

0298	0471	0770	1030	1031	1032	1033	1034	1035	1036	1037

1038	1040	1042	1044	1045	1046	1047	1050			

K48: Container ∟ ⊔ (*cross-sectional view*)

0303	0857	0929								

K49: Mark/ Indicator/ Here ╳ (*cross-shaped symbol marks the spot*)

0303	0310	0547	0551	0854	0906					

K50: Illness 疒 (*building with outer wall crumbling*)

0305										

K51: Roof 宀 (*cover of building*)

0316	0317	0318	0319	0321	0323	0324	0325	0326	0327	0328
0330	0332	0333	0334	0335	0336	0340	0376	0629	0763	0979

K52: Buttocks 𦣻 (*overhead view of plump rump*)

0327	0511	0911	0912							

K53: Claw ⺥ (*sharp pointed fingers*)

0349	0467	0585	0655	0858						

K54: Open Hand 彐 (*extended fingers*)

0353	0390	0453	0739	0829	0830	0832	0839	0842	0949	1000
1029	1034									

K55: Bending ⸌ (*downward angle*)

0360	0537	0739							

K56: Net 罒 (*wire mesh*)

0373	0922								

K57: Bowing 卩 (*hands on thighs with torso bent*)

0380	0470	0956	1041						

K58: Clothes 衤 (*long wide sleeves and sash of kimono*)

0400	0408	0410	0414	0419	0420				

K59: Bent Body 尸 (*upper body bent forward*)

0411	0418	0553	0644	0793					

K60: Disintegrate 歹 (*flesh falling off bone*)

0415									

K61: Fire ⺣ (*flames from gas jets*)

0430	0432	0433	0434	0435	0437	0439	0880	0901	

K62: Twenty 廿 (*ten plus ten*)

0433	0476	0505	0909						

K63: Ornate ⿱ (*design adorns crown*)

0486	0710	0855	0872	0882					

K64: Short Thread 幺 (*strands from skein*)

0495	0518	0590	0620	0813	0819	1033				

K65: Platform 丌 (*stool with two legs*)

0499	0515	0710								

K66: Pieces/ Parts/ Marks 乂 (*four distinct ones*)

0518	0792	0923								

K67: Bird 隹 (*beak and plumage*)

0522	0901									

K68: Hill 阝 (*sloping mound*)

0526	0527	0528	0529	0530	0531	0533	0534	0535	0537	0538
0539	0540	0541	0542	0543	0544	0546	0856	1056		

K69: String 丨 (*long thin length*)

0536	0926	0927								

K70: Discreet 夋 (*person covers mouth*)

0540	0560									

K71: Pig 豖 亥 (*flat snout on four-legged mammal*)

0556										

K72: Full 畐 (*food from field fills one mouth*)

0565	0917	1024								

K73: Ornate Roof ⺮ (*roof with intricate design*)

0592										

K74: Bamboo ⺮ (*spiky leaves of shoot*)

0606	0946	0947	0948	0949	0950	0951	0952	0953	0955	0957
0958	0959	0960	0961	0962	0963	0966	1064			

K75: Between 来 (*split two persons*)

0622	0868	0980								

K76: Hacksaw 乍 (*handle and toothed blade in frame*)

0678	0759									

K77: Again 亦 (*cut top twice*)

0745	0779	0941								

K78: Gone 莫 (*sun sinking behind big plants*)

0777	0796	0919								

K79: Ladder 其 (*rungs and legs of extension ladder*)

0787	0896									

K80: Tool/ Stick ｜ (*short thick implement*)

0829	0830	0832	1029							

K81: Village 阝 (*boundary of rural area*)

0837										

K82: Dog 犭 (*side view of furry creature*)

0862	0865	0866	0867	0868	0870	0871	0872	0873	0876	0878
0879										

K83: Alcohol/ Wine 酉 (*large jug with stopper*)

0876										

K84: Ice 冫 (*two frozen drops*)

0884										

K85: Bent Arm マ (*at elbow to flex bicep*)

0944										

K86: Brush 亖 (*handle with bristles*)

0949	1034									

K87: Head 頁 (*turtle head peaks out from shell*)

0967	0968	0969	0970	0971	0972	0973	0974	0975	0976	0977
0978	0979	0980	0981	0982	0984	0985	0987			

K88: Accumulate 冓 (*plants and plants again*)

1005										

K89: Excessive 昌 (*beyond border opening are two more openings*)

1027									

K90: Beast 豸 (*horns, legs and tail*)

1028									

K91: View 䀾 (*eye looking ahead and laterally*)

1046									

K92: Align 侖 (*books aligned under one cover*)

1063									

APPENDIX 2

Secondary pronunciations and acronyms

Course Number	Kanji	Pronunciation	Acronym (meaning)
0001	一	ITSU	ITself Single Unit (one)
0017	日	JITSU	Journal ITS Unit (day)
0026	工	KU	Kommon Undertaking (work)
0059	板	BAN	Bulletins Attain Notice (board)
0064	人	NIN	Normal INdividual (person)
0094	夫	FUU	Fraternal Uncle Union (man)
0103	拍	HYOO	Hit Yet On Object (beat)
0107	右	YUU	Your Usual Utterance (right)
0114	台	TAI	Tall Atop It (platform, stand)
0118	合	GAT	Get ATtached (fit, combine)
0118	合	KAT	Konnect AT (fit, combine)
0132	己	KI	Kalled Individual (self)
0143	性	SHOO	Sense Has Of Oneself (sex)
0153	月	GATSU	Greet Annually Twelve Such Units (month)
0158	易	I	Intelligible (easy)
0166	正	SHOO	SHOw Omission (correct)
0176	示	SHI	SHall Indicate (show)
0184	井	SHOO	Sunken Hole Of Oil (well)
0187	封	HOO	Holdings Of Overlord (fief)
0217	素	SU	Simply Unadorned (plain)
0233	大	TAI	Tremendously Ample Individual (big)

0240	牙	GE	Grinder Elongated (fang)
0269	米	MAI	Main Agricultural Item (rice)
0297	行	GYOO	Get YOurself Out (go)
0298	役	EKI	Enter Kombat Intent (battle)
0320	子	SU	Someone Underage (child)
0322	元	GAN	Great ANcestor (origin)
0324	定	JOO	JOin Onto (fix); Just Opt On (decide)
0339	妄	BOO	Behavior Obviously Overhasty (rash)
0343	如	NYO	Not Your Opposite (like)
0369	貧	BIN	Bankrupt INdividual (poor)
0394	冥	MYOO	Mysterious YOur Observation (hidden)
0431	畑	hatake	HArd Tilled Area KEpt (dry field)
0435	無	BU	Be Unborn (not, without)
0450	鈴	RIN	RINgs (bell)
0489	留	RU	Restrict Utterly (stop)
0490	恵	E	Endow (favor)
0505	世	SE	Sphere Earthly (world)
0518	率	SOTSU	Soldiers Ordered To Stand Up (command)
0534	除	JI	Just Isolate (exclude)
0623	下	GE	Ground Existence (down)
0633	治	CHI	Can Heal Injury (cure)
0635	泌	HI	Habitually Issue (secrete)
0640	去	KO	Kurrent Once (past)
0677	伴	BAN	Besides ANother (accompany)
0678	作	SA	Something Assemble (make)
0685	供	KU	Kontribute Unto (offer)
0937	強	GOO	GOrilla Ordinarily (strong)
0954	弟	DAI	Dad's Affiliated Inferior (younger brother)
0981	頭	ZU	Zone Uppermost (head)
1033	後	KOO	KOnsequent One (after)
1042	御	GYO	Great You Operate (control)

APPENDIX 3

Secondary meanings and acronyms

Course Number	Kanji	Meaning	Acronym (pronunciation)
0011	寸	little	Small UNit (SUN)
0015	斗	measure	Total Ounces (TO)
0017	日	sun	NIght CHases It (NICHI)
0021	兆	trillion	Count HOnestly Overwhelming (CHOO)
0028	汁	juice	JUice Unaltered (JUU)
0035	沢	abundant	TAKe Unlimited (TAKU)
0053	材	material	Zebrawood Actually Is (ZAI)
0055	斤	weight	KIlogram Number (KIN)
0060	田	paddy	Drenched ENclosure (DEN)
0063	相	mutual	Shared Observation Of (SOO)
0073	代	replace	Deploy Another Instead (DAI)
0079	支	branch	Short Hardwood Item (SHI)
0081	伐	cut down	BAyonet Thrust SUddenly (BATSU)
0083	本	book	Holds One's Notes (HON)
0086	払	clear away	Free Up The SUrface (FUTSU)
0087	丁	block	Corners HOmes Off (CHOO)
0090	折	bend, fold	Straight Edge Turn Smoothly Under (SETSU)
0103	拍	beat	Hit Yet On Object (HYOO)
0106	口	open	KOver Off (KOO)
0111	加	join	Konnect Another (KA)
0121	号	sign	Gives One Omen (GOO)

0126	品	quality	Highest INdicator (HIN)
0133	忌	mourning	Keening Indicates (KI)
0138	忍	stealth	Now INconspicuous (NIN)
0142	生	birth	SEminal Instance (SEI)
0143	性	sex	Sense Has Of Oneself (SHOO)
0153	月	month	Greet Annually Twelve Such Units (GATSU)
0158	易	easy	Intelligible (I)
0173	至	extreme	Set HIghest (SHI)
0175	坊	boy	Brother Of Other (BOO)
0176	示	altar	Stand Honors Immortal (SHI)
0177	社	shrine	SHared Altar (SHA)
0181	里	distance	Range Indicator (RI)
0183	幸	luck	KOntingency Opportune (KOO)
0187	封	fief	Holdings Of Overlord (HOO)
0212	系	system	Komplex Entirely Interconnected (KEI)
0214	糾	examine	Karefully You Uncover Understanding (KYUU)
0217	素	plain	Simply Unadorned (SU)
0222	紋	pattern	MOtif Needlework (MON)
0226	納	accept	NOw Obtain (NOO)
0226	納	store	Next Occasion Open (NOO)
0228	細	minute	Small And Intricate (SAI)
0237	芸	skill	Great Expertise Illustrates (GEI)
0243	苦	bitter	Keenly Unsweetened (KU)
0249	壮	grand	SO Overpowering (SOO)
0250	荘	solemn	Serious Opulent Occurrence (SOO)
0275	有	exist	Your Undying Urge (YUU)
0278	肝	vital	Key ANatomically (KAN)
0288	胆	gall	TAkes Nerve (TAN)
0294	脱	escape	Danger Avoidance That SUcceeds (DATSU)
0298	役	battle	Enter Kombat Intent (EKI)
0308	故	reason	Kause Of (KO)
0309	致	cause	CHange Induce (CHI)
0324	定	decide	To Establish Irrefutably (TEI)
0339	妄	rash	Behavior Obviously Overhasty (BOO)
0340	安	cheap	Amount Niggardly (AN)
0341	好	good	KOngenial Origin (KOO)
0342	妃	princess	Herself Imperial (HI)

0348	爪	fingernail	Tips Snatch Unsuspecting MEal (tsume)
0360	負	defeat	Failure Utter (FU)
0375	貴	noble	Klass Inheritance (KI)
0388	金	money	Konvertible INcome (KIN)
0388	金	metal	Kommon INgot (KIN)
0399	食	eat	Sample HOt KUisine (SHOKU)
0401	表	surface	Hard YOur Outside (HYOO)
0402	長	leader	CHief Of Old (CHOO)
0410	被	cover	HIde (HI)
0417	喪	mourn	SOrrow Offer (SOO)
0422	灯	lamp	Table Object Often (TOO)
0435	無	without	Be Unborn (BU)
0470	服	obey	FUlly Komply Usually (FUKU)
0476	度	time	Distinct Occasion (DO)
0481	祭	worship	SAcrificial Invocation (SAI)
0488	界	boundary	KApacious Intersection (KAI)
0489	留	stop	Restrict Utterly (RU)
0501	番	number	Born As Numeral (BAN)
0501	番	watch	Behold ANother (BAN)
0502	畳	fold	Join Over Oneself (JOO)
0505	世	world	Sphere Earthly (SE)
0514	卑	humble	Handiwork Inferior (HI)
0518	率	command	Soldiers Ordered To Stand Up (SOTSU)
0522	準	semi	JUst Nearly (JUN)
0525	載	load	Ship Ample Imports (SAI)
0526	防	defend	Barrier Obstructs Opponents (BOO)
0534	除	exclude	Just Isolate (JI)
0540	険	steep	Kliff ENcounter (KEN)
0541	陰	negative	Indicating Not (IN)
0542	隆	high	Rise Yields Ultimate Upgrade (RYUU)
0550	判	seal	Helps Affix Name (HAN)
0552	制	system	Sequence Establishes Interaction (SEI)
0556	刻	time	KOunt Kontinuous Units (KOKU)
0568	私	I	Signifies HImself (SHI)
0570	和	Japan	Western Asian (WA)
0573	科	course	Kurricular Attribute (KA)
0595	励	strive	Really Exert Intensely (REI)

0606	筋	thread	Keenly INtertwines (KIN)
0618	甲	shell	KOver Outer (KOO)
0629	密	secret	Mostly ITS Unknown (MITSU)
0633	治	cure	Can Heal Injury (CHI)
0640	去	past	Kurrent Once (KO)
0641	法	method	Helps Official Operation (HOO)
0643	注	pour	Continues Heavily Upon Us (CHUU)
0662	柄	handle	Holds Essential Items (HEI)
0674	任	entrust	Normally INvest (NIN)
0675	仮	false	Klassify Artificial (KA)
0680	何	how many	Konfirms Amount (KA)
0707	指	point	Straight Hand Indicates (SHI)
0710	挙	perform	Komplete Your Operation (KYO)
0733	唱	recite	State HOnestly Openly (SHOO)
0737	布	spread	Fabric Unfurled (FU)
0739	急	sudden	Katches You Utterly Unprepared (KYUU)
0741	怠	neglect	To Attend Indifferently (TAI)
0754	悪	evil	Abhorrent KUstom (AKU)
0756	意	thought	Ideas (I)
0761	昆	descendants	Kin Offspring Numerous (KON)
0777	暮	live	Becoming One (BO)
0788	涯	shore	Ground Along Island (GAI)
0790	街	town	Governed Area Incorporated (GAI)
0792	塁	base	Run Upon Infield (RUI)
0805	威	threaten	Intimidate (I)
0814	裁	cut	Skin Apply Incision (SAI)
0817	足	suffice	Satisfy One's KUriosity (SOKU)
0821	床	floor	Step HOrizontally On (SHOO)
0823	序	order	Join Onward (JO)
0836	廃	abolish	HAve Invalidated (HAI)
0840	廉	cheap	Reduced ENtity (REN)
0842	当	this	Talk Of One (TOO)
0844	参	participate	Share Activity Now (SAN)
0861	器	container	Kitchen Implement (KI)
0864	状	form	Just Observe Outline (JOO)
0864	状	letter	Just Official Order (JOO)
0891	破	tear	Hold Apart (HA)

0892	砲	gun	Hostile Overpowering Object (HOO)
0904	市	market	Sellers Hype Items (SHI)
0906	希	rare	Kase Infrequent (KI)
0913	逓	successive	Travel Every Interval (TEI)
0934	侯	marquis	KOunt Overlord (KOO)
0940	弾	spring	Directly Arise Now (DAN)
0942	豆	miniature	TOy Object (TOO)
0947	符	tally	Final Unit (FU)
0950	等	equal	Twin Of One (TOO)
0955	第	ordinal prefix	Degree Arranging Inflection (DAI)
0957	節	season	SEparate Time Special Unit (SETSU)
0958	管	pipe	Konveys ANything (KAN)
0960	箇	item counter	Kounts Articles, Kounts Objects (KA, KO)
0967	頂	receive	Catch Hold Of Offer (CHOO)
0968	頃	about	KOncerning ROughly (koro)
0978	領	territory	Region YOu Oversee (RYOO)
0979	寡	widow	Keeps Alone (KA)
0982	頼	rely	Rest Assured Intent (RAI)
0987	願	request	Go Ask Now (GAN)
1001	閑	quiet	KAlm Nature (KAN)
1003	円	yen	Exchange Note (EN)
1004	再	twice	Second Addition Identical (SAI)
1009	礼	propriety	Rules Elicit Integrity (REI)
1031	征	subjugate	Sternly Enforce Invasion (SEI)
1042	御	control	Great You Operate (GYO)
1047	徴	summon	Court Held Official Order (CHOO)
1053	連	consecutive	Repetition ENsues (REN)
1061	軸	axis	Just Intersects Kore Unbroken (JIKU)
1064	範	limit	Hinders Advance Now (HAN)

READINGS INDEX

The Readings Index lists the kanji in this volume alphabetically for ease of reference. As is true throughout the course, *on* (Chinese-derived) readings are set in capitals and *kun* (native Japanese) readings appear in lowercase. To the right of each reading is the character itself, followed by the course number.